THE FLYING GRUNT

The Story of Lieutenant General Richard E. Carey, United States Marine Corps (Ret)

Alan E. Mesches

CASEMATE

Philadelphia & Oxford

Published in the United States of America and Great Britain in 2023 by
CASEMATE PUBLISHERS
1950 Lawrence Road, Havertown, PA 19083, USA
and
The Old Music Hall, 106–108 Cowley Road, Oxford OX4 1JE, UK

Hardcover Edition: ISBN 978-1-63624-258-3
Digital Edition: ISBN 978-1-63624-259-0

A CIP record for this book is available from the British Library

Printed and bound in the United States of America by Integrated Books International.
Typeset in India by DiTech Publishing Services.

For a complete list of Casemate titles, please contact:

CASEMATE PUBLISHERS (US)
Telephone (610) 853-9131
Fax (610) 853-9146
Email: casemate@casematepublishers.com
www.casematepublishers.com

CASEMATE PUBLISHERS (UK)
Telephone (0)1226 734350
Email: casemate-uk@casematepublishers.co.uk
www.casematepublishers.co.uk

Front cover: Cherry Point Marine Corps Air Station Wing Commander Major General Richard E. Carey prepared for a training flight (Carey family collection, 1977)
Back cover: Lieutenant General Carey (left without helmet) participated in an exercise held at 29 Palms, California. (Carey family collection, 1982)

To the Chosin Few. May we always remember your courage and sacrifice in Korea during the harsh winter of 1950.

To my grandchildren: Emily, Owen, and Jack.

Contents

Acknowledgements

For aiding in the editing of this book, I would like to thank the following:

Mike McCollum
Allen H. Mesch, author
Emily M. Meschertson, Smith College, Class of 2024
Jane L. Mesches
Frankie L. Pittman

For their assistance in developing story lines and overall encouragement for this project, I would like to thank the following:

Ed Fitzmaurice
Bill Signs
Frank Walker
Warren Wiedhahn

Preface

Up from the enlisted ranks, Marine 2nd Lieutenant Richard Edward Carey led platoons and served as intelligence officer in Korea. After participating in the Inchon landing in September 1950, Carey led his troops to Seoul. Two months later, as an intelligence officer, Carey learned where Chinese Communist Forces (CCF) were about to attack on the Hagaru-ri perimeter in North Korea. Outnumbered eight-to-one, enduring subzero weather and blinding snow, at East Hill near the Chosin Reservoir, Carey hurled grenades at the Chinese. Holding East Hill aided the Marines as they broke through the Chinese trap and moved to the port at Hungnam.

On March 23, 1951, a badly wounded Carey refused treatment at an aid station. "I have a job to do," he said. Despite mortar wounds, Carey continued leading his troops. It was his seventh near-death experience in 189 days. Finally, Carey's commander ordered him to an aid station. While his actions earned Carey a Silver Star, the wounds ended his time in Korea.

Always wanting to fly, Carey won a slot in Marine Corps aviation and earned his wings as a fighter pilot. In 1967, Carey again faced Communist forces. In Vietnam, he flew 204 sorties, mostly as an F-4 fighter pilot. Carey earned the Distinguished Flying Cross and 16 Air Medals during the Vietnam War.

Believing that his career had stalled as a lieutenant colonel in 1970, Carey looked at retirement. An opportunity to earn his college degree relaunched Carey's career. Over the next nine years, Carey earned four promotions and rose to three-star general. Carey led the evacuation of some 100,000 South Vietnamese out of Saigon to the United States. Carey completed his 38-year military career as Commanding General at Quantico, Virginia. He continued serving in retirement as a member of an Ohio Governor's cabinet and led the effort to build monuments honoring those who served at the Chosin Reservoir.

Many would call Lieutenant General Richard E. Carey USMC (Ret) a warrior. That is fact. This book will cover both the warrior and the human sides of General Carey. One hundred hours of face-to-face meetings with the General, Carey's papers, speech copies, oral histories, Marine Corps documents, and interviews with fellow Marines and family members, along with newspaper stories, went into the research for this book. The General answered tough and deeply personal questions. No subject was off-limits. The General wanted the book to be right. I hope that I met his standard.

CHAPTER I

The Early Years

According to the General, his family had a long history of military service. The Careys descended from Irish immigrants who arrived in Massachusetts in the early 1700s. Eventually, they migrated to the Ohio Territory prior to statehood. The General's ancestors included two Union soldiers who served in Ohio units during the American Civil War; one died at Shiloh, Tennessee, and the other died at Chickamauga, a campaign fought in Tennessee and Georgia. A member of the Carey family served in the Spanish American War.

The General's father, Timothy Francis Carey, served in France during World War I. Many of his cousins served in World War II. The General's father entered service in July 1917 from his home in Ironton, Ohio, located along the Ohio River in the southeastern part of the state. A troop ship took him to France where he served in St. Mihiel and Meuse Argonne, earning promotions to the rank of corporal.

Like so many doughboys, Timothy Carey was a mustard gas victim from his World War I service in France. The mustard gas disabled Timothy Francis Carey. The effects of mustard gas ended his career as a teacher (and prevented him rejoining the Army during World War II). Limited employment opportunities combined with the economic tumult of the Great Depression hampered his opportunities to earn a living. He married Marie Schlosser in 1922 when she was 18 and he was 26, according to the 1930 U.S. Census. The couple's daughter, Rosalie, was born in 1923. Five years later, on January 10, 1928, the future general entered the world in Columbus, Ohio.

Although Timothy Carey tried a couple of business ventures as a contractor and running a painting business, he ended up with little money and often had his family living in rooming houses. Pride prevented him from seeking help. They struggled on until, when Rosalie was 14 and Richard nine, Marie walked out on the family. His childhood environment helped create a value system for young Richard who would grow up to become a highly decorated three star-Marine Corps general.

Young Richard Carey sat on Santa's lap. (Carey family collection, 1933)

For two years, Richard Carey lived on his maternal grandparents' 300-acre farm in Grove City, Ohio, milking cows and undertaking other farm chores. During summers, he carried water jugs for the farm workers while riding a pony. During one stretch, Timothy Carey and his children lived with Carey's paternal grandfather, John Carey, in Columbus. Carey described his father as "very intelligent and very, very caring," adding that "he took care of me". He said he would have wanted his father in his platoon. Carey's father did not remarry but his mother did. Carey did not see Marie again until he joined the Marine Corps. Carey's mother and second husband lived in the Cleveland area. With her second husband, Robert Dietrich, Marie had two sons (twins) and four daughters. Dietrich, who worked for Coca-Cola, gave 12-year-old Richard an opportunity to earn money at Ohio State football games in Columbus, picking up Coca-Cola bottles during the games.

During the years following the Careys' divorce, Rosalie stayed in touch with her mother. In the decades that followed, all of Marie Schlosser Carey Dietrich's children connected with the General after his return from the Korean War. He said that he wanted to see his mother and began communicating with his siblings. Eventually one of his half-brothers, Gerald, nicknamed "Blackie" because of his wavy black hair and 17 years the General's junior, served in the Marine Corps for four years, including a tour of duty in Vietnam.

"Now, we're very close. There's no half-brother or half-sister," said General Carey. In 2021, the General's sister Bev flew from her home in Florida to spend two weeks with the General in Texas. She calls him every day to check on him. General Carey said that his brothers and sisters "respected" him.

Early indicators of General Carey's resolve were evident when he started attending high school. Determining that West High School offered the best opportunity for him, Carey walked a round trip of 10 miles a day until the spring term of his sophomore year of high school when his father moved the family to within 2 miles of the school. Due to his participation in varsity sports along with other extra-curricular activities, Carey seldom came home during daylight. He became both a good student and an athlete. At West High, he won the respect of peers when he earned leadership roles as the team captain in three sports. During his junior year, Carey captained both the wrestling and track teams. In addition, he played half back on the football team as a sophomore. His running ability caught the attention of the cross-country coach, and he became a distance runner on that team, captaining it as a sophomore. He won both track and cross-country events at the city and district levels, and also participated in state meets. His best event was the half-mile: "I always loved to run," he said.

For two years, Carey took part in the Spanish Club and earned membership into the "W" Association for the school's varsity athletes who earned their letter.[1] While in high school, he developed his strong Christian faith. He served as president of Hi-Y at West High, an affiliate of the YMCA. Carey also was president of the Columbus-wide Hi-Y.

Participation on the wrestling team would have long-term implications for Carey. He wrestled as a 165-pound middleweight. In one meet, West High did not have heavyweight. Rather than have the heavyweight match end in a forfeit, Carey stepped up and volunteered to wrestle the opposing school's heavyweight wrestler. While he battled his much heavier rival, Carey lost the match after his opponent put him in a body lock. He was hurt but did not know at the time how badly he was injured. After the match, Carey went to his girlfriend's house. When leaving to go home he passed out from what he later learned was internal bleeding and ended up in the hospital. The young athlete later returned to a track meet, anchored the mile relay that his team won and then became sick again. Doctors determined that he had suffered a ruptured kidney. Surgeons who met with Carey and his father recommended an operation to remove the damaged organ. The doctor told him, "Well, your chances are, you know, pretty good, but I can't really say that you're going to completely heal because it's pretty badly torn."[2] Demonstrating both his resolve and stubbornness, the 16-year-old refused to let the doctors operate. Carey firmly believed that he would heal and would not give up his kidney. He also acknowledged that he was "head strong" at that point in his life.

Because of the damaged kidney, he recuperated at home. Unable to attend classes at West High School, Carey home-schooled himself during his senior year by getting his assignments and books brought to him. Not only did he complete his final year of high school at home, but Carey also earned membership in the National Honor Society. Requirements for National Honor Society membership included scholarship, leadership, service, and character. Those traits stayed with Carey at each juncture of his life.

General Carey told on himself when he said that he originally tried to enlist in the Marine Corps in 1944. At age 16, the recruiter told him that he was too young to enlist without parental permission. That day, he was late getting home. When asked why he was uncharacteristically late, young Carey admitted that he attempted to enlist in the Marine Corps. Smiling, when he shared the story 77 years later, General Carey acknowledged that his 21-year-old sister was very upset with her brother about that. Rosalie had the dual role of big sister and surrogate mother. The General also described the Marine who declined to let him sign up for the Marine Corps as an "honest recruiter."[3]

In June 1945, Carey and his fellow West High seniors received their diplomas at their graduation ceremony. While the war in Europe had ended with Germany's surrender on May 7, Japan continued the fight in the Pacific. Many American soldiers serving in the European Theater of Operations (ETO) boarded troop ships that took them across the Atlantic, through the Panama Canal into the Pacific. They headed for Japan during the summer. In July, just a few weeks after graduating from West High, 17-year-old Richard Carey entered military service. That began a 38-year career that would take him around the globe as he rose from a raw recruit to lieutenant general in the United States Marine Corps (USMC). Carey explained that he might have enlisted sooner, but he and Rosalie needed to arrange care for their ailing father.[4]

The young enlistee knew that he wanted to be a pilot, so he signed up for the Navy's V-5 program, which offered recruits two years of training and a path toward becoming a military pilot. The Navy planned to conduct Carey's training at the University of Cincinnati, one of many college campuses hosting military instruction during World War II. More than 60,000 Navy pilots earned their wings between 1942 and 1945.[5] However, with the end of World War II came the close of the V-5 training: the Navy did not need any more fliers. Carey declined what he termed the Navy's strong push for him to enter their Officer Candidate School at Ohio State University located in his hometown of Columbus. He accepted a discharge and for two months drove a truck for Retail Merchants Delivery in Columbus during the busy holiday season.

Carey still felt obligated to the country; he wanted to serve and earn the GI bill college funding program. He also had a long-term goal of becoming a medical doctor. He recruited four friends to join him, and with his buddies

General Carey's Marine Corps career began at Parris Island. Carey is in row two, third from the left. (Carey family collection, 1946)

went to the Marine Corps recruiting station in Columbus. They all got through the verbal test, then Carey learned that all of the slots were full. Not deterred from joining the Marines, he took a train to Indianapolis where there were still slots. Three of his four friends went to boot camp for basic training at the Marine Corps Training Depot at Parris Island, South Carolina. His friends started their training two days before Carey's arrival, and he did not see them while at Parris Island.

Since 1915, Marine recruits have gone through boot camp at Parris Island. When asked how he did at boot camp, the future general quietly but proudly said, "I aced boot camp." He expressed pride in the fact that Marine Corps boot camp is at least three weeks longer than the Army's initial training. Despite the South Carolina heat and humidity, Carey said that he was in "superb physical shape." Prior to entering the service his preparation for track, cross-country, wrestling, and football combined with his 4–10-mile round trips to school contributed to his physical condition.

He earned the slot of platoon guide during the 13 weeks of training in the summer of 1946. Selected by the drill instructor (DI), Sergeant Kozak, the platoon guide served as the go-between with the DI and the platoon. The platoon guide also carried the unit guidon or flag.

Boot camp, especially his DI, left a lifelong impression on the future lieutenant general instructor. He shared this memory of his DI:

> The Marine Corps teaches leadership. I mean, I remember in boot camp our DI pounded on that. I remember that. Old Kozak; Sergeant Kozak. If he walked in the room today, I would stand at attention.[6]

Carey's initial encounters with the Navy and Marine Corps demonstrated that his superiors saw leadership skills in a young man then only a few months past his 18th birthday.[7] After 13 weeks in the Marine Corps at boot camp, leadership became part of the young private's core values. Leadership would carry him throughout his career.

Overview of the Marine Corps

As a young man, Richard E. Carey entered a small and unique service with a rich history and tradition. Marines consider themselves the best. The Marine Corps continues to have an air, land, and sea component. These words from the Marine Corps Hymn describe the members of the Corps:

> We fight our country's battles
> In the air, on land, and sea.
> First to fight for right and freedom ...

After nearly 250 years of service, the Marine Corps remains the military's smallest service branch. There is no Marine Corps Academy. Graduates of the United States Naval Academy may choose to become officers in the Marine Corps. Awards and medals presented to Marines reference the Navy. The Marines' recruiting advertisements played on their smaller size as a unique selling proposition for candidates with this slogan—"Marines—the few, the proud."

All Marine officers are riflemen, not career specialists. Officers who come from Officer Candidate School, Reserve Officer Training Corps programs, or the United States Naval Academy receive training on a wide range of military specialties at MCB Quantico, Virginia. Newly commissioned officers continue training through a lengthy program known as The Basic School (TBS).

The Marine Corps became part of the U.S. military on November 10, 1775, some seven months before the United States' declaration of independence on July 4, 1776. Since then, Marines have answered the call in every conflict that faced their country.[8] They have fought pirates along the Barbary Coast and battled to the "halls of Montezuma," in Mexico.[9] In the American Civil War, fought between 1861 and 1865, Union forces included Marines who fought at the battle of Bull Run in Virginia. Other Marine units served with the Navy.[10]

Before World War I, Marines served in the Spanish-American War, Philippine Insurrection, and the Boxer Rebellion in China. Nine years after the Wright Brothers' first flight in 1903 at Kitty Hawk, North Carolina (about 190 miles from MCB Camp Lejeune), Marines added aviation to their mission in 1912. In World War I, Marine aviators flew bombing runs over Belgium and France. On the ground in France during World War I, the Fourth Marine Brigade, known as "Devil Dogs," fought in battles at Belleau Wood, Soissons, St. Mihiel, Blanc Mont, and Meuse-Argonne.

Battles across islands in the Pacific brought victory to the United States in World War II and more recognition to the Marine Corps. Marines fought and died on Guadalcanal, Bougainville, Tarawa, New Britain, Saipan, Guam, Peleliu, Okinawa, and Iwo Jima.[11] The famed photograph of Marines raising the American flag over Mt. Suribachi on Iwo Jima captured the hearts and minds of Americans. In Ohio, young Richard Carey learned that older brothers of his friends served on Iwo Jima. "They were my heroes," he said in 2021.

During the second half of the 20th century, Marines served in Korea and Vietnam. In the Korean War, Marines, including Second Lieutenant Richard E. Carey, landed at Inchon on September 15, 1950, drove to take Seoul and heroically battled sub-zero temperatures along with hordes of CCF soldiers at the Chosin Reservoir. In Vietnam, after withdrawal of troops in 1973, Marines guarded U.S. assets including the Embassy in Saigon. Then Brigadier General Richard E. Carey led the evacuation of Vietnamese refugees and Embassy staff in 1975. The last four military deaths connected to the war in Vietnam were Marines.

In 1983, a terrorist truck bombing in Lebanon killed 241 service members including 220 Marines, 18 sailors, and three soldiers. The attack hit their barracks. Following the 9/11 attacks in 2001, Marines served in Iraq and Afghanistan. During the August 2021 evacuation of Americans and Afghanistan supporters of the United States, 13 service men and women died. Eleven of the 13 were members of the Marine Corps.

Three core values drive the Marine Corps—honor, courage, and commitment. For a Marine, honor means:

> Honor guides Marines to exemplify the ultimate in ethical and moral behavior. Never lie, never cheat or steal; abide by an uncompromising code of integrity; respect human dignity and respect others. Honor compels Marines to act responsibly, to fulfill our obligations and to hold ourselves and others accountable for every action.

Courage requires:

> Courage is the mental, moral, and physical strength ingrained in Marines. It carries us through the challenges of combat and aids in overcoming fear. The inner strength enables us to do what is right, to adhere to a higher standard of personal conduct and to make tough decisions under stress and pressure.

Commitment requires:

> Commitment is the spirit of determination and dedication found in Marines. It leads to the highest order of discipline for individuals and units. The ingredient enables constant dedication to Corps and country. It inspires the unrelenting determination to achieve victory in every endeavor.

All Marines live by the Latin phrase "Semper Fidelis." That translates into the words "always faithful." Marines shorten the phrase to "Semper Fi." Those words end meetings and conversations. Written correspondence includes s/f.[12]

A higher percentage of total Marines lost their lives in World War I, World War II, the Korean War, and the Vietnam War than the Army, Navy, and the Air Force. In Vietnam, for example, the Marines accounted for 25 percent of total deaths although they made up just 9 percent of the total U.S. force.[13]

Marines have not always been respected within the military. The Marine Corps comes under the Secretary of the Navy. No Marine held a four-star rank until World War II. Even President Harry S. Truman showed a lack of respect for the Marine Corps.

On August 29, 1950, President Truman received a letter from California Republican Congressman Gordon L. McDonough urging him to place a Marine on the Joint Chiefs of Staff. President Truman responded with an attack on the Marine Corps. In his reply to Congressman McDonough, the president said:

> For your information, the Marine Corps is the Navy's police force and as long as I am President that is what it will remain. They have a propaganda machine that is about equal to Stalin's.[14]

The following week, President Truman issued a written apology and addressed the Marine Corps League's September 6 national meeting in Washington, D.C. As he introduced the president to the Marine Corps League, General Clifford B. Cates, Commandant, said, "We in the Marine Corps appreciate courage—especially personal courage." President Truman told the audience, "When I make a mistake, I try to correct it."

Sea Marine

From Parris Island, Carey's next assignment took him to San Diego, California, for Marine Sea School where he became a sea-going Marine. On board ship, the Sea Marines Detachment, according to Carey, "provided discipline of the Navy." Sea Marines ran the brig that served as the ship's jail. Carey's first post-training orders put him on the USS *Boxer*, an aircraft carrier that deployed out of the bay area in Oakland, California. On board the ship, Private Carey ran the brig, served as company clerk since he knew how to type, helped run the ship's store, and was the orderly for the ship's captain and admiral. The *Boxer* was a command ship with a fleet admiral on board (the captain commands the ship with or without senior officers aboard). An orderly served in the role of an assistant. Carey stood watch outside the admiral and captain's quarters in case they needed anything. He also accompanied the captain when he attended events on shore. Carey's responsibilities as the company clerk included personnel assignments, administration, and payroll. He also was responsible for clothing, equipping, and feeding 100 men. In addition, Carey captained the gun tub where he led 12 men in preparation for air defense combat. In 1947, according to the General's papers, he passed the corporal's exam with a score of 99 percent. No wonder the General saved that test paper. While serving on the *Boxer*, Carey won the ship's middleweight boxing championship. He had learned to box at a YMCA in Columbus where he often worked out while in high school. His YMCA coach told him that he could be a boxer.

Commissioned in 1945, the *Boxer* served on what Naval historians called "normal peace time duty" in the Pacific while Carey's detachment was on the ship.[15] The young Marine's brief time in the Navy's V-5 program had convinced him that he wanted to fly. While on the *Boxer*, the future Marine aviator saw aircrew members up close, which only solidified that desire.

By 1948, the one-time three-sport high school captain who became platoon guide in boot camp had moved quickly through the ranks. Shortly after he reached his 20th birthday, Carey had already advanced from private to sergeant in only two years. Carey's leadership skills drew the notice of his detachment first sergeant, James Gillis, as well as his commander, Major Warren Morris. First Sergeant Gillis taught Carey to "Never forget my origin [from the enlisted ranks] or dedication to my troops." He also thought enough of Carey to trust him as a babysitter for his eight-year-old son Jim. The younger Gillis would go on to join the Marine Corps, make the service a career, and retire as a full colonel.

Major Morris told then Sergeant Carey, "You ought to be an officer." That conversation took place shortly after an eventful evening when Carey accompanied the ship's captain, Stanhope C. Ring, when he went ashore in a gig. The gig, known as the captain's taxi, was a smaller craft that took the captain (a naval captain equals the rank of a Marine full colonel) from the ship to shore.[16] As the pair returned to the *Boxer* in the evening, the gig struck a sandbar. Corporal Carey called an enlisted sailor on board who helped him work the gig around the sandbar to get the captain back on the ship.[17] The captain told Major Morris that Carey was "a good Marine, a leader." Initially, the young sergeant declined Morris' offer, telling the major about his plan to go to college and then become a doctor. The major persisted. The conversation lasted about an hour and Carey finally relented. Morris wrote a letter of recommendation that gained Carey entry into what he called "a program for a special type of Marine."[18]

Private Carey's first assignment after boot camp on the *Boxer*. Carey (end of row at far left) stands for inspection aboard the *Boxer*. (Carey family collection, 1947)

After getting the recommendation of Major Morris, Carey agreed to apply to Officer Candidate School (OCS). He took and passed several tests. Within a month, he headed from California to Quantico, Virginia, about 35 miles south of Washington, D.C. Quantico covers more than 55,000 acres and is one of the Marine Corps' largest installations.

Just before his OCS class began, Carey suffered an attack of appendicitis. He underwent surgery in the base hospital and spent three days recuperating there. By the time he had recovered, the OCS class was already underway. In Carey's case, school leaders decided that this "special type of Marine" could skip the 90-day training based on his record and experience. Over the next three months, Carey served on guard duty and worked on special projects. He then joined the class for a challenging nine-month training program known as The Basic School (TBS) as a second lieutenant. All newly commissioned Marine lieutenants went through the TBS program exposing them to everything in the Marine Corps. There were more than 300 lieutenants in that TBS class. The group included graduates from the Naval Academy, Reserve Officer Training Corps (ROTC), colleges, and former enlisted Marines. Overall, the one-time sergeant who never attended college finished seventh in that class, placing second in leadership and 15th in academics. According to General Carey, approximately 100 members of his original TBS class members dropped from the program. "The Basic School was a very important part of my development," he said.[19]

At 21, on April 13, 1949, Richard Edward Carey earned the gold bars of a Marine Corps second lieutenant with a date of rank of June 4, 1948. He would eventually earn eight more promotions. In 1949, after he completed TBS, Lieutenant Carey

The General said that he "always liked to run." Carey ran relay for Quantico Marines while at The Basic School in 1949. (Official photograph, Photographic Services, MCS, Quantico, VA, 1949)

Second Lieutenant Richard E. Carey runs relay for Quantico Marines while at TBS in 1949. Carey is at the far right. (Official photograph, Photographic Services, MCS, Quantico, VA)

received his first assignment as an officer. His orders directed him to report to 1st Battalion, 4th Marines (known as 1/4) at Camp Lejeune, North Carolina. Opened in 1941 near the beaches between Wilmington and Morehead City, the setting provided a perfect location for amphibious training. The camp was named in honor of a past Marine Corps commandant, Lieutenant General John A. Lejeune. The historic mission of the camp that continues today is to "maintain combat-ready units for expeditionary deployment."

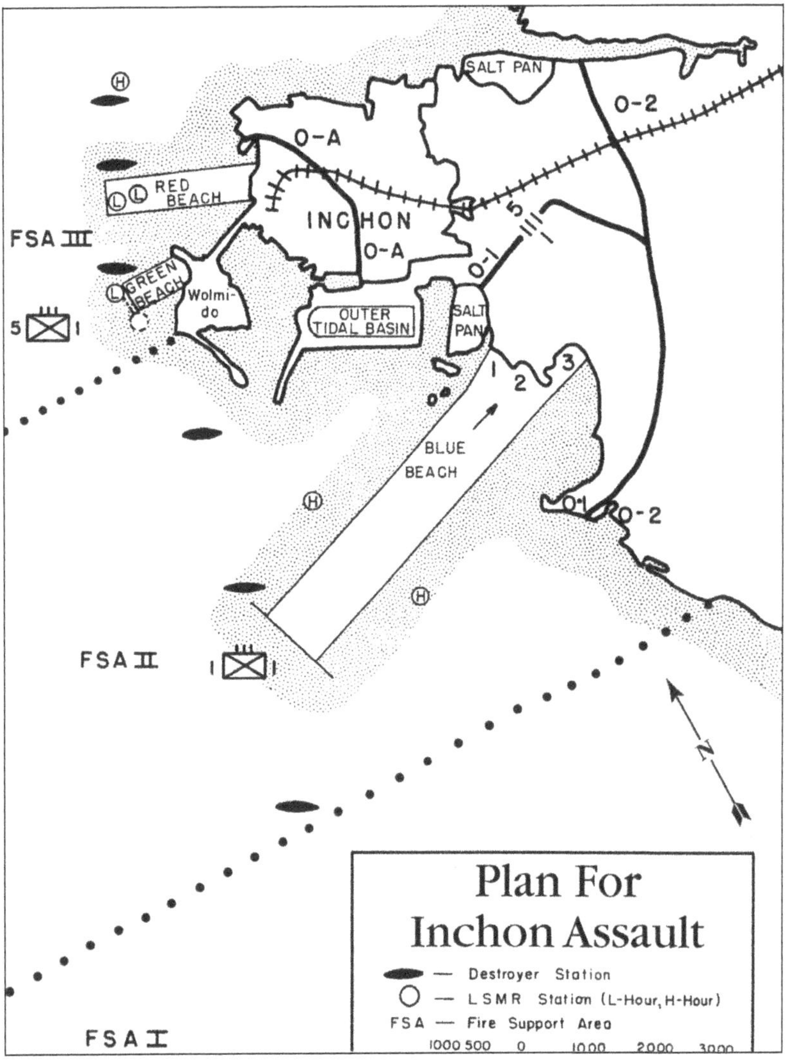

Carey and his platoon were part of the Inchon, Korea, landing in September 1950. The map shows the plan for the Inchon Assault. (United States Marine Corps History Division)

CHAPTER 2

On to Korea

Five years after the end of World War II, American service members entered a new conflict, facing a new enemy: communist forces. During World War II, allies of the United States included China and the Soviet Union. In the Korean War, the United States faced their former allies as the enemy. North Korea received military hardware from the Soviets while the Chinese crossed into North Korea with hundreds of thousands of soldiers.

In 1945, combined totals of the armed forces of the United States stood at just over 12 million. With the end of the war, the numbers rapidly declined and by 1950, the number of active-duty military members had dropped to just under 1.5 million.[1] To boost troop strength with the advent of the Korean War, the military called up the reserves and utilized the draft. Neither were popular options. By 1952, the number of Americans serving in uniform topped 3.6 million. Only World War II had seen more people serving in the military. The 1952 Korean War total military strength surpassed the number who served in World War I by 738,000 and the peak number in Vietnam by nearly 90,000.[2]

On June 25, 1950, Lieutenant Carey was planning his future outside of the Marine Corps. Newly returned to Camp Lejeune after a tour in the Mediterranean, he looked forward to finally going to college. 1/4 had reconstituted as 1st Battalion, 6th Marines (1/6). Carey became platoon leader of 1st Platoon, Alpha Company, 1st Battalion, 6th Marines and served with a battalion landing team as part of an amphibious task force deployed to the Mediterranean between 1949 and 1950. In that role, the lieutenant led special operations and once commanded 150 Marines.[3]

His two-year active-duty commitment was ending. The young officer was filling out paperwork with two objectives—go to college and spend four years in the Marine Corps Reserve—when a friend told him that North Korea had just crossed the 38th parallel into South Korea. The comment from his friend not only changed Carey's short-term plan, but also affected the next 33 years of his life: "I tore up my papers right there." When asked why he made the life-altering decision, the General simply said, "I am a Marine."[4]

Shortly after deciding to remain on active duty, Lieutenant Carey assisted with a court-martial (the military justice system for trials) at Camp Lejeune. His involvement with the court-martial ended with a call to the battalion headquarters where he received orders to take 1st Platoon, Alpha Company, 6th Marines, via train with the 2nd Division's equipment to the 1st Marine Division (1stMarDiv) in California. That equipment eventually went to Korea. Carey received $3,000 in cash to purchase food for his troops. As the train did not offer meal service, Lieutenant Carey went to the caboose one stop in advance of each mealtime to send ahead orders for 50 meals. The food came from Harvey House, a food service company that sold food along railroad stops.[5] Carey placed meal orders three times a day for seven days as the train wound across the country. General Carey recalled going north from Camp Lejeune into Kentucky. Then the train went to St. Louis and headed west to California. Along with the caboose, he said the train had freight cars that carried the Marines' equipment and a Pullman section used by his troops.[6]

During July 1950, Carey was at MCB Camp Pendleton, California, for training prior to joining the fight in Korea. The Marines trained 18 hours a day in the foothills of Santa Margarita Mountains; Carey described it as "good training" for Korea. "There was a lot of emphasis on physical training," he said, "that's why they had 18-hour days." The Marines also held exercises on tactics including attacking and defending areas. While they were not part of the formal training, Carey mentioned the value of having World War II veterans on hand during training. In his interview for an oral history with Dr. Laura Calkins of Texas Tech University in Lubbock, Carey said, "Those vets lived through it [World War II]. They provided tips that you don't get out of a book."[7] Later, he explained that it was best "to learn from the experience of the guy who had been there before." He called the insight of the World War II Marines "invaluable."[8] Based on their experience in World War II Pacific battles, the vets emphasized the need to react and adjust to circumstances on the spot.[9] General Carey acknowledged that there was no cold-weather training, although his unit received emphasis on the importance of cold-weather gear.

On August 4, 1950, the Marine Corps reactivated 3rd Battalion 1st Marines. Carey's platoon went from 1st Platoon, Alpha Company, 6th Marines to 1st Platoon, George Company 3/1.

Following training at Camp Pendleton, Carey moved south to San Diego to load the USNS *Simon B. Buckner*, the ship that would eventually take him to Korea.[10] Marines and sailors worked together to load the vessel. Lieutenant Carey ensured the equipment was loaded correctly on the ship.

In June 1950, North Korea attacked South Korea in an attempt to control the entire peninsula of Korea. Landing at Inchon would catch the North Koreans by surprise. The success of the Inchon landing resulted in the recapture of Seoul and drove the North Korean forces back to North Korea.[11]

From San Diego, the *Buckner* sailed to Yokosuka, Japan where the Marines needed to pick up additional equipment for Korea. The trip took seven days.[12] Training continued at the Marine base at Camp Otsu, just south of Yokosuka. This time, Carey said that nighttime training was the focus. The Marines also trained on conditioning, hiking, scouting, patrolling, and company field problem-solving activities. In addition, they rehearsed for the landing at Inchon.[13] Again, Carey had the task of loading the *Buckner*. The loading process, known as combat loading, put the equipment needed first in Korea at the front of the deck. That equipment went on the ship last. Lesser priority items had to go in the back and came off the ship last. Logistics training at The Basic School now had a practical application for the young lieutenant.

Before Lieutenant Carey and his team could begin loading, a typhoon delayed the start of the process from September 5 to September 7. Lack of motor transportation caused further delays in loading. At the port in Yokosuka, about an hour south of Tokyo, Lieutenant Carey put paper templates on the floor of the ship's deck to show the correct placement of each piece of equipment. While on his knees putting the templates down, the young officer met the most decorated Marine in the Corps' history with five Navy Crosses, the nation's second highest award for heroism in combat—Colonel Lewis B. "Chesty" Puller. He felt a tap on the shoulder and said, "Just a minute." "What the hell do you think you're doing, lieutenant?" hollered the colonel. Carey explained that he was setting up the equipment placement. Colonel Puller told him to "throw away the blanking paper dolls and you'd get it done." Puller retired as a lieutenant general. Carey described Puller as "something else." He added that Puller connected well with the troops and described Puller in Korea as someone who reacted to the situation. He also added that Puller "did not respect the Chinese capabilities."[14]

While Carey and his fellow Marines trained in Japan, the 1st Marine Brigade had quickly pushed into the Pusan Perimeter at the southern tip of Korea on August 17, 1950, stopping the North Korean Army from driving Allied troops out of Korea.[15] That earned the brigade's nickname of "Fire Brigade."

On September 10, the *Buckner* left Yokosuka and headed to port at Inchon, South Korea. One day away from Inchon, another typhoon hit. Waves estimated to be more than 50 feet high pounded the ship, but the *Buckner* weathered the storm and, the next day, reached its destination. A Marine Corps Special Action Report after the war pointed out that the port was not ideal. The report concluded, "Nature and man contributed little toward making Inchon a good port to mount out of." There were no dock facilities and no nearby open areas for staging vehicles. The General pointed out that in his view, the North Koreans did not expect U.S. forces to land there due to high tides. As a result, General Carey said, "The North Koreans did not protect the port at Inchon. It was a surprise."

Most importantly, the landing at Inchon worked. One thing that the Marines knew—if they attempted to land earlier than 5:40 p.m. on September 15, 1950, they would be bogged down in mud. Since Carey's ship arrived early in the afternoon, his platoon held a debarkation exercise.[16] Before leaving Japan, the Marines had loaded a pallet of 2×4 boards on the ship, according to then Private First Class Bob Harbula, a machine gunner who served with Carey as part of George Company, 3rd Battalion, 1st Marines (3/1). The boards would form ladders to aid the Marines, as they had to climb a seawall once they arrived at Inchon.[17]

The Marines who landed at Inchon "were loaded down like pack mules" with supplies and ammunition.[18] One private said that he carried a special pack that held four cans of ammunition instead of two cans. Each can weighed 18 pounds.

As he looked back on the first moments after he and his platoon landed in Korea, Carey explained they soon took enemy fire. The platoon went directly to the beach away from the seawall. Other units used the makeshift ladders. The General talked about confusion and smoke on the beach. General Carey said the confusion came from the noise. Smoke came from burning buildings, and what he called "combat smoke" resulted from bombs and the firing of weapons.[19] Due to those factors, Carey's platoon, 1st Platoon, G (George) Company, 3rd Battalion, 1st Marines (3/1) ended up in a creek bed around which the North Koreans had placed concertina wire, also known as barbed or razor wire. Members of his platoon with wire cutters began cutting through the obstacle. Not everyone carried wire cutters, Carey explained; there were not enough cutters to go around and even Carey did not have any. A member of his platoon standing next to

Carey began cutting through the wire. The General recounted, "[He] took a round in the forehead. I grabbed his wire cutters and started cutting myself through the wire." The General said of that day, "God was watching out for me." A deeply religious man, General Carey acknowledged that during combat he felt the hand of God. For the 22-year-old second lieutenant, that was the first of seven narrow escapes from death during his 189 days in Korea.

Already, within hours of reaching Korea, Carey had to handle the death of a member of his platoon. "You can never be trained to know that. It startles you. No way to be prepared. You try to imagine that it will happen and you do your best with it." The General explained TBS covered that situation during operational training. Although a fellow Marine had lost his life, Carey said that he had to "Take care of the mission right now. Accomplish what you are supposed to accomplish." His platoon made it out of the creek bed and moved on to their next objective, Radio Hill. They began receiving enemy shellfire. A bullet shot Carey's radio off his shoulder. That was the second near miss for the lieutenant during his first hours in Korea.

Two more members of his platoon died. Then Carey learned the shelling had come from the U.S. Navy. In retrospect, Carey said, "Well, I was a little perturbed, but that's war." By evening, Carey's platoon held Radio Hill and he received a replacement radio. During the first hours after the landing, the 3rd Battalion suffered 19 casualties. Four men, including the three from Carey's platoon, died and 15 were wounded.[20]

The next day Carey's unit headed for Seoul. They made the 20-mile trek on foot. Even in the first days in Korea, senior Marines put Carey in a leadership role. Carey described his early assignment when he said, "My platoon was sent forward again. I don't know what it was, but I was always kind of the chosen one." When asked to assess, from his perch as a three-star general, why Lieutenant Carey went out as the point, he said, "Leadership picked me to do the hard things. I proved myself in battle in the beginning. I gained the hill (Radio Hill) before it was expected. The goal was to get there as fast as possible and save as many guys as possible." Private First Class Bob Harbula, who served as a machine gunner with Lieutenant Carey as a member of George Company, described Lieutenant Carey as "an up front leader" who was trusted by the men.[21]

Positive response to the Inchon landing came within the military and from the media. Navy Lieutenant Joseph Wright said this about the 1stMarDiv's landing on Inchon: "I've never seen such courage." Lieutenant Wright, a 14-year veteran of the Navy, served in the Pacific during World War II. His ship, the USS *Whiteside*, helped bring equipment for use by the Marines from Japan.[22]

New York Times military analyst Hanson Baldwin said the tides at Inchon "were right." Baldwin, a Pulitzer Prize recipient, graduated from the United States Naval Academy. At the time of the landing, the North Koreans had not heavily mined the harbor. Baldwin praised General Douglas MacArthur when he wrote, "The Inchon landing of September 15 was a great gamble and General MacArthur deserved major credit for its success."[23]

The Marines, including Lieutenant Carey, landed at Inchon at 5:30 p.m. (Korean time). Within 30 minutes of landing, they were 2 miles into the city of Inchon. Two hours later, they were pushing toward Seoul.[24] According to *The Salt Lake City Tribune* on October 26, 1950, the 1st Marine Division landing at Inchon "turned the tide of the war." An editorial in the *Charlotte News* described the Inchon landings this way: "Then came the Inchon landings and the Korean War did an about-face. Defeat swiftly turned into victory, a brilliant and impressive victory that removed many of the bitter memories of those grim first weeks."[25] General MacArthur pledged that the Inchon invasion "will end the war in Korea by winter and save 100,000 lives."[26] That statement turned out to be inaccurate by nearly three years.

On Carey's second day in Korea, while on the road to Seoul, his platoon encountered a platoon of 20 North Korean soldiers. Carey spotted the enemy's platoon leader. He pulled out his .45-caliber pistol. His North Korean counterpart surrendered. Due to the actions of Lieutenant Carey's platoon, five North Koreans died and 15 became war prisoners of the Americans. A Marine intelligence team quickly interrogated the captives, "because of their shock of being taken prisoner," Carey said. That brief exchange with the North Koreans formed Carey's opinion of the enemy soldiers. He said they were not seasoned soldiers and, in his view, they lacked the will to fight.

For leading the capture of 15 POWs, the Marine Corps awarded Carey the Bronze Star Medal for Valor. Colonel Lewis B. "Chesty" Puller presented the award to 2nd Lieutenant Carey in 1950. (Carey family collection)

For leading the capture of 15 POWs on his second day in Korea, the Marine Corps awarded Carey the Bronze Star Medal for Valor. Shortly after that, Colonel Puller and Lieutenant Carey would meet again at an awards ceremony. As it turned out, General Carey explained, he ended up being the lone officer receiving an award that day. Puller, once an enlisted man, who according to Carey did not necessarily like officers, said, "What the hell are you doing here?" The lieutenant replied that he was there for an award. Later, Colonel Puller asked Carey if he was the lieutenant loading the ship up in Japan. "Yes sir," Carey replied. The colonel had remembered the young officer. General Carey said that Colonel Puller talked separately with each Marine who received an award that day and taught him that no problem was ever too big. According to Colonel Puller, problem solving required two things—strong decisions and dedication.

At 10 a.m. on September 17, 1950, George Company including Carey's platoon, moved toward Seoul. The next day, George and Item Companies from 3/1 took hill 123 (numbers assigned to a hill equaled the height of the hill in meters above sea level) despite undergoing heavy mortar fire.

On his third day in Korea, Carey's 1st Platoon rendezvoused with the battalion. Again, Carey took point. He rode with a unit of tanks and sat on one of the tanks. Speaking about this experience, Carey said that he spotted a North Korean T-34 tank sticking out of the window of a roadside building. He yelled "tank" to the commander. The tank commander fired and took out the tank, but the movement knocked Carey off the tank and on to the ground. After that, the platoon spotted a North Korean motorcycle with an officer riding in the sidecar. Several members of the platoon fired and killed the North Koreans. Carey's unit continued down the road. As they approached a hill, the North Koreans began firing at Carey's platoon. The lieutenant had gathered his platoon behind a building to develop a plan to stop the North Koreans when one of his men pointed to the road. Walking down the middle of the road was none other than the commander of the United Nations forces, five-star General MacArthur. Carey said MacArthur was dressed in his khaki-colored uniform, wore his sunglasses, and carried his trademark corncob pipe. North Koreans continued firing. Carey leaped up, grabbed MacArthur, and pulled him to the ground behind a building. "What the hell do you think you are doing lieutenant?" yelled the man who outranked Carey by 11 steps. Lieutenant Carey told General MacArthur that he was trying to keep him alive. General MacArthur told him, "Lieutenant, the bullet isn't made that can kill me."[27]

Seeing MacArthur on the line "bolstered my confidence," the General said. In hindsight, General Carey saw the move "as an unnecessary risk. That was why I pulled him down." In a June 2021 email, staff members at the MacArthur Memorial in Norfolk, Virginia, said that there was "a vague recollection of a story about something like this happening to MacArthur in Korea, but no hard evidence or documentation." MacArthur did ask what Carey he planned to do about the enemy action he faced. Lieutenant Carey briefed the general on his next steps and MacArthur told him that sounded like a good plan.

Carey's platoon fought its way through another 10 miles to Seoul. By September 21, 3/1 reached the highway toward Seoul and inflicted heavy casualties on the North Koreans. The Marines killed an estimated 200 enemy soldiers and captured 25 POWs. There Carey saw General MacArthur for the second time. MacArthur called the 22-year-old junior officer to his jeep and asked him, "Throw down any generals, lately?" He added, "Keep up the good work."

Seventy-one years after his two brief meetings with General MacArthur, General Carey made a few observations about the man who became a brigadier general during World War I and had the word "general" in his title for 33 years. "MacArthur thought he was God," said General Carey. He described MacArthur as someone who thought he did not make mistakes and did everything right. He added that MacArthur was "in love with himself and overconfident."[28]

Carey's unit pushed forward to Yong Dong Po, arriving at the Han River just outside of Seoul. At Yong Dong Po, the North Koreans offered heavy resistance as they defended Seoul. Lieutenant Carey put his platoon sergeant, Staff Sergeant Gerald Tillman, in for a Silver Star for his actions that day. In the write-up that generated the medal, Lieutenant Carey described the sergeant's "exceptional leadership" and the fact that he "put himself at more risk than he had to" for his platoon. Carey shared his thoughts about the medals process during an interview for the Texas Tech Oral History Project. "The Marines are pretty tough on that. They are tougher than the Army is. I don't say that maliciously, it's just a fact." He later added, "You don't get medals handed out [in the Marine Corps]; you've got to earn them."

George Company, including Lieutenant Carey's platoon, took the lead into Seoul after crossing over the Han River on September 25 in a Landing Vehicle, Tracked (LVT). The LVTs permitted amphibious travel over water. Once in Seoul, the Marines faced enemy fire from the North Koreans that included snipers. They met additional resistance coming from North Koreans in a school building. Carey took his troops to the hills located behind the school, he said. The unit faced what General Carey described as intense fire. The gunnery sergeant in his company took a hit to the stomach. Carey carried the much larger Marine about 200 yards to the command post which had a battalion aid station located nearby. There, a fellow Marine noticed Carey's blood-covered uniform. He asked Lieutenant Carey if he had also been wounded. Carey explained that the blood came from the gunnery sergeant's wound and that he would return to the line after bringing the wounded man in for treatment. That night, the North Koreans counterattacked with tanks and infantry. The Marines battled back and took out four enemy tanks. Positioned near one of his unit's tanks, Carey suffered a ruptured eardrum from the noise. (By 2005, General Carey said, he had a 90 percent hearing loss in that ear.) Sent back to the rear, Carey and his platoon had two days of rest. That rest period did not include hot meals nor a shower, but he had time to write family members.[29]

While in Seoul, Carey and a wounded sergeant, 23-year-old Gene F. Lilly from Oklahoma, briefly rested on a curb as they waited for a corpsman. A bullet went between the two. Carey and Lilly stood up to move away but as the pair stood up, a bullet struck and killed Sergeant Lilly.[30] That was another near miss for Carey.

Just 10 days after arriving at Inchon, Carey's platoon reached Seoul. On September 28, the battalion received orders to protect the route into Seoul for General MacArthur's reentry into the city. The entire battalion guarded Seoul's Po Boulevard for MacArthur and the United Nations group. George Company guarded the presidential palace grounds.[31] After that, Carey's platoon spent a night in South Korean President Syngman Rhee's presidential palace. President Rhee was not home that night.[32] The general said, "The way it happened, we were in a fight and needed to rest in a secure place." He did acknowledge that he took it upon himself to go there. General Carey described the evening at the place as "peaceful and comfortable."[33]

Seoul

Carey's platoon drove forward through Seoul to cross the 38th parallel. They faced, he said, only sporadic resistance from the North Korean soldiers. While battlefield casualties and the loss of friends and fellow Marines had an impact on the young officer, civilian deaths were even more upsetting to Carey. Just north of Seoul, the platoon came upon bodies of women and children. According to the General, the communist forces had massacred them. All of the victims suffered gunshot wounds to the back of the head. After crossing the 38th parallel, the platoon received orders to return to Inchon. This time, they made the trip in trucks instead of on foot. By then, the one-time 165-pound high school wrestler's weight had dropped to about

130 pounds. Carey described his platoon as dirty, tired, and worn out. The Army's First Cavalry Division replaced the Marines. While the Marines rode packed onto trucks, the soldiers traveled in two-man jeeps. To add insult to injury, one soldier yelled out, "Oh, it's the raggedy ass Marines." A member of Carey's platoon took offense to that soldier's comment. He tossed a grenade at the soldier. Although Carey's troop did not pull the pin on the grenade, the loudmouth soldier dove into the water. There were no other disparaging comments directed at the Marines.[34] General Carey admitted that he thought he knew who threw the grenade but said that he was not sure.[35]

A Look Back

In the after-action report, signed by Carey's battalion commander Lieutenant Colonel Thomas L. Ridge, conclusions included the following: the enemy organization was "impossible to determine," due to the ignorance of POWs. He said that enemy equipment included Russian-made rifles. Ridge pointed out that the only time the North Koreans wore helmets came during their lone offensive attack near Seoul at Yong Dong Po. 3rd Battalion casualties equaled 23.7 percent of the unit including 34 who died in action. The North Koreans had 637 soldiers killed in action. Ridge's report also covered planning, morale, combat efficiency, and included recommendations.[36]

Regarding planning, Ridge pointed to a lack of pre-Inchon landing intelligence when he explained that the 15-foot seawall and mudflats were "not usually encountered in normal beach assault." The report pointed out that the LVTs had capacity for 30 men; there was no allocation for equipment. Another conclusion related to carrying equipment. Ridge's report suggested taking supplies such as field shoes and utility clothing to the troops after they reached their location rather than carrying those items with them. The report said the morale of 3rd Battalion was "excellent."[37]

On to Wonsan

Back at Inchon, Carey and his troops took showers, ate hot meals, and received clean uniforms—Army uniforms, though, due to a lack of Marine uniforms. They prepared for the invasion of Wonsan. For a few days, the platoon stayed on a landing ship tank known as an LST, where the Marines ate fresh bread and drank cold beer. Then, Carey's platoon received rations for their trip to Wonsan—corned beef hash and potatoes packed in cans along with #10 cans of cherries. That was it. The resourceful lieutenant, who had made friends with the commander of the *Buckner* while crossing the Pacific Ocean, went to see him. Quickly, the commander helped Carey out with additional food. He provided steaks, pork chops, canned vegetables, bacon, and eggs. One of Carey's runners, Private Peter P. ("Waz") Wasylczak, who according to the General could get just about anything, "found" some baking powder and baking soda that the platoon needed. The food provided by the *Buckner* lasted for the 10-day LST trip to Wonsan. Carey helped fix their last meal on the ship when he flipped pancakes for their breakfast. The troops appreciated Lieutenant Carey's efforts to get them better food, even the large cans of cherries. More than 60 years later, Corporal Orace Edwards joined General Carey for dinner and confessed that he "swiped" one of the cans and ate them. The General laughingly said, "You stole my cherries." Mr. Edwards said those cherries made him sick and he never ate them again.[38] However, he had nothing but respect for his platoon leader:

Orace Edwards (left), a member of Carey's platoon at Wonsan, confessed to stealing canned cherries. (Courtesy of Orace Edwards, circa 2015)

> I lucked out when I got Carey as an officer. He was the best second lieutenant in the Marine Corps. That was proven when he stayed in and retired as a lieutenant general. He was a mustang. He went in as a private and worked his way up. We caught him in his first assignment as an officer. I believe that was divine providence, too.[39]

Regarding Wonsan, Lieutenant Colonel Ridge's report summarized the lack of planning and intelligence. That was similar to his evaluation of the Inchon landing. He pointed out that his battalion received only a "very small amount of intelligence or preliminary planning for movement to Majon-ni."[40]

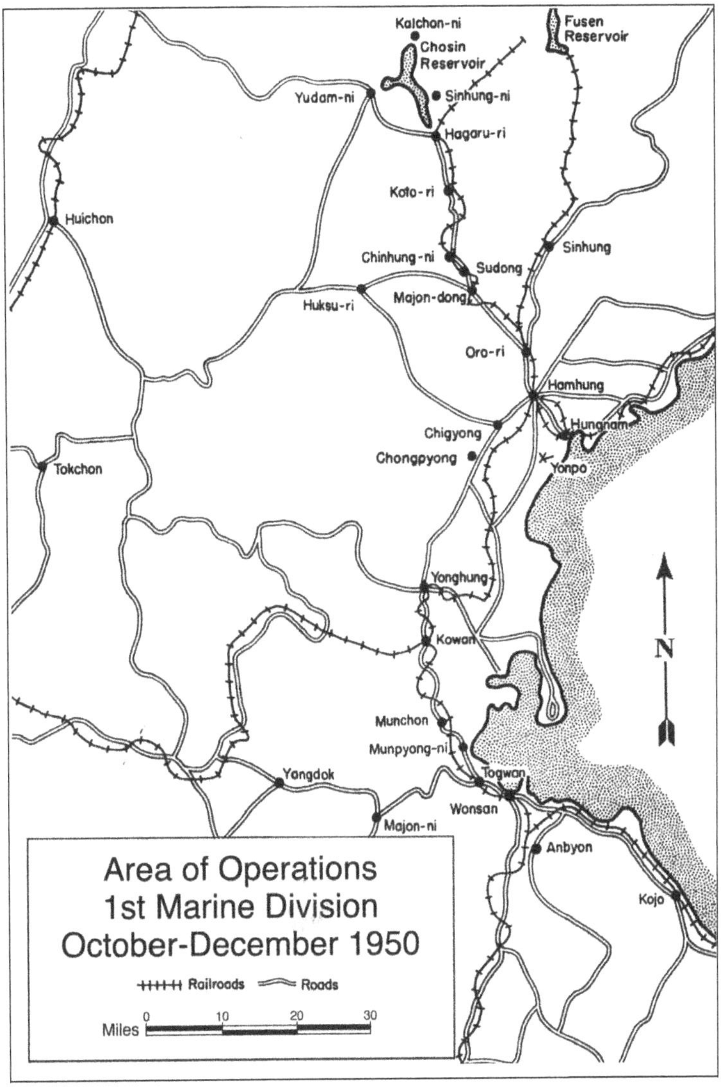

The 1st Marine Division operations went from Majon-ni to Wonsan and up to the Chosin Reservoir. From the Reservoir, 1stMarDiv reached the coast at Hungnam. (United States Marine Corps History Division)

CHAPTER 3

A New Role—Chosin Reservoir Campaign

Carey's First Enemy Contact in North Korea

On October 27, 3/1 received orders to move out to Majon-ni, 29 miles west of Wonsan. Lack of transportation delayed the move by a day but the next morning the battalion, minus 1st Platoon, George Company, began the trip to Majon-ni in trucks, arriving during the afternoon. Meanwhile, Lieutenant Carey's 1st Platoon, George Company followed the battalion, escorting a large Caterpillar bulldozer through enemy territory at night. The bulldozer was to be used to build an airfield at Majon-ni.

3/1 relieved Republic of Korea (ROK) Marines at Majon-ni and immediately set up a defensive perimeter. Carey's platoon made return trips to Wonsan, taking with them POWs previously captured by the ROKs and bringing necessary supplies back to Majon-ni.

3/1 faced no enemy action until November 2. Then, enemy forces frequently attacked battalion units at Majon-ni, on the road west to Pyongyang, and hit 3/1's supply convoys on the road to and from Wonsan with both small arms and automatic weapons fire. The enemy killed 10 Marines and wounded 26 others. The next day 3/1 took the high ground around Majon-ni while the North Koreans struck with "extensive night fire." The battalion hit back, using 81mm mortars and 105mm howitzers. Only one Marine suffered wounds. On November 6, the battalion heard a civilian warning of a pending attack on Majon-ni. Shortly after 5 a.m., trip flares and booby traps exploded as enemy forces approached. Within 90 minutes, the North Koreans retreated, and the Marines took 81 POWs who had surrendered.[1]

During his time in Majon-ni, Carey had the opportunity to observe his South Korean (ROK) Marine allies up close during their training. Despite the freezing temperatures of approaching winter, ROK Marine non-commissioned officers (NCOs) led their troops in outdoor exercises. In the cold, the ROK

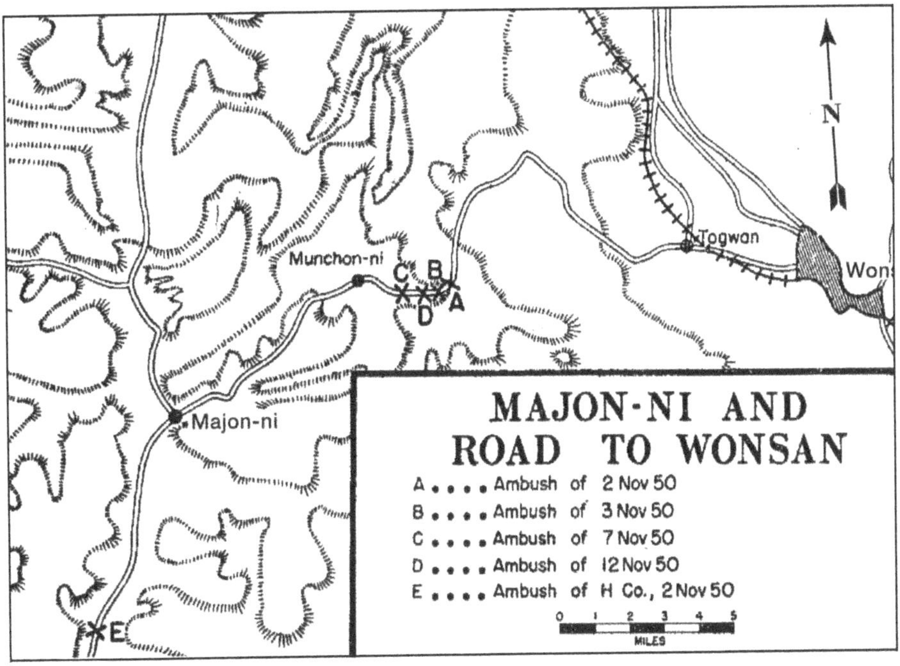

Carey's platoon shuttled POWs from Majon-ni to Wonsan. Carey's commander gave the lieutenant and his platoon a rest on November 2, 1950. Carey dodged death when his replacement platoon leader died in an ambush attack. (United States Marine Corps History Division)

Marines removed their shirts. Carey also noted the discipline of his allies. One ROK Marine failed to adhere to that discipline and as a result, one of his superiors shot him.

On a personal note, General Carey spoke about a fellow platoon leader, Second Lieutenant James "Jim" D. Beeler, a 1949 U.S. Naval Academy graduate who played football for the Midshipmen. After graduating from the Naval Academy, Beeler had options to remain in the Navy or to join the Marine Corps. When George Company's commander, Captain Carl L. Sitter, gave Carey's platoon a rest from shuttling POWs to Wonsan, Beeler's platoon took over. Beeler, from Jewell, Kansas, told Carey, "That's great. I got a Purple Heart here and want to mail it back."

Again, the hand of God played a role in General Carey's life. North Koreans ambushed Beeler's platoon and killed him on November 2. Posthumously, Beeler received the Silver Star Medal. Carey said that when Marines found Beeler's body, there was a spoon rammed through his neck and his Purple Heart stuck in his teeth. General Carey pointed out the difference between North Koreans and Chinese Communist Forces. He said the North Koreans "didn't fight according to rules." The Chinese, he explained, "were pretty straightforward."[2] Had Beeler's platoon not replaced Carey's platoon, the future general might have been an ambush victim.

Poignantly, Beeler, while on the ship to Korea, had told Carey that he thought he would die in the war.[3]

On November 14, a unit of the 15th Infantry Regiment, 3rd U.S. Army Division arrived to relieve the 3/1 Marines at Majon-ni. The Marines boarded trucks for a return trip to the 1st Marines Command Post (CP) at Wonsan where they awaited transportation 70 miles north to Chigyong.[4] On November 17, 3/1, including George Company, moved by train from Wonsan to Chigyong. At one point, the train stopped while Army engineers worked on repairing the train track. While this was happening, Carey organized a "survey" of Marine rifles. The Marines swapped their rifles for brand new ones that were part of the Army's supply. Carey, Captain Carl L. Sitter, George Company First Sergeant Rocco Zullo, and Staff Sergeant Gerald Tillman also ended up with new field jackets that they found in some other boxcars on the train.[5] 3/1 had no contact with the North Koreans during the next six days that included Thanksgiving on the 23rd at Chigyong.

George Company remained stuck at the Chigyong-Hungnam area, pulling guard duty while awaiting transportation to 1stMarDiv headquarters at Hagaru-ri, located at the southern edge of the Chosin Reservoir. It was then that Second Lieutenant Carey's company commander, Captain Sitter, had a new assignment for him. Since two of George Company's three platoon leaders had already died in action, Sitter told Carey, the sole surviving platoon commander in George Company, that he (Carey) had done enough frontline duty. Sitter told Carey that Battalion S-2 (Intelligence) needed beefing up to prepare for advancing Chinese troops. The battalion reassigned Carey to 3rd Battalion S-2. In the Marine Corps, those serving in Intelligence at regiment and below are in S-2; and those at division level and up are in G-2. Carey did not want the new position; he wanted to remain as George Company 1st Platoon commander. Seventy years later remembered he "was very disappointed."

Carey detached from his old platoon and joined the rest of 3/1 still at Chigyong. Years later, General Carey said, "We had a nice meal on Thanksgiving." During Thanksgiving, planning started for 3/1 to move from Chigyong to Hagaru-ri, where it would be responsible for the defense of 1stMarDiv headquarters.

Carey quickly learned why the battalion S-2 section needed to be "beefed up." On November 24 at Koto-ri in his new role as 3/1's S-2, Carey met Lieutenant Colonel William Frederick Harris, new battalion commander of 3rd

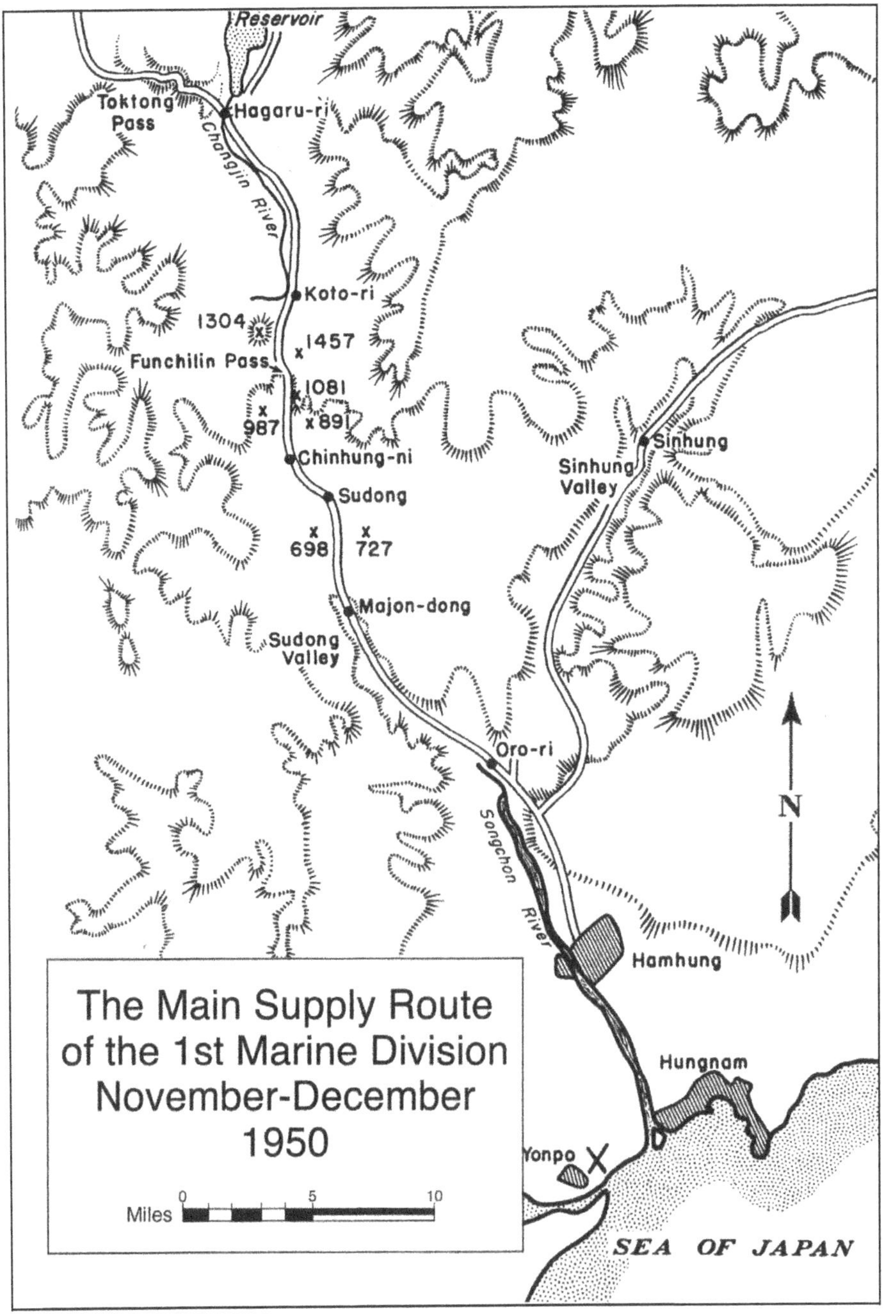

The winding and often single lane route made up the 1st Marine Division's Main Supply Route between November and December 1950. (United Sates Marine Corps History Division)

Battalion, 7th Marines (3/7),[6] and Harris' executive officer (XO) and battalion intelligence officer (S-2), First Lieutenant Richard Crowley. Carey received a situation report (SITREP) outlining intelligence about a CCF army deployed around Hagaru-ri, 3/1's destination, 11 miles north of Koto-ri. Prior to that on October 31, 7th Marines commander Colonel Homer Litzenberg sent a reconnaissance team to the ROK 26th Regiment Command, in anticipation of relieving the regiment near Sudong. Those Marines had reported seeing 16 Chinese Communist Forces POWs captured by the 26th (ROK) regiment. Interrogation of the 16 prisoners revealed the 124th CCF Division had deployed to defend the Chosin Reservoir, while the 126th CCF Division had moved east of Chosin and the 125th CCF Division had moved to the western flank of the 124th.[7] From November 2–4, the 7th Marines had battled the 124th CCF Division and decisively pushed them back north.[8] Without question, 1stMarDiv leaders knew they were up against an overwhelming number of CCF troops. Chinese forces outnumbered them by 8:1.[9]

This intelligence about CCF units surrounding Hagaru-ri, together with debriefs from North Korean civilian "line crossers," would prove crucial in the fight to protect the future 1stMarDiv headquarters at Hagaru-ri.[10]

On November 24, 1950, Carey, along with a driver, a platoon scout, and Lieutenant Crowley headed out on a reconnaissance mission along the main supply route (MSR) from Chigyong to Koto-ri to Hagaru-ri as part of his S-2 assignment. On the road to Hagaru-ri, Carey's team observed burned out enemy T-34 tanks that the 7th Marines had destroyed. The road had several hairpin turns which provided enemy forces with ambush opportunities. Carey noted that Marine engineers worked to improve the roads, facing enemy fire as they worked. That part of the MSR to Hagaru-ri would soon earn the name of "Hell Fire Valley." As Carey and Crowley drove up the MSR, they noted each unit established a complete perimeter defense; as Carey said, "the enemy would find the Marines well prepared defensively." However, Carey was still unsure about his new assignment: "I had little formal training in intelligence and therefore it was necessary at times to more or less feel my way."[11]

At Hagaru-ri, Carey noted what he described as "one huge hill" on the eastern edge of town, completely dominating the village and the road leading to Koto-ri. The hill would later become known to history as "the infamous" East Hill.[12]

3rd Battalion, 1st Marines Fights at Hagaru-ri

With planning completed on November 25, an advance detail of 3/1 departed Chigyong-ni for Hagaru-ri, over 80 miles north. The next day the rest of the battalion followed, although George Company remained at Chigyong due to a transportation shortage.[13] It took four hours to load the equipment and supplies on trucks. An insufficient number of trucks delayed the start of the trip by four hours and the first of three groups did not leave until 11:30 a.m. The MSR to Hagaru-ri was a single dirt lane. In addition, the battalion faced combat delays between Chinhung-ni and Koto-ri and arrived at Hagaru-ri without George Company on the evening of the 26th.

Carey's S-2 team consisted of nine men: intelligence chief, assistant intelligence chief, four scouts, an interpreter, an intelligence draftsman, and a clerk. According to Carey, his intelligence chief and senior NCO, Technical Sergeant James E. Sweeney, had "extensive knowledge." However, Sergeant Sweeney went to a rifle company due to a need for NCOs. Carey made the decision to assign his scouts to companies to ensure that men in each of the companies were acquainted with the S-2 representative to improve communication. In addition, S-2 members were used as replacements in How (H) and Item (I) Companies.[14]

At Hagaru-ri, three days into his role as Battalion S-2 on November 27, Lieutenant Carey met with seven Korean civilian line crossers who went out to gather intelligence that included information about the location and timing of the arrival of Chinese Communist Forces at Hagaru-ri. CCF attacked the 5th and 7th Marines at Yudam-ni, 16 miles northwest of Hagaru-ri, during the evening of the 27th and early morning on the 28th. The enemy also attacked the U.S. Army's 31st Regimental Combat Team (RCT), 10 miles northeast of Hagaru-ri. When Marines at Hagaru-ri learned of those attacks, they knew that they were fortunate that the Chinese did not hit Hagaru-ri on the 27th. More importantly, they knew that Hagaru-ri was the next CCF target.[15]

When his line crossers returned during daylight on the 28th, Carey learned of a pending night attack by the Chinese at the southwest perimeter of Hagaru-ri. After determining where the CCF were massing, Carey calculated that the attack would start at 9:30 p.m. on the 28th. In his post-action report, Carey explained how he arrived at the estimated attack time. Line crossers reported that the enemy was 5 miles away. Since the enemy, believed to be the size of a regiment, would move at dark and night fell at 6 p.m., Carey and his team used that time as a likely starting point. They concluded it would take two hours to get in attack position. The enemy ate after dark, so cooking and eating added another 30 minutes to the travel time. Carey said, "Organization for the attack during nighttime requires careful planning and silent execution." That took more time and Carey added another hour for the movement of enemy forces.[16] With this intelligence information, Carey

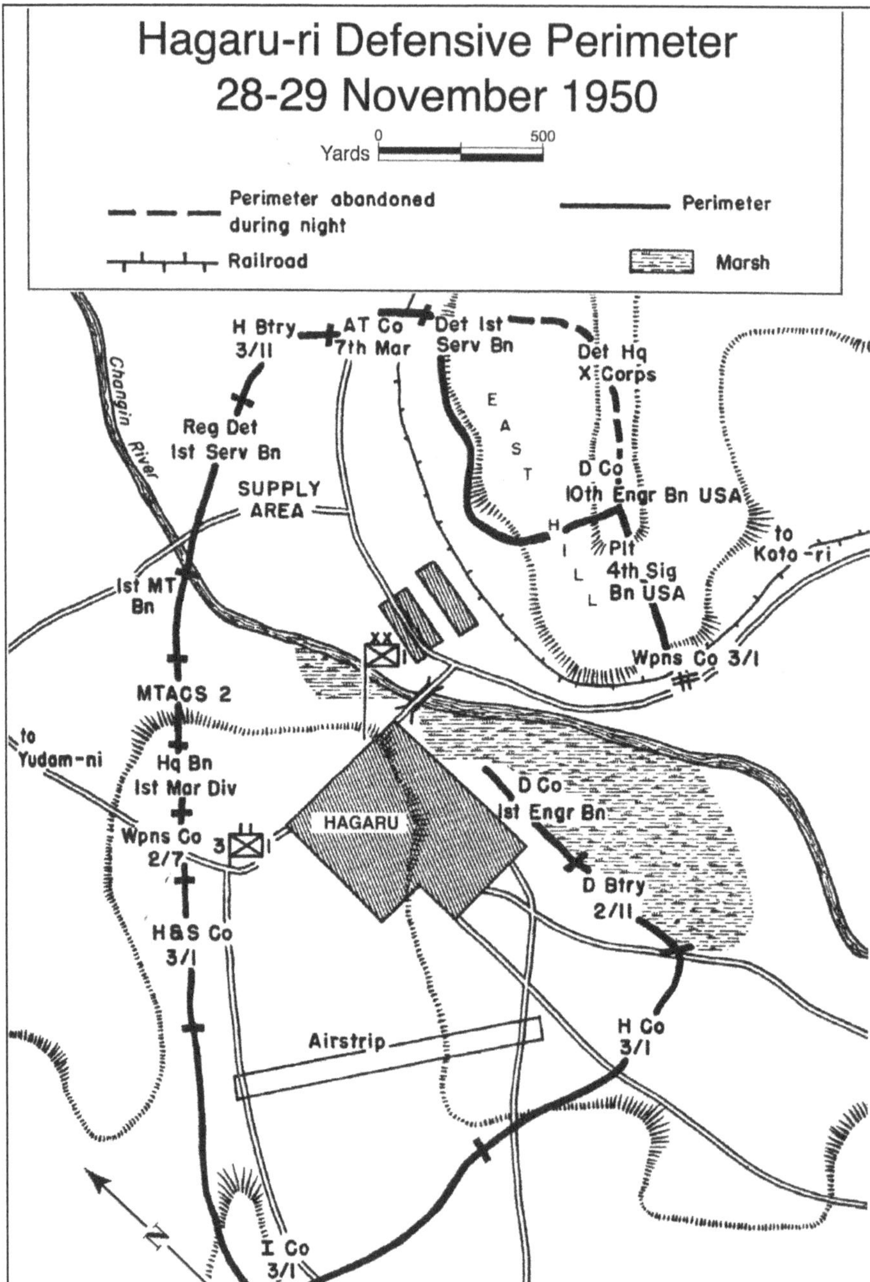

Line crossers provided 2nd Lieutenant Carey with intelligence about the Chinese Communists' planned attack on Hagaru-ri on November 28, 1950. (United States Marine Corps History Division)

briefed his battalion commander, Lieutenant Colonel Ridge, and 1stMarDiv commanding general, Major General O. P. (Oliver Prince) Smith, at the 1stMarDiv Command Post.

The Chinese hit the southwest perimeter of Hagaru-ri at 10:30 p.m. the night of the 28th. To help battle the large numbers of Chinese soldiers coming at them, innovative Marines developed a booby trap using five-gallon cans of gasoline. General Carey outlined the process when he said:

> We had two ways to set them off. The first way called for detonating a white phosphorus grenade by pulling a wire attached to the pin on the grenade, detonating the five-gallon can of gasoline. Secondly, we also put a block of C-2 [explosive material] under the five-gallon gasoline can with a wire attached to a blasting cap in the block of C-2. If pulling the wire to the pin didn't work, we would set off the C-2. Either way, the booby trap lit up the battlefield. That's how you could see where they (CCF) were.[17]

The airfield at Hagaru-ri also was the scene of another near miss for Second Lieutenant Carey that night. As the engineers built the airfield, he crossed over it while reviewing the results of the failed attacks on the southwest perimeter. He left H Company's lines to check out I Company, knowing that I Company had come under heavy enemy fire during the attack.

Three times during the night of November 28, the enemy nearly killed Carey. As Carey moved across the airfield at Hagaru-ri, he saw another person. He thought it was an American but actually came face to face with a very large, armed Chinese soldier. As Carey pulled out his weapon, the enemy moved away from Carey in the snow and disappeared before Carey could shoot him.

Again, that night while moving to I Company Carey had a second near miss when a mortar round landed near him. While he was not hit with shrapnel, the concussion knocked Carey unconscious. The Marines from Item Company left their lines, brought Carey into a tent behind the lines, and revived him.

In the third narrow escape on the night of November 28, Carey again barely missed losing his life. He climbed down into a foxhole in the Item Company lines, joining a former Basic School classmate and close friend, Second Lieutenant Charlie Maddox, a one-time Master Sergeant. Shortly after Carey climbed out to continue his line check, a mortar landed in the foxhole, killing Maddox.[18]

While Carey was at the airfield that night, he saw the work of the engineers and was struck by their bravery: "These engineers were working under lights and at no time ceased work despite the fire of the enemy or his close proximity."[19]

The 1st Engineer Battalion, led by Lieutenant Colonel John Partridge, had a 60 percent casualty rate as they built the airstrip at Hagaru-ri. The engineers also widened and lengthened an airstrip at Koto-ri. Both airstrips were large enough to handle C-47 transport aircraft.[20]

General Carey explained years later that one platoon from How Company was almost "wiped out." While the Marines continued taking casualties, they hit hard at the Chinese and captured a company. Lieutenant Carey went to interview the captives' commander. In his role as Battalion S-2, Carey spoke with the company commander through an interpreter. He was stunned when the captured officer said, "If you feed us, we will fight for you."[21] Carey did not take him up on the offer. Seventy-one years after that incident, General Carey remained upset by the officer's willingness to quit fighting for his country in exchange for food. Angrily pointing out that the Marines went days without food, General Carey said the enemy commander was "a traitor." In the General's view, that soldier lacked good training and was not loyal to his country. That disloyalty bothered the General, even though the soldier was his enemy. His voice grew angry as he recalled the long-ago event. He still could not accept any soldier selling out his country.[22]

Since the Chinese hit the perimeter at 10:30 p.m., his fellow Marines joked to Carey that he was an hour off on his first intelligence briefing to a general. The next morning, the 29th, his battalion commanding officer, Lieutenant Colonel Ridge, teased Carey, asking how he got the point of attack right but missed time of attack by an hour. Carey responded, "That's easy, Colonel, the Chinese fight at night so they weren't on daylight-saving time."[23]

Even the U.S. Army, not always complimentary to the Marine Corps, offered praise for Carey's use of the line crossers to establish the timing of the Chinese attack. The Army's report said:

> Lt. Col. Thomas L. Ridge, commander of the 3d Battalion, 1st Marines, and officer in charge of the defense of Hagaru-ri, was well informed of the location, size, and intent of the 58th [CCF Division], though not of its numerical identity. His S-2, 2nd Lt. Richard E. Carey, had had phenomenal success over the past two days with two Korean agents. By interrogating civilians coming into Hagaru-ri from the countryside, the agents learned of the approach of the Chinese. By making a circuit of the high ground around Hagaru-ri, they next determined the enemy's location and approximate size, and while mingling among Chinese troops they heard boasts that the division would occupy Hagaru-ri on the night of the 28th. The roadblock to the south was discovered during the afternoon of the 28th by a platoon of infantry and three tanks who were turned back by enemy fire when they attempted to patrol the road to Koto-ri.
>
> Figuring the time it would take the Chinese to reach Hagaru-ri after dark; Carey predicted that the first assault would come around 2130. On this and Carey's other findings Colonel Ridge based his plan of defense. Using his own battalion, which was still short Company G, and a hodgepodge of other Marine and Army units, he fashioned a four-mile perimeter around the Jangjin [Koreans called the area Jangjin. During World War II the Japanese called it Chosin] River flats in which Hagaru-ri was located.[24]

Task Force Drysdale

After the initial attack on Hagaru-ri on the night of the 28th, General Smith did not believe the under-strength 3/1 could hold Hagaru-ri if it was furiously attacked by the Chinese again. Smith, from his division's command post at Hagaru-ri, ordered Colonel Puller to send infantry reinforcements with tanks from Koto-ri. Puller quickly put together Task Force Drysdale. The task force had the objective of bringing reinforcements 11 miles up the MSR from Koto-ri to Hagaru-ri.

George Company, left behind when the rest of 3/1 moved to Hagaru-ri on the 26th, arrived from Chigyong at Koto-ri on the 28th, on its way to join the rest of the battalion defending Hagaru-ri. The task force, therefore, included the following: 150 members of George Company 3/1, 240 British Royal Marines (RM) from 41 Independent Commando, Royal Marines, and B Company, 31st Regiment, U.S. Army. The 31st Regiment had been making its way up to join what would eventually become Task Force Faith, east of Chosin. Drysdale's task force left Koto-ri at 9:30 on the morning of the 29th with about 900 men and 29 tanks. The task force received its name from British RM Lieutenant Colonel Douglas B. Drysdale. Colonel Drysdale led from the front.

Lieutenant Colonel Drysdale's initial plan was to have his Royal Marines attack Chinese forces dug in along the right side of the MSR, then have George Company pass through the British Marines and attack Hill 1236 looming over the east side of the MSR about a mile and half north of Koto-ri. It was during this attack on Hill 1236 (known as "Telegraph Hill" by the men of George Company) when 1st Platoon Staff Sergeant Gerald Tillman was killed. Tillman had been Lieutenant Carey's platoon sergeant from his time at Camp Lejeune and with 1/6 when Carey served in the Mediterranean. Carey said, "Tillman was the best platoon sergeant in the division in my opinion."[25]

Around 1 p.m. on the 29th, Marine tanks from Company D, 1st Tank Battalion, and a platoon of Sherman tanks from 1st Marines Anti-Tank Company, that had arrived at Koto-ri earlier that day, caught up with the task force.[26] The force had to push through the roadblocks and thousands of Chinese troops who held the high ground on both sides of the road while moving up the MSR. Chinese forces surrounded Drysdale's troops and enemy fire wounded Drysdale.

In a 2014 presentation, General Carey described that day when he said, "All hell broke loose." Carey's old company, George/3/1, took heavy casualties. Among the casualties was Corporal Orace Edwards, 1st Platoon,

George Company's "canned cherries thief." He received wounds from an exploding truck.[27]

In Hell Fire Valley the Chinese cut Drysdale's task force into three parts. CCF action along the road delayed the arrival of the first third of Drysdale's task force, about 300 men and 16 tanks (including George Company), at Hagaru-ri until midnight of the 29th. Earlier, at 3 p.m. on the 29th, Puller sent B Company, 1st Tank Battalion up the MSR from Koto-ri to bring back as many survivors as possible from the bottom third of the column; they made it back with 12 tanks. Army infantrymen and some Marines, caught in the middle third, fought until they ran out of ammunition. In the early morning of the 30th, the Chinese captured several Marines and soldiers, including then Marine Major John N. "Jack" McLaughlin, a man Carey would come to know during his career. The major spent nearly three years in captivity, at one point he was placed in solitary confinement for four months.[28] General Carey described McLaughlin as "very personable and a helluva Marine."[29]

Those British Marines in the middle of the task force, who eluded capture, continued their mission. British Royal Marines continued arriving at Hagaru-ri throughout the day of the 30th by eluding the enemy that cut them off and surrounded them on the road up from Koto-ri. The remaining troops caught in the middle third of the task force either slipped away during darkness or were eventually forced to surrender.

While the arrivals in Hagaru-ri consisted of only a third of Task Force Drysdale's beginning roster, and just over half of its tanks, this was enough to save Hagaru-ri from annihilation, according to General Smith.

Gordon Payne, a surviving member of Drysdale's task force, had just completed his training when 41 Independent Commando British Royal Marines formed in August 1950. As a Royal Marine, he held the rank of Marine-1 and served as heavy weapons specialist. Payne's responsibilities included mortars and machine guns. According to Payne, when the task force formed up, Lieutenant Colonel Drysdale gathered his men, gave them their assignments, and told them, "It's not going to be a walk in the park." He described Drysdale's leadership style as "strict, but fair." Payne described his experience on November 29 and 30:

> After our truck had been knocked out by a mortar bomb the six of us that survived decided to follow the convoy that had gone on ahead. Staying well to the left of the road we eventually ran into an enemy position. After shooting our way out we crossed a river and spent the rest of the night making our way towards the lights at Hagaru-ri, arriving there at daylight on the 30th, all suffering various degrees of frostbite.[30]

Payne had this impression of the U.S. Marines: "We always got on with them very well and found them to be courageous."[31] Lieutenant Colonel Drysdale said this about the Boxer Rebellion and Korean War ties between British and U.S. Marines:

> This was the first time that the Marines of the two nations had fought side by side since the defence of the Peking Legations in 1900. Let it be said that the admiration of all ranks of 41 Commando for their brothers in arms was and is unbounded. They fought like tigers and their morale and esprit de corps is second to none.[32]

Payne remained with 41 Commando through March 1951 when he returned home for further treatment of his wounds from a ricochet bullet. Like many others who served in Korea, he also suffered from frostbite.[33]

Drysdale's actions won accolades from the Americans who fought with him. In 1955, the United States awarded him the Silver Star. On July 15, 1955, *The London Gazette* carried this statement from Admiralty, Whitehall, S.W.1 regarding the award to Colonel Drysdale:

> The QUEEN [Elizabeth II] has been graciously pleased to give unrestricted permission for the wearing of the following decorations bestowed by the President of the United States of America for gallant and distinguished service in operations in Korea:—Silver Star Medal (to) Douglas Burns Drysdale.

In August 2021, General Carey learned that Lieutenant Colonel Drysdale received the Silver Star. The General spoke highly of the Royal Marine who led a group of both American and British Marines when he took charge of the task force. General Carey described Colonel Drysdale as "a real competent individual in combat and leader with a dry sense of humor."[34]

On November 30, Lieutenant Carey heard that George Company's First Sergeant, Rocco Zullo, had lost his life in Hell Fire Valley. The enemy shot Zullo, who operated a .50 caliber M-2 heavy machine gun mounted in the back of the George Company truck, at the last CCF roadblock located at the junction of the MSR leading into Hagaru-ri.[35] Wanting to pay his respects to the New Hampshire native with the booming voice, Carey found corpses placed outside 3rd Battalion Headquarters at Hagaru-ri. He approached Sergeant Zullo's body. Then, in the cold air, Lieutenant Carey saw the first sergeant's breath. Quickly, he had Zullo's body brought inside for medical attention.

Many in George Company thought that Zullo had died in Hell Fire Valley. Not only did he not die that day, Zullo lived nearly 65 more years before he died at the age of 97. By 1950, Zullo, who served in China prior to World War II and fought in Guadalcanal and Peleliu in WWII, was a 13-year veteran of the Marine Corps. Zullo was the recipient of the Silver Star, Bronze Star, and Purple Heart.[36]

Former Private Bob Harbula talked about attending a George Company reunion in 1990. He said that he had not seen anyone from George Company in almost 40 years. Then Harbula heard that familiar New England accent. Harbula talked about the conversation. "I said Rocco, I thought you were dead." Zullo responded, "Do I look dead?"

The Attack on East Hill

CCF's initial assault on Hagaru-ri's southwest perimeter on the night of the 28th had failed. Major Reginald Myers, 3/1's XO, led a counterattack that stopped the CCF attack on East Hill on the 29th. The Chinese then massed a large force to take East Hill.

The CCF were described by Lieutenant Colonel Ridge as well trained, highly disciplined, and skillfully led. An estimated 120,000 Chinese troops attacked the Marines, their main objective to annihilate the 1stMarDiv. The enemy believed that if the Marines were destroyed, the UN would pull out of the war. Captured CCF documents pointed to two tactics in the attack. First, Chinese forces sought to surround the Marines. Then they could cut off supplies and limit chances for retreat. That happened to Task Force Drysdale between Koto-ri and Hagaru-ri. Second, the enemy attack used a triangle formation to destroy the Marines' organizational integrity by using roadblocks along with cover and concealment.[37]

> Cover gives you protection from bullets, fragments of exploding rounds, flame, nuclear effect, and biological and chemical agents. Cover can conceal you from any observation. Cover can be natural or man-made. Concealment is anything that hides you from enemy observation. Concealment does not protect you from enemy fire. Concealment, like cover, can be natural or man-made.[38]

Chinese soldiers crossing the Manchurian border each carried three pounds of rice and 80 rounds of small arms fire ammunition. Unlike the American forces who received airdrops, it appeared that China did not have an organized resupply process. They just kept sending more and more soldiers. The Chinese soldiers did not have steel helmets, basic toiletries or, in some cases, gloves. As General Carey commented, "They only had what they could carry."

He described the CCF attack style as using human waves. "The advanced element of the Chinese would have rifles and some automatic weapons, not very many. However, directly behind them would be another element with burp guns. Anybody that turned tail and ran, they would shoot them." The

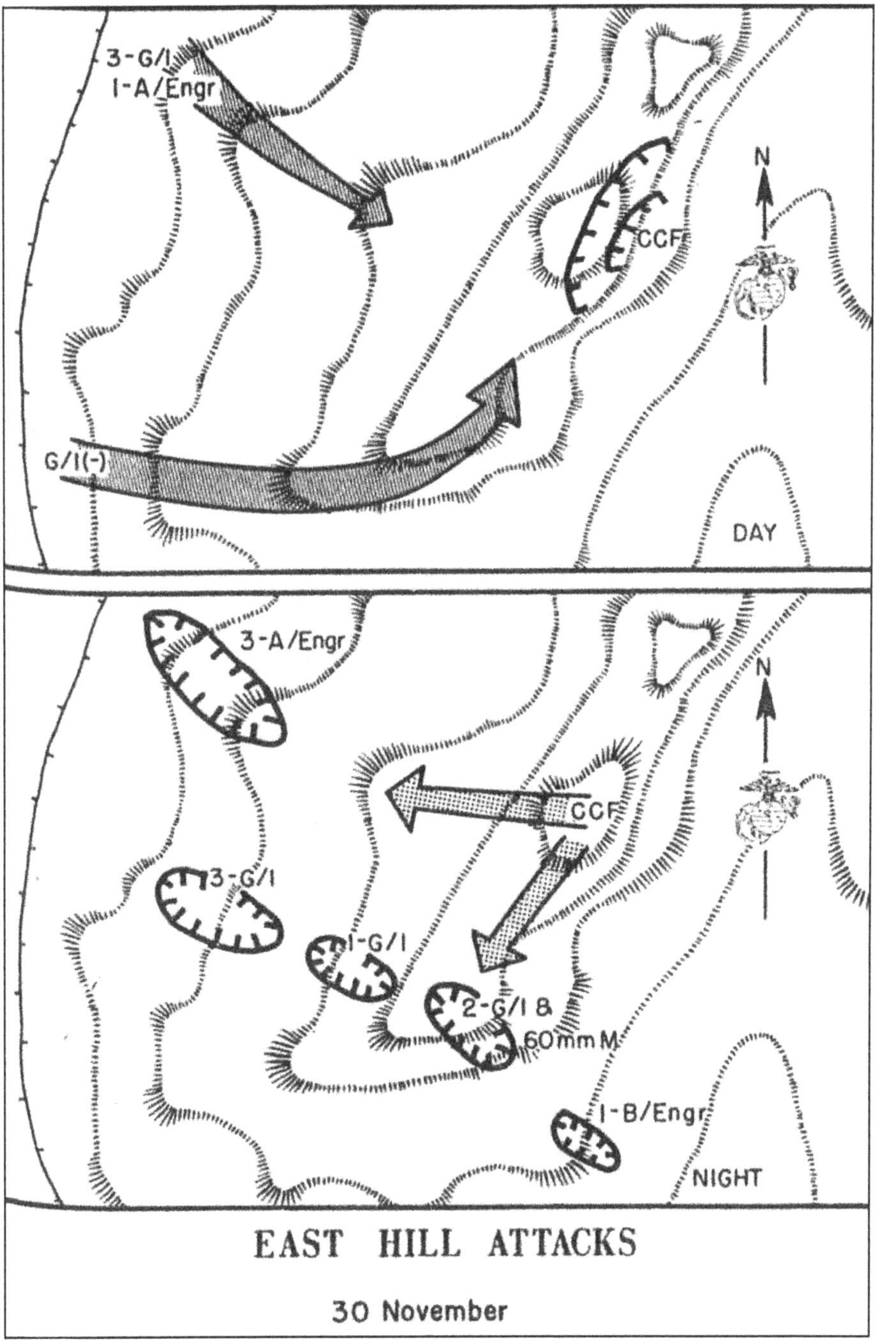

From East Hill 2nd Lieutenant Carey, threw grenades to slow the advance of Chinese Communist forces. (United States Marine Corps History Division)

Chinese forces "took a lot of casualties," he added.[39] Some of the Chinese second wave did not have weapons. "They picked them [up] from fallen first wave troops."

Reflecting on East Hill, General Carey pointed out that the line crossers, most of whom had been in the Nationalist Chinese Army, were "one of the most important things that happened." He praised their support as "heroic and significant" when on the 30th they advised Carey where the Chinese were massing for the attack on East Hill. That intelligence enabled the Marines to organize major artillery and air strikes on the Chinese assembly points. Carey learned from captured POWs that most of the Chinese units at Hagaru-ri took a number of big hits from the Marines and that their "combat effectiveness had been reduced at least 50 percent."[40]

"I had faith in the division when they sent line crossers to us," General Carey said in answer to a question about how he knew that those providing intelligence were reliable and trustworthy. Years later, General Carey said that he did not know what happened to six of the seven line crossers who aided the East Hill battle. He learned that one line crosser served as a double agent. "Well, we killed him later on," General Carey said. While wearing the uniform of a Chinese officer, the double agent lost his life to American forces in early December on the road to Koto-ri during the withdrawal.[41]

More than 70 years after that battle, General Carey modestly explained, "East Hill was very important."[42] After the CCF's initial unsuccessful assault on Hagaru-ri's southwest perimeter on the night of the 28th, Chinese forces then attacked East Hill on the 29th. Again, the Marines stopped the CCF. The CCF then placed the heaviest concentration of their troops in the area against East Hill on November 30. Since enemy forces had failed to stop all of Task Force Drysdale on the road from Koto-ri to Hagaru-ri, the surviving combat available men of George Company also moved to East Hill on the 30th.

To aid in the battle for East Hill, General Carey said he organized a reaction platoon, consisting of 70 cooks, bakers, and others including band members, to form a blocking platoon. The men took additional ammunition, the lieutenant picked up a rifle and grenades, and they moved up the hill as the dark of night fell on November 30. Years later, General Carey referred to those Marines as "heroic." He added, "Those that I took upon the Hill with me did a good job."[43] One-time Private Bob Harbula agreed that the unit that Lieutenant Carey put together "fought like Marines."[44]

At this point another blessed moment occurred in Second Lieutenant Carey's life. The wounded, but still very much in command of 41 Commando, Lieutenant Colonel Drysdale happened to be in the CP as Carey prepared to head up to East Hill with his 70-man scratch platoon and three boxes of grenades. Seeing the young lieutenant in only a field jacket, he asked Carey, "Where's your parka, lad?" When Carey replied he did not have one, Drysdale then said, "Then take mine," and removed his bloody parka and gave it to Carey. Carey, hauling one of the boxes of grenades, proceeded to East Hill with his reaction platoon. Halfway up the hill Carey decided to take a break to catch his breath. While sitting next to his box of grenades, a sniper took a shot that hit nearby. Carey, not moving, then felt a jolt when a sniper's second shot hit him square in the front of his cartridge belt. Carey decided to get moving as fast as he could up the hill. When he later checked his belt buckle, he saw the bullet had hit the center front of the belt, traveled along the belt around his waist, then exited exactly at the center rear of the belt. He did not receive a scratch. When he came off the hill two days later, he gave the parka back to Drysdale, who saw the bullet holes in the front and back. With characteristic dry humor, he asked, "Where's the blood, lad?" Carey replied, "God was on my side."[45]

Disturbing to Lieutenant Carey was the lack of leadership in his old platoon. His replacement as 1st Platoon leader in George Company became "a battle casualty psychologically," the General explained. Captain Sitter, commanding officer of George Company, needed a new platoon leader. He said, "I want Carey." That did not result in a straight-up change of position for the lieutenant. Carey now had two jobs. In addition to serving as platoon commander, he continued his assignment as the battalion's S-2. In less than two weeks, the lieutenant was temporarily back in the fight with his old platoon.[46]

When Carey arrived at the hill with his replacement troops, he saw his old platoon coming down the hill. Carey turned them around and brought them back up the hill along with the 70 troops he assembled from battalion headquarters. Company Commander Captain Sitter[47] ordered Carey to take over both the first and second platoons. The captain placed the majority of the 70 men from the reaction force in the platoons Carey commanded.[48]

Although George Company reached the crest of East Hill at about 4 p.m. on the 30th, it could not completely close the gap to its left. Four hours later, George Company heard Chinese bugle calls and at 8:30 p.m., they spotted enemy flares. Chinese small arms fire began shortly before midnight.[49] As day turned to night, the Chinese had a greater advantage since the Marines did not get air support at night. In addition, on East Hill, the enemy soldiers badly outnumbered the Marines. Conditions were appalling. The troops endured a wind chill factor that once dropped to an estimated minus 65 degrees. Frozen ground reached 19 inches deep making entrenchment of fighting holes (foxholes) almost impossible. At times, Marines stacked dead Chinese soldiers around their fighting holes as protection from both the enemy and the elements.

Carey moved between two platoons on East Hill on the 30th through the night of December 1. At one point, he found Staff Sergeant Jack P. DeLoach in a foxhole. DeLoach had taken over 2nd Platoon when his lieutenant suffered wounds and required evacuation. DeLoach, originally from Georgia, suffered shrapnel wounds before Carey arrived. He had blood pouring over his eyes making it difficult for him to see. Despite his wounds, DeLoach opened grenade canisters out of the fresh supply brought by Carey and his reaction platoon and handed them one by one to Carey. Lieutenant Carey pulled the pins and hurled them at the advancing CCF. While all this was going on, Carey at one point watched a Marine pilot fly away. He said to DeLoach, "That guy's going back to Japan. He is going to have a steak tonight and a shower. When this is over, that's what I'm going to do."[50] Carey's comment was not just a random thought. By that time, he had already submitted his application for aviation training.

At that point, Carey thought, "I'd better get busy if I want to see tomorrow." DeLoach eventually went to the battalion aid station. Staff Sergeant DeLoach survived and lived more than 40 years after that night. Lieutenant Carey recommended the staff sergeant for a Silver Star; DeLoach received a Bronze Star instead. In September 1990, DeLoach wrote about his memories of that battle. That was when General Carey learned that no one ever put the staff sergeant in for the Purple Heart. Carey made sure that DeLoach received his Purple Heart. DeLoach wrote that an enemy grenade caused the facial wounds he received while heading back to East Hill with additional ammunition before he ran into Carey.

The Chinese were driving toward the ridgeline of East Hill. Lieutenant Carey's team held off the Chinese attack and restored the line until George Company was safe. Half of his old platoon lost their lives. "A lot of people died, bled to death," Carey explained. Snow and cold affected the troops. C-rations froze at night and thawed during the day. Water came from melted snow.

Just before 2:30 a.m. on December 1, George Company's left flank was in trouble. By 8 a.m., they regained the main line of resistance. "We held the hill," said General Carey. "Some of the best Marines I knew didn't make it," he added.[51]

The attacks on East Hill continued from December 2 to December 5, when 3rd Battalion, 5th Marines (3/5) relieved George Company. None of the attacks reached the intensity of those of November 30 through December 1. Lieutenant

Carey left East Hill on December 2. He returned to the battalion CP and resumed his duties as the battalion S-2, while George Company continued to battle the Chinese for control of East Hill for three more days. Had they had not stopped the Chinese at East Hill 1stMarDiv would not have been able to survive and reach Sea of Japan's coastline at Hungnam.[52] In his post-analysis written after going to Hungnam, Carey said that the enemy "failed to exploit his advantages on the nights of the 28th and 30th of November."[53]

Supply

The Air Force and Marine aviators airdropped supplies during daylight hours of December 2 to aid the badly outnumbered Marines. As a result, the Chinese had more success at night when not facing air power. In one happy accident, when isolated members of the 7th Marines began running low on mortar rounds, they requested resupply. The code name for 60mm mortar rounds was "Tootsie Roll." The Marine radio operator sent that request to the Air Force in Japan. Unfortunately, the airman receiving the request apparently failed to check his code sheets. Knowing the request was urgent, the airman called for a supply of Tootsie Rolls, the popular candy. The Air Force dropped pallets of Tootsie Rolls for Fox Company, 2nd Battalion, 7th Marines (F/2/7). Isolated, Fox Company guarded Toktong Pass, the key to keeping the road from Yudam-ni to Hagaru-ri open. The candy turned out to be a blessing to the Marines. Tootsie Rolls were portable, did not take up a lot of room, and provided quick energy. The Marines who received the candy shared it with other Marines, General Carey said. In addition, the tubular shaped candy also filled holes in bullet-riddled equipment such as radiators, gas tanks, and tires.[54]

After receiving the candy, the Marines again started the process to get the ammunition that they still needed. A second call got them the ammo. Private Robert L. Atkins, a truck driver with the 1st Engineer Battalion, 1stMarDiv said that Tootsie Rolls "were just about all I lived on," because his food froze. He added that Ellen Gordon, the president of Tootsie Roll Industries, attended his battalion's reunions.[55] (In 1950, Mrs. Gordon was the 18-year-old daughter of the founder of Tootsie Roll. She worked at the company when the Air Force dropped Tootsie Rolls to the Marines at the reservoir.) Over the years, Mrs. Gordon attended Chosin Few annual reunions and always brought plenty of Tootsie Rolls.

Retired Gunnery Sergeant Harry K. Peterson confirmed the lack of food in Korea. Sergeant Peterson, an ammunition technician with the

1st Ordnance Battalion of the 1stMarDiv, said his food froze and he was unable to heat it. As a result, he often ate only fruit cocktail, crackers, and other dry rations.[56]

A later study even indicated some Americans at the Chosin Reservoir died of starvation. One 23-year-old Marine private lost his life from an enemy bullet on December 8 near Koto-ri. His remains were returned to the United States in 1954 and later identified by the Defense POW Accounting Agency (DPAA). Researchers discovered that the private ate a starvation diet consisting of mustard seeds and a form of a wild rose: he had been hungry and foraged for food. The food eaten by the private was worse than what captors fed POWs and was "pretty much inedible unless you are absolutely starving."[57]

After East Hill

A significant directive came on December 2 when General MacArthur ordered X Corps troops (including the Marines) to return to Hungnam. At about the same time, engineers completed the airfield at Hagaru-ri. That airfield provided support for transport aircraft carrying the wounded out and bringing in supplies and equipment.

In the first week of December, Marine aviators evacuated more than 2,600 men from Hagaru-ri. Enemy POWs provided information about their heavy casualties. The POW officers "reported they doubted if a major attack could again be initiated without reinforcement(s)." The Marines captured so many enemy soldiers that they expanded the size of the stockade. In addition, enemy forces shared one thing with their American counterparts: the CCF suffered from frostbite too.[58]

General Smith, 1stMarDiv commanding general, met with reporters on December 4. Smith said, "We are not retreating. We are attacking in another direction."[59]

Korea was not Carey's first encounter with General Smith. Smith led the training program at Quantico when Lieutenant Carey went through TBS two years earlier. In 2021, General Carey acknowledged that he did not have any direct interaction with Smith at Quantico. Carey explained that General Smith was "the big boss" at Quantico and he (Carey) was a second lieutenant. He pointed out, "[At the Chosin Reservoir] once again, General Smith was the big boss and I was still a second lieutenant."

A few days later, Colonel Puller backed up General Smith's comments, when meeting with a reporter. The colonel said, "Remember whatever you write, that was no retreat. All that happened was that we found more Chinese in front of us, so we about-faced and attacked."

Media coverage, however, did not always take this line. "Allies Flee from surging Chinese," was the headline in the *Columbus (NE) Telegram* on December 4. The *Kansas City (MO) Times* stated on the same day that, "It was learned on responsible authority that top government and military officials now regard the immediate military situation with unrelieved anxiety." "U.S. losses are heavy in Korean War," headlined an Associated Press story in *The Sun Times* in Owen Sound, Ontario, Canada on December 5, while a few days later on December 13 the *San Francisco Examiner* announced, "Allies reported fleeing Northeast Korea by sea; U.S. Britain favor truce."

On December 5, when George Company was relieved on East Hill, the company moved to provide perimeter defense at the west end of the airstrip. Meanwhile, 3/1 prepared to break out with the rest of the division. The point unit of the 1stMarDiv convoy, commanded by Lieutenant Colonel Ray Davis's[60] 1/7, left Hagaru-ri on the morning of December 6, moving down the MSR on the 64-mile trip. 3/1, including its S-2, Lieutenant Carey, was positioned toward the tail end of the convoy and left Hagaru-ri the morning of December 7. They arrived in Koto-ri in the late afternoon that same day.[61]

By midnight on December 7, traffic clogged up on the single-lane dirt MSR, delaying arrival into Koto-ri of the division rear guard. Sergeant Peterson served as part of an eight-man rear guard on the road to Koto-ri. The sergeant said that he and his men were "very watchful" as they moved down the mountain. Sergeant Peterson described the trek as "spooky."[62]

Facing bitter cold the night of the 8th at Koto-ri, General Carey said the men prayed. In the darkened sky appeared a single star. General Carey said, "We then knew that it signified that we were going to make it out." Later, that star became the logo of the veterans of the Chosin Reservoir campaign. Those who spent the night at Koto-ri never forgot that shining star. "It is cherished as the Star of Koto-ri," General Carey said. Nearly 70 years later, the memory of that star would come into play with the dedication of the National Chosin Few Monument. General Carey and fellow veterans of the Chosin Reservoir campaign wear Star of Koto-ri lapel pins to distinguish themselves as "The Chosin Few."

At around midnight on December 8, a Chinese force, estimated to be nearly 1,000 soldiers, struck the division at Koto-ri. The Marines fought back leaving the Chinese with 300 casualties including 50 dead and 250 wounded.

On December 9, the division buried their dead from battles from Yudam-ni to Hagaru-ri to Koto-ri in a mass grave scraped out of the frozen ground by bulldozers.

Then 3/1, as part of the division, moved out of Koto-ri going south on the MSR to Funchilin Pass.[63] Watson Crumbie, then a staff sergeant, recalled that the temperature dropped to 50 degrees below zero that day.[64]

Honoring the Fallen

As Section Leader of Graves Registration for 1/7, Staff Sergeant Robert B. Gault described his work during a July 10, 1951, interview for the Korean War Project by the USMC History Division. Gault, a Chicagoan with a love for football, entered the Marine Corps in 1948 and arrived in Korea for the Inchon landing. The staff sergeant's plainspoken language showed the passion and dedication that he had for his work—work that earned Gault a Commendation Ribbon with a "V." (The Commendation Ribbon was re-designated a Navy Commendation Medal in 1960 and in 1990 changed to the Navy and Marine Corps Commendation medal.) Gault's citation signed by General Smith recognized his courage. In part, the citation read:

> Regardless of danger or personal fatigue, he repeatedly volunteered to go forward of the friendly front lines to remove the dead. On numerous occasions, it was necessary for him to kill to drive off enemy snipers before his mission could be accomplished. At times when he was pinned down by enemy small arms and automatic fire, he courageously fought his way out and continued on his mission.

Gault's efforts to find the 3/7 commander, Lieutenant Colonel Harris, last seen on the MSR near Koto-ri, demonstrated his approach to his task. During his interview with the History Division, Gault described the search for Harris:

> We searched the area. We even went against orders. We were not supposed to go—and we went out anyway because all the boys wanted to find Colonel Harris.[65]

One unidentified wounded Marine Corporal commented, "Whenever a wounded man froze to death, we took him off the truck and left him on the road." The Graves Registration unit would pick up the bodies.[66] Graves Registration identified all of the dead before the burial, Gault explained. They did not declare a Marine dead until identified. The Marines considered anyone unidentified as MIA.[67]

In describing the mass-grave burial, Gault said his five men laid the bodies out in rows, placed ponchos over them, and covered the graves. Chaplains from each faith spoke at a brief ceremony attended by General Smith and a number of other Marine senior officers.[68] Gault saw Colonel Litzenberg cry at the burial sites. "It was one of the saddest days in Marine Corps history."[69] Unlike other burial sites, there were no religious symbols or flowers placed that day.

While General Carey and those who lived through Koto-ri always remembered the star in sky, they never forgot those Marines buried in the frozen earth of North Korea.

Breaking Out from Chosin

Along with enemy fire and frigid temperatures, UN forces moving down the MSR faced another obstacle: the Chinese had destroyed the bridge over the Funchilin Pass, 5 miles south of Koto-ri. The Marines called for the Air Force to drop eight Treadway bridge sections out of C-119 transport aircraft, known as flying boxcars. Treadway bridges were floating (or pontoon) bridges—no one had ever tried dropping them out of an aircraft before.

Time worked against the Air Force and Marines. Each section of the bridge weighed 2,500 pounds. A test drop at Yonpo Airfield destroyed one bridge section. Aircrew members then attached two large parachutes to each bridge section, in case one fell off. C-119 pilots from 62nd Airlift Squadron of the 314th Troop Carrier Group, led by Squadron Commander Lieutenant Colonel Royal S. Thompson, dropped down to 800 feet, which made the C-119s easier targets for the CCF. However, pilots did drop eight sections after testing. Thompson led the eight C-119s while wearing his signature non-uniform red beret, according to his daughter, Sandy Thompson Carroll.[70]

Severe damage from the drop made one section unusable and the CCF captured another section. Engineers used the remaining six sections to span the gap. Lieutenant Colonel Partridge's engineers replaced the bridge on the morning of December 9,[71] enabling the division to continue moving south.[72] According to General Carey, "The Treadway bridge pieces over the blown-out section at Funchilin Pass saved 1,700 vehicles and many thousands of Americans, British, and Korean troops. Coming out with us was also a long, long line of North Korean citizens who wanted to go south for freedom."

General Carey said of the Chosin Few's journey, "The odds were so terrible. God brought us out. We did not do it ourselves. That had to be God." Nine members of the North Texas Chapter of the Chosin Few (NTCF) became ordained ministers after surviving their Chosin experience.[73] They shared General Carey's strong Christian faith.

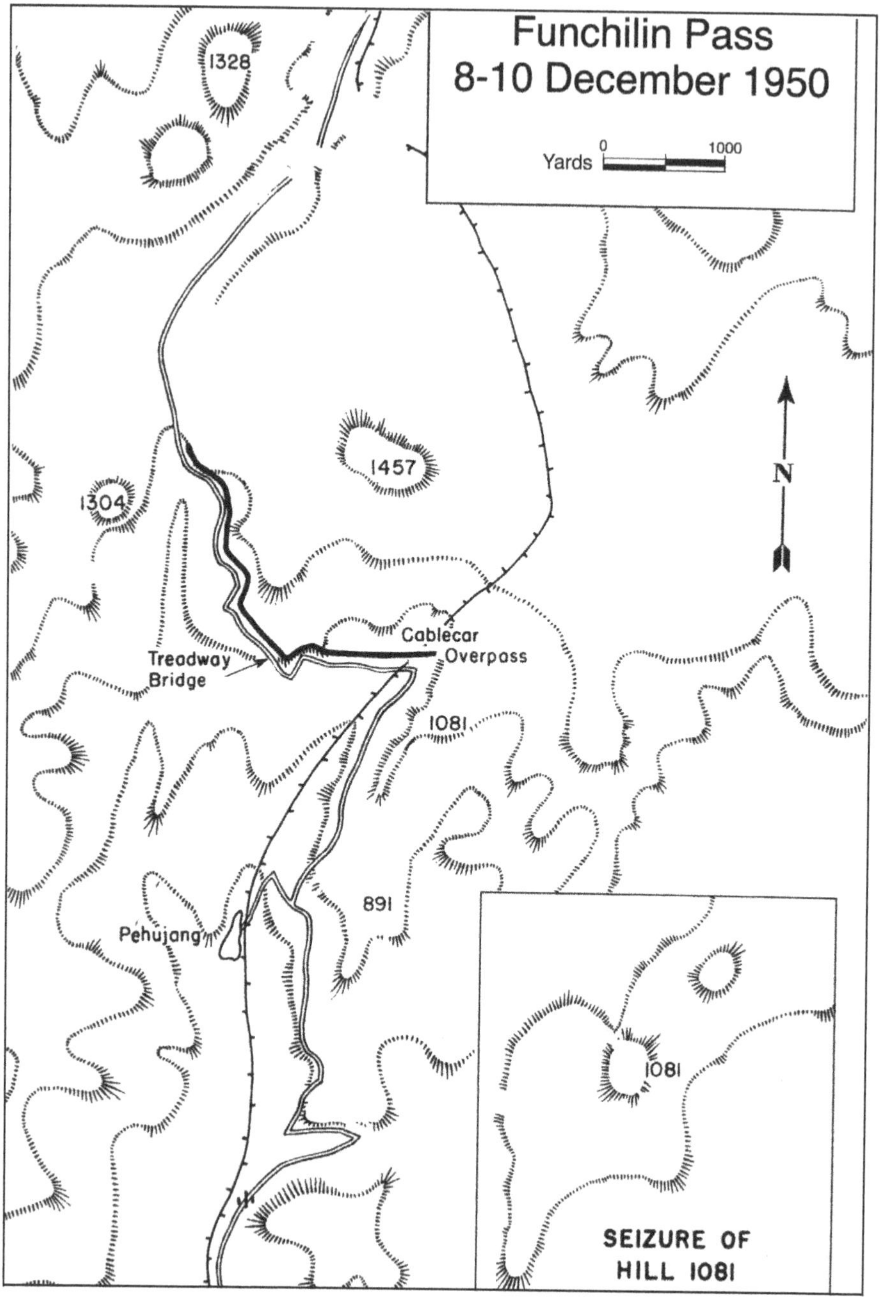

Air Force C-119s dropped sections of Treadway bridges. Marine engineers placed the sections that permitted troops and equipment to cross the Funchilin Pass in December 1950. Captain Robert H. Barrow's A/1/1 benefited from the blinding snow as they took Hill 1081. (United States Marine Corps History Division)

Carey praised the aid and protection that the division received from Captain Robert H. Barrow, company commander of Alpha Company, 1st Battalion, 1st Marines (A/1/1). Barrow's company came up the pass as Carey's battalion came down with the rest of the division. A/1/1 climbed Hill 1081 single file in a blinding snowstorm and surprised the CCF. Barrow said, "Had it not been snowing, we would never have taken 1081." A/1/1 spent two nights on the hill in minus 25-degree weather.[74] The captain's company "kept us from being decimated," General Carey said.[75] Barrow's leadership at Funchilin Pass between December 9 and 10 earned him the Navy Cross.

Although 1stMarDiv faced sniper fire, it continued to Chinhung-ni and on to the Hamhung/Hungnam area. Some of the division units boarded trucks and others took trains from Chinhung-ni south 43 miles to Hamhung. On December 12, the division handled "routine administrative tasks" and prepared to board ship at Hungnam. Despite all the Marines had gone through at Hagaru-ri, there was another assignment—loading the ships. 3/1 left camp the next afternoon at 1:30. The battalion reached the loading area at 3 p.m. and began loading the USS *Buckner* at 8 p.m.

The Marines came out of Chosin, according to a December 12 story by Keyes Beech, a Chicago Daily News Service reporter, "as an organized unit with most of their equipment." They brought out all of the wounded and many of the dead. They buried those who they could not bring back in the battlefields.[76]

Reporter Fred Sparks followed the Marines from near Hagaru-ri to Hungnam. Sparks wrote about the Marines' refusal to surrender and their leadership. He described the unshaven faces covered in dirt, frozen and disfigured lips, frozen canteens, and those huddled in the back of open trucks. He predicted that the mission "will forever be an inspiration to those of us who saw them.[77]

General Carey remembered that he did not shave for 15 days. "I had a beard," he said. Payne, the Royal Marine, said Commandos shaved "every day when possible." He even shaved using "a canteen cup half full of warmish coffee."[78] Carey also pointed out that the only Marines who rode in trucks were the wounded. The General said that he walked.[79]

From General Carey's perspective, the Chosin Reservoir proved that the Chinese Communists could not defeat the forces of the United Nations. "The cost was high for both sides," he pointed out, and listed several examples. A Marine rifle company from the 7th Marines that started with 220 men at Yudam-ni ended up with only 20 able to fight. The Marines suffered 4,000 battle casualties plus 8,000 non-battle casualties, with frostbite the main cause of non-battle casualties. The Chinese suffered at least 50,000 battle and non-battle casualties.[80] The General also offered these explanations for the success of the UN forces despite facing significantly higher numbers of enemy soldiers: "We had the advantage of air and the Chinese had no air or artillery. We had the will to win … I think in reality, the Chinese had been so decimated at that time that it kind of appeared to us that they really wanted to let us out because they were taking so many casualties."[81]

As General Carey reflected on his experience at the Chosin Reservoir, he said that it was "because of the spirit of the Marines. They had to fight, win, and eventually fight their way out." He pointed out that Marines took care of each other: "That was instilled in the beginning. They learned it from the drill instructors. They were motivated in boot camp."[82] Private Atkins, then 20, exemplified that spirit when he spoke about moving down the mountain. Atkins, originally from Lubbock, Texas, said, "I knew we were gonna get out of there. Never entered my mind (that) we wouldn't get out of there. We were all gonna get out."[83] In addition, the division was led top to bottom by WWII combat veteran officers and senior NCOs.

CHAPTER 4

Reflections on Chosin Reservoir

Americans had rallied behind the military in World War II. The attack on Pearl Harbor in Hawaii united the nation. The war in Korea, by contrast, never generated popular support. The United States, for the first time in history, fought a war that did not result in a victory. In fact, returning service members did not receive parades honoring their sacrifice. Many referred to Korea as the "forgotten war." Yet, for Richard E. Carey, the Korean War established him as a leader. His service in Korea led to 33 more years in the Marine Corps. His heroics in Korea became part of his legacy. Military leaders recognized that service when he retired.

In 1950, the total Marine Corps force stood at just under 75,000. Officers, including Lieutenant Carey, totaled 7,254. At the peak, with reservists, there were 261,000 members of the Marine Corps on duty during the Korean War. By the end of the conflict in Korea, 4,267 Marines died and another 23,744 (including Lieutenant Carey) suffered wounds. The Marines accounted for 20 percent of all American military casualties in the Korean War.[1]

General Carey's Report

After his time at the Chosin Reservoir, Carey wrote a 26-page undated report from his memory of events from November 23 to December 6, 1950. The yellowing pages remain in his files to this day. At the start of his report, Carey wrote that he would try "to recall certain points strictly from memory."

Lieutenant Carey's report, after coming out of the Chosin Reservoir battle, included several recommendations regarding intelligence. First, the intelligence team needed people "highly trained in all phases of the collection and deployment of intelligence." He said that his section did an "adequate job." The unit's biggest weakness was the lack of training, according to Carey.

He recommended more formal training and classroom work in the United States. In his report, Carey pointed to a need for selection of personnel specifically for the intelligence billet. Unfortunately, Lieutenant Carey explained, many in Korea assigned to intelligence wanted to return to rifle companies (himself included). He also pointed out that they did not have enough interpreters. Finally, Carey said, "Peacetime should be devoted to the training of all personnel in the ways of a potential enemy. Knowledge gained through battle is invaluable, but often very expensive." Overall, Carey pointed out that the report included his views and recollections. He also mentioned that many times he took off his intelligence hat and moved back to his duties with his old rifle platoon.[2]

Through the Eyes of Veterans

Media coverage about the Korean War years after the fighting ended highlighted the Chosin Reservoir. In September 1985, *Marines*, an official publication of the U.S. Marine Corps, interviewed a veteran of the Chosin battle, then Sergeant Major Ernest W. Arthur. The sergeant major was in his 39th year of service, having begun his career at age 17 in 1946. Arthur said this about his Chosin experience: "I didn't think about the things that went on at the Chosin (Reservoir) until years later. I look at everything said and written and find myself thinking it must have really been tough. But, while I was there, I just figured 'this is part of the job.' "[3]

More than 40 years after the Korean War, one-time Corporal Russell Roemmele, who served as a machine gunner in 1/7, 1stMarDiv, described the Chosin fight in a newspaper column he wrote for *Bloomfield Life*, a New Jersey paper. Roemmele's commentary was written in his capacity as co-chairman of an effort to raise funds for the Korean War Memorial built in Washington, D.C. He also served as president of the New Jersey Chapter of the Chosin Few. Describing his fellow Marines who fought at the reservoir, Roemmele said, "They did not for a moment consider surrendering. No one ever thought of deserting. We endured days under enemy fire, and each day friends would fall in the ice and snow."[4]

Another Chosin veteran did an interview with Diana Sevanian, a reporter for *The Signal* in Santa Clarita, California, in 2001. Don Henry lied about his age, enlisted in the Marine Corps at 16, and served with the 1stMarDiv at the Chosin Reservoir. "Chosin was a hellish place to be. Though severely outnumbered, we fought a heroic battle," he said. Mr. Henry, who spent

32 years in the Marine Corps Reserve added, "The Korean War should not be forgotten." He offered praise for General Smith.[5]

On the 60th anniversary of the battle of Chosin, Candace Page of the *Burlington Free Press* in Vermont interviewed Dave Erkson, a Marine corporal when in Korea. He served as machine gunner in 2nd Battalion, 5th Marine Regiment (2/5) at the reservoir. Erkson recalled sleeping fully clothed in an unzipped sleeping bag despite subzero temperatures. He explained that the zipper on the sleeping bag could stick in the cold if he had to exit in a hurry. Erkson, 80 at the time of the interview, was only 20 when he was at Chosin. He described one encounter that he had with the Chinese. A fellow Marine roused him from his sleep to show him an enemy soldier standing 10 feet away. Erkson's machine gun jammed. His friend held off the enemy with an M-1 rifle while Erkson cleared his weapon. Later, Erkson realized that a bullet had dented his helmet. Erkson said that during the battle "mobs" of Chinese attacked. "We did pretty well. We did not come out on our hands and knees. We came out with our heads up. I can't say I liked it up there, but I'm proud of what we did." Erkson made a career of the Marine Corps. He retired as a gunnery sergeant after 22 years of service.[6]

On November 10, 2010, more than 250 Korean War veterans went to Seoul, Republic of Korea to commemorate the 60th anniversary of the Chosin Reservoir battle. ROK Defense Minister Kim Tae-young spoke. He said, "Today we have the great honor to be in the presence of the heroes of this battle. The Republic of Korea will always remember you." U.S. Army General Walter L. Sharp, Commander, United Nations Command, Combined Forces Command and U.S. Forces Korea also spoke. The general praised those who served at the Chosin Reservoir when he talked about the outnumbered service members who fought "in the bitter cold." General Sharp added, "We owe you a debt of gratitude that cannot be repaid."[7]

Rayburn Blair, a Chosin Reservoir Marine veteran who served with 3/1and later became a Christian minister, wrote a poem that appeared in the July-August-September 2021 issue of *The Chosin Few Digest*. It included these lines:

> Yes, we slept, working, looking, and even talking
> The last few miles out of Chosin, I slept walking,
> After much of the firing had stopped, but remembered
> Nothing of events or time it took. Yet no one noticed.
> I must have been doing my job whether asleep or just blacked out, I do not know.

The words Mr. Blair used in his poem summed up what Carey and his fellow Chosin Few Marines went through.

The Impact of Chosin

Tootsie Rolls helped Marines survive the Chosin Reservoir. Ellen Gordon, President of Tootsie Rolls Industries, received a plaque from General Carey honoring the company's support for the Chosin Memorial. (Carey family collection, 2017).

In a post-9/11 address to a group from the Daughters of the American Revolution (DAR), General Carey compared the Chosin Reservoir campaign to General George Washington's winter at Valley Forge, Pennsylvania. The General told the DAR the battle at the Chosin Reservoir "does not receive its just due." In his speech, General Carey said that at Yudam-ni on November 27, 1950, the Marines faced blowing snow, with a wind chill factor of 65 degrees below zero. To keep engines from freezing over, the vehicles continuously ran. Water in their canteens froze. Weapons froze. Even the food froze. Eventually "Tootsie Rolls," General Carey said, "were the main staple." Four days earlier, General Carey said, the Marines received orders from General MacArthur, ordering them "to boldly advance up the mountain road to the Chosin Reservoir, then to advance to the Yalu River, and then be home by Christmas."

In his DAR speech, General Carey also pointed out that after pushing back to the sea the fighting was far from over for the Marines. In January 1951, he prepared for additional battles. General Carey also quoted from an open letter written by Ed Bertholet, a Marine veteran of the Korean War. Mr. Bertholet said,

> Sadly, in today's American education practices, the Korean War is reduced to a five-paragraph description in our history books. Servicemen returning from Korea were lost in our population as we were intent upon getting on with our lives. Our numerical rate of return was an insignificant impact on everyday American life. Many of our classmates from high school did not even know we had been gone. The Korean veterans had no voice or spokesman to tell our story. The Korean War has been the only war in American history that does not have even one song dedicated to it. What was the impact of the Korean War? The communist philosophy "conquest by force of arms" was controlled and defeated. We preserved a free people and nation, South Korea, as we know it today. The Korean War was catalyst for the eventual downfall of communism as a major threat to world peace. Korea was the opening engagement of the cold war era. The forgotten war is a testament to patriotic service equal to that of any generation of Americans. We have given the unique and lasting contribution of our silent generation to the honor of our country.

On September 10, 2000, General Carey and fellow Chosin Few Marine Corps veterans gathered for a reunion marking the 50th anniversary of that battle. Interviewed by a reporter for the *Herald Democrat* in Sherman, Texas, General Carey commented on the Chosin Reservoir:

> Yeah, we have reruns of what happened and the stories start to stretch, but this is a bond we share that makes us special. When they named it "The Chosin Few," they named it right. The hell we went through together, that's what brings us here today.[8]

1stMarDiv Commanding General Major General O. P. Smith at gravesite on December 13, 1950, where he paid tribute to Marines killed from Yudam-ni to Hagaru-ri. (United States Marine Corps History Division)

In 2013, the General received a certificate of appreciation from Secretary of Defense Leon E. Panetta honoring the 60th anniversary of the Korean War truce. The words on the certificate included:

> In recognition of honorable service during the Korean War in defense of Democracy and Freedom. Through your selfless sacrifices, the tide of communism on the Korean Peninsula was halted and liberty triumphed over tyranny. The Department of Defense and the people of American and Korea are forever grateful.

CHAPTER 5

After Chosin Reservoir

Following Koto-ri in December 1950, Second Lieutenant Carey and his unit went to Chinhung-ni. There the Marines joined forces with an Army unit to form a defensive perimeter. Then, the troops boarded a train to the Hamhung/Hungnam area where they went to a bivouac also called a rest camp. The General remembered that he slept for 18 hours and ate hot meals. For the first time since Thanksgiving, he ate food that did not come out of a can. However, moving from the Chosin Reservoir to the sea did not mean the war ended. Despite General MacArthur talking about ending the war by Christmas of 1950, Americans faced enemy fire in Korea until late July 1953.

Along their way to Hungnam, the Marines picked up abandoned Army equipment such as 105 howitzers, trucks, and jeeps. With a smile, General Carey made this comment about the equipment, "Many of those vehicles were repainted and made Marine. Finders keepers, I guess," he said.[1] General Carey acknowledged, with a mischievous grin, that while the Marines might not always have all the equipment they needed, they always had paint.

Following a brief rest period, the battalion members regrouped. They prepared to load the remaining equipment on ships in Hungnam Harbor.

LVTs took Carey's group to a familiar ship—the *Simon B. Buckner*, the ship that brought him to Korea. The *Buckner's* crew prepared the ship for members of the Marine Corps and the Army for their three-day trip to Pusan. With the large number of Marines and Army troops, the ship lacked enough bunks for everyone. As a result, sleeping required a rotating schedule. To help make that work, the *Buckner's* cooks kept the chow line open all day. As far as sleeping quarters for himself, Carey, the one-time Sea Marine, had an alternative. He knew the warmest place on the ship was the boilerplates, so he slept there during that trip. After arriving in Pusan, the Marines offloaded the ship and went to Masan, an agricultural area also known as the "bean patch." They remained in Masan for about five weeks.[2]

With the holidays approaching, Carey again received a command task. His reputation for getting things done led to a beer run. He had to obtain beer for the battalion from an Army depot. To aid his effort, the lieutenant, still the battalion S-2, borrowed the runner and ultimate George Company scrounger, Private Wasylczak, better known as "Waz." Getting beer appeared to be a much easier task than fighting Chinese and North Koreans, until the two Marines arrived at the depot. First, the soldier at the depot claimed he did not have authorization to sell beer to Marines. Second, their vehicle that would bring the beer back to the unit went missing. Waz came up big when he helped Lieutenant Carey get an Army officer's rank insignia—larger than the rank insignia that Marine officers wore. With "borrowed" rank insignia, Carey's beer "purchase" won approval. Then, Waz commandeered a replacement vehicle large enough to carry the beer.

Before he left for the beer run, Carey received a bottle of homemade wine from his grandfather in Ohio. He left it on his bunk in Masan. When he returned, the bottle was gone. It turned out, Carey later heard, the chaplain needed the wine for communion.[3]

While at Masan, the Marines received replacement troops and more equipment. Carey continued in his S-2 assignment. As plans got underway for an attack, Lieutenant Carey was working on a map, when in walked Eighth Army commander Lieutenant General Matthew B. Ridgway.[4] The general asked Carey for a briefing. Carey said that he was certain General Ridgway already knew the Marines' plans. The lieutenant noticed two things about General Ridgway. First, he was, as General Carey said in 2005, "a true combat warrior who carried grenades on his shoulder straps." Second, he described General Ridgway as "a down- to-earth-guy." The lieutenant remembered his 15–20-minute meeting with the general. "That impressed me that a man of his position would take that much time with a lowly second lieutenant. He did what a 'leader' is supposed to do."[5]

Heavy Machine Guns—New Assignment

For three days after meeting with General Ridgway, Carey remained with the battalion headquarters Company as the S-2. He then received a new assignment as commanding officer of Heavy Weapons Platoon, 3/1. Major Edwin H. (Ed) Simmons, who commanded the 3/1 Weapons Company, already knew Carey from their time together in 1/6 at Camp Lejeune and recommended Carey take over the heavy machine guns platoon. Simmons later became the battalion operations officer (S-3). [6]

In his new position, Lieutenant Carey led the heavy Machine Gun Platoon. The platoon had six Browning .30 caliber water-cooled heavy machine guns. Each gun had a gunner, assistant gunner, and four ammunition carriers. Cans of ammunition weighed between 25 and 30 pounds. Leading this platoon turned out to be Lieutenant Carey's last ground combat assignment in the Korean War.

Acknowledging that he would have preferred going back to a rifle company, the General later said that he grew to like his new assignment. There was one Weapons Company for each infantry battalion. The General explained the role of the Heavy Weapons Platoon in the weapons company along with the rifle companies, when he said, "Of course, what we usually did in the attack is we assigned a section of .30 caliber water-cooled 'heavies' to each of the three rifle companies." There were two heavies per section. He added, "A section of heavies was used in setting up the platoons' bases of fire."[7]

Mid-morning on March 23, 1950, Carey was with How Company, 3/1 when the battalion operations officer made an emergency call to him. "Item Company was in a buzz saw of a fight," the operations officer told Carey as he requested two more heavy machine guns. Carey and his men joined with Item Company for the attack on a hill against the Chinese.[8] The lieutenant and two of his men moved toward the top of the hill known as Hill 550. As they prepared to position their guns, the gunner and his team placed the machine gun on a tripod. General Carey explained the role of the weapons unit: "The rifle company commander would utilize the heavies in the base of fire because they provided a high sustained rate of fire and they were good for long distance. Their tripod was such that you could pretty well zero in on targets and provide a lot of fire. So they were very valuable weapons in the attack."[9]

Wounded—Heading Out of Korea

As Carey set up his teams, an enemy mortar landed near him. The force of the mortar round blew Carey off the ridge of Hill 550. Within 10 yards of him were two of his men. Both of them died from mortar wounds. Again, Carey felt the hand of God. Briefly knocked unconscious, Lieutenant Carey suffered from shrapnel wounds and a broken left wrist. The mortar round bent Carey's left hand back toward his elbow. That should have been enough for him to seek medical attention, but Carey's men wrapped his handkerchief around his wounded wrist and he did not head to the aid station. Carey remained in the fight. The corpsman who gave Carey morphine told him that he needed to go the aid station. Carey responded, "Yes, but not until my job is done."[10] Despite the pain from his wounds, Lieutenant Carey went back to continue the battle for Hill 550. He positioned the guns and stayed with Item Company as they continued the attack that drove the Chinese from the next hill.[11] Item Company's commander, Captain Joseph R. "Bull" Fisher, ordered him to the aid station. The General described Fisher as a "blood and guts type guy."[12] That description was well earned.[13]

Finally, Carey walked, unaided, about 500 yards down the hill to the aid station. While Lieutenant Carey was at the aid station, medics cleaned out the shrapnel and placed him in an ambulance that took him back to Masan. Doctors at the aid station told him that they could not fix the wound to his hand there and he would probably have to go back to the United States. If that happened, the disappointed young officer knew that would end his combat tour.

Lieutenant Carey went to a hospital ship where doctors did "an amazing job" of straightening out his hand. As the General explained, he later took up golf and needed a good left hand to swing the club. He ultimately played to a 13 handicap that had him consistently scoring in the mid-80s. Colonel James M. Pendergast, USMC (Ret), a fellow golfer who served under Carey in two assignments during the 1970s and 1980s, described the General's golf game as "highly competitive." He added that the General "never learned the meaning of a 'gimmee putt.'"[14]

Carey was on the hospital ship for a short stay. From there, doctors sent him to a military hospital in Yokosuka, the port he had left a little more than six months earlier to prepare for the Inchon landing in Korea. He arrived there in early April. Initially, the medical staff at Yokosuka attempted rehabilitation of his hand so that he could return to Korea. When the doctors in Japan could do no more for his hand, the lieutenant flew back to the States to a hospital in Mare Island, California. The injuries to Lieutenant Carey ended his combat time in Korea.

Although Carey had great success in combat as a "grunt" (infantry), he still wanted to be a pilot. In fact, Carey was waiting to hear the status of his application for aviation training.

Carey spent most of May and June 1951 in California. There, he underwent two operations on his left wrist and received a long-term cast that he wore for two months.[15] From California, Lieutenant Carey drove his car to Great Lakes Training Center, located on Lake Michigan about 40 miles north of Chicago. He explained that he drove the 2,100-mile trip using only his right hand. Fortunately, his Ford had an automatic transmission. He only spent one night on the road as he wanted to get to Great Lakes as soon as possible. The base, opened in 1911, serves as the Navy's only boot camp and was the closest Navy hospital to Columbus, his hometown. After being nearly 6,800 miles from home, Carey was now only 360 miles away from Columbus, Ohio. At Great Lakes, he received additional rehabilitation on his hand and wrist. The lieutenant left the hospital in late July with 30 days' leave. Carey then returned to Ohio. He saw his family for the first time in nearly two years.

Return to Parris Island

In September 1951, Carey went back on active duty. It had been nearly six months since the mortar round injured him. Promoted to first lieutenant by that time, Carey received orders for his next assignment. He left Columbus and drove back to Parris Island where he had begun his Marine Corps career as a recruit in 1946. He returned to the Marine Corps boot camp as a decorated combat veteran and an officer. Five years earlier, recruit Carey had trained under a drill instructor (DI) Sergeant Kozak. In his new assignment, Carey led a company of DIs, although Kozak was no longer at Parris Island. Carey's role was to make sure that the DIs did not "get out of hand with the training." In his view, DIs were the "heroes" of the Marine Corps. Since the DIs reported to him, General Carey said there was one thing that he did not appreciate about the job. He missed not having direct contact with the troops in this assignment and did not like that.

On the Way to Marine Aviation

While at Parris Island, Carey made multiple contacts to Headquarters Marine Corps about his aviation application. He was persistent, yet all that he heard was, "It's under consideration."[16] Meanwhile, the lieutenant continued working with the DIs. Part of the training process of recruits was weeding out those with attitude problems or lack of discipline. Those recruits received an early discharge from the Marine Corps, according to the General. After two months at Parris Island, the 23-year-old with nearly six years of service received his dream assignment—aviation training at Pensacola Naval Air Station in the Florida panhandle. Persistence had paid off—his career path was about to change. His orders for October 1, 1951, read in part "for duty involving flying under instruction as a Naval Aviator with the Naval Air Base Training Command for a period of about 18 months."

189 Days Launched a Career

Korea launched Carey's career. A one-time "grunt," Carey headed for flight training. Tested in battle over 189 days, and as a leader in desperate situations, the young officer succeeded. Senior officers recognized his courage. They recognized him as a "doer" with great potential. No matter where Carey's career in the Marine Corps took him, Korea would always be his base, his ground zero, and his launching pad. In many ways, his Korean War experience, particularly at the Chosin Reservoir, defined Carey as a Marine leader. He survived near-death experiences. Never did he quit, nor did he let his fellow Marines quit. At no time did Carey lead from the rear. No challenge was insurmountable. Throughout it all, Carey maintained his faith in God.

CHAPTER 6

Aviation Career Begins

After arriving at Pensacola, the now first lieutenant learned that his efforts as a machine gun platoon commander on March 23, 1951, had earned him recognition with the awarding of the Silver Star Medal. He received the medal at Pensacola. The citation he received read:

> The President of the United States of America takes pleasure in presenting the Silver Star to Second Lieutenant Richard Edward Carey, United States Marine Corps, for conspicuous gallantry and intrepidity in action against the enemy as a Machine Gun Platoon Commander of Weapons Company, Third Battalion, First Marines, FIRST Marine Division (Reinforced), in action against enemy aggressor forces in Korea on 23 March 1951. Although painfully wounded in the arm by enemy shell fragments when an accurate hostile mortar barrage inflicted heavy casualties on his platoon, Second Lieutenant Carey refused to be evacuated and continued to direct effective fire on the enemy in support of the company's assault elements. After skillfully reorganizing his platoon, he personally supervised and directed the evacuation of the wounded men in his unit before permitting himself to be evacuated. By his courageous leadership, marked coolness under fire and inspiring devotion to duty, Second Lieutenant Carey contributed materially to the success achieved by his company and upheld the highest traditions of the United States Naval Service.

He also received the Purple Heart on April 10, 1951, for the wounds that he suffered on March 23. Along with the Silver Star and Bronze Star, Second Lieutenant Carey earned four battle stars for his wartime service in Korea.

The aspiring Marine pilot quickly learned he faced new challenges. First, he had to pass the flight physical. The lieutenant had three potential physical liabilities that could keep him from getting through the exam. Two challenges came from his time in Korea. His recent injury left him with a weakened left hand, a condition that stayed with him throughout his life. Second, he suffered from frostbite. Then there was the ruptured kidney he had suffered in high school. Lieutenant Carey simply did not mention any of those issues. He managed to pass the physical exam. His next obstacle in the training program turned out to be one of his instructors, a Navy officer. Before he faced the instructor, he had to pass one examination for the five-week pre-flight course. The course normally took 10 weeks, but if a candidate could pass the test in five weeks, then he could begin flight instruction. Classes covered flight requirements, flight engineering, weather, and navigation. "Navigation was the key," the General said. The instructors gave the navigation exam last. Once trainees passed the navigation exam, they could move on to the next section of their flight-training program. Failure meant the candidates had to take a 14-week course. Lieutenant Carey passed all five of the exams. One of his friends from Korea, E. E. "E-Square" Smith ended up taking the longer route. ("E-Square" Smith would play a role in Carey's personal life in the early 1960s.) Another friend from Korea, Hank Commiskey, who was the Marine Corps' first Medal of Honor recipient in Korea, also had to take the 14-week program.[1] While his friends went through the 14-week program, Lieutenant Carey went to a grass field called Pace Field in Wallace, Florida, located about 10 miles from Pensacola. There Carey continued flight training.

Despite a warning from a naval flight instructor that he never gave an "up" (passing grade) to a Marine, Captain Carey earned his wings as a Marine aviator. (Carey family collection, 1953)

By then, Carey received notice that he had been selected for promotion to captain. While he could not pin the silver bars of a captain on his uniform, he could soon expect promotion orders. Carey met one of his instructors, a Navy lieutenant. A Navy lieutenant holds the equivalent rank of a Marine Corps captain. The initial meeting did not go well for Carey. His instructor told him that he never gave a Marine Corps pilot "an up." In other words, the instructor did not pass Marine Corps pilot candidates. For a man from a broken home who grew up in poverty, walked a 10-mile round trip to school, survived a ruptured kidney, rose from the enlisted ranks, avoided death at least seven times in 189 days, suffered frostbite, and survived serious wounds, this was just another challenge. Lieutenant Carey was one of three aviator candidates working with the Navy instructor. He was also the lone Marine trainee in the group. Carey looked straight at his instructor and said four words, "I will show you." There were 18 primary flights ahead in an SNJ, also called T-6, a training aircraft.[2] For the first 17 flights, the Navy lieutenant flew with Carey providing instruction and critiques along the way. He sat directly behind Carey during those flights. Trainees took tests during the sixth and 13th flights. The General explained that the trainees passed the test or they washed out as an aviation candidate. Lieutenant Carey made both of the cuts. His 18th flight would be his first solo with the lieutenant observing on the ground. The General explained what happened on his solo flight. There were no problems, although the instructor tried to give him a negative or a "down" for dealing with cross winds. He mentioned that he became friends with other instructors and told them about his issues with his instructor. They, as the General put it, talked to "the head man." After his solo flight, Carey had a new flight instructor.

After soloing, Lieutenant Carey completed preliminary flight training. Next up came formation flying. Two trainees flew at the same time. One pilot was in the lead and one was on the other's wing. Then the young pilots switched roles. Looking back, General Carey said, "In those days at that stage, it's precarious flying." He added that the instructors were "edgy" during formation training flights. Every flight received a grade throughout the training program. During the process, pilot-trainees could only get two "downs" or negatives. If a trainee received a down, they had to take a recheck flight evaluated by another instructor. Two "downs" meant that a trainee had to face a review board to determine whether they were fit for aviation. Lieutenant Carey received one down for flying during a crosswind. He passed the recheck and did not receive another down.

Instrument flying rules (IFR) followed formation flight training. The U.S. Federal Aviation Administration's (FAA) *Instrument Flying Handbook* defines IFR as:

> Rules and regulations established by the FAA to govern flight under conditions in which flight by outside visual reference is not safe. IFR flight depends upon flying by reference to instruments in the flight deck, and navigation is accomplished by reference to electronic signals.[3]

With the instructor in the back seat, General Carey explained, the trainee went under a cloth hood that permitted the flyer to see only the instruments. Trainees could use only instruments for approaches, landings, and flying a specific route. The instructor served as a safety valve to prevent possible collisions with another aircraft. The General said that he had "no problem" with instrument flying. After that, the next training section covered tactics. In addition to practicing carrier landings, Lieutenant Carey and his fellow trainees worked maneuvers including wingovers, Lufbery circles, and Immelmanns.

In a wingover maneuver, the pilot takes the airplane into a steep climb followed by a vertical flat turn that is similar to turning a car. Pilots use Lufbery circles as a defensive position. When flying in formation, pilots form a defensive circle providing each aircraft with protection from enemy aircraft. Immelmanns are maneuvers allowing the pilots to reposition their aircraft. When doing an Immelmann, the pilot flies straight up, turns around, and comes back; in other words, the pilot does a vertical 180-degree maneuver.

The ability to do carrier takeoffs and landings determined if the pilot made the grade. According to General Carey, carrier landings required precise flying. Initially, pilots practice carrier landings by landing on outlines on the ground before attempting to land on a carrier deck. There was very little margin for error and Carey described the initial landings as "scary." He added:

> The thing about carrier landings that make it more frightening than anything else and particularly in your early stages of your training is, in essence, you're what we call "hanging on the prop." You are only about two or three knots above stall speed. You are very slow, extremely slow, and cocked up. That is a very uncomfortable position to be in. If you don't react quickly enough, why, you're dead.

Lieutenant Carey completed the carrier-landing portion of his training and became an aviator. He finished in the top 2 percent of his class and graduated in 13 months in what was supposed to be an 18-month program in December 1952. Carey did not have to take any "reflies." His days as a "grunt" ended with successful completion of flight school. Part of his graduation from pilot training, Lieutenant Carey said, included a stop at the commander's office where the commander pinned on Carey's wings. Then, he participated in a Marine aviator tradition. His fellow pilots pinned on another set of wings and pounded Carey's chest until the wings penetrated his skin. That happened, the General said, "So you'd remember." That pinning tradition ended in the 1990s. The General expressed his disdain for the change, when he made this comment, "The Marines did that to a point where the mommas complained so much about their little boys getting hurt that they had to quit." He added that he thought the wing pinning "was an honor."[4]

Following training at Pensacola, Carey went to Corpus Christi, Texas, for advanced tactical training in early 1953. He trained on an attack aircraft known

Captain Carey, standing at the far left, with fellow aviators during advanced training at Corpus Christi, Texas. (Carey family collection, 1953)

as AD. The AD, also known as the Sky Raider, succeeded the Corsair used in Korea. Carey completed 150 hours in the AD; mostly formation flying. Since the AD was a single-seat aircraft, Carey did primary instrument checks in the SNB-Sikorsky Navy Bomber. The instructor sat in the other seat for safety reasons. In advanced tactical training, Carey also practiced bombing runs with mini-bombs.[5]

On March 16, 1953, Carey received a memo from the chief of Naval Air Advanced training at Naval Air Station Corpus Christi that stated, "You are hereby designated a Naval Aviator." Captain Carey had achieved the dream that began with his brief participation in the Navy's V-5 program nearly eight years earlier. He had earned his wings.

Next, he moved from training to the operational side of Marine aviation. Assigned to Marine Corps Air Station (MCAS) El Toro, located about 11 miles from Irvine in southern California, he had a new job and a promotion, his fifth promotion after seven and a half years. At El Toro, he was now Captain Carey, assistant operations officer for a Marine Corps squadron with the 3rd Marine Air Wing (3rd MAW). There, aircrew members prepared for their assignment to Korea as the war continued. Primarily, Captain Carey again flew the AD Sky Raider, a close-air-support aircraft. Close air support meant the pilots dropped their bombs near the ground action and in many cases just in front of the troops. In looking back at his AD Sky Raider time, the General explained the aircraft with propellers 13 feet in diameter served as a "workhorse." Built by Douglas between 1945 and 1957, the aircraft carried large bombs and could absorb ground fire, making it suitable for close air support.[6]

In addition to primarily flying the AD Sky Raider, the captain had the opportunity to fly the F9f Cougar, a fighter jet. More than a half- century later, the General reflected on his F9f experience with this observation: "I think I was principally born to be a fighter pilot." He also appreciated the thrill of one-on-one combat. The General compared that to his experience as a wrestler in high school or as a boxer at the YMCA in Columbus and onboard the *Boxer*.[7]

General Carey explained the process of close air support and how it tied back to his time as part of the ground forces. A forward air controller, known as FAC, was on the ground. The FAC would call in the target and often marked the target for the pilot. The pilot then dropped bombs at that spot. His experience in Korea gave General Carey a good understanding of the roles of pilots and Marines on the ground. He explained that relationship this way, "You get the feeling when you're supporting troops in the attack, for example, or in a defense where they are one-on-one with the enemy. You're helping them directly and you get good feedback from them."[8]

In addition to his own flight training, Captain Carey's assignment as assistant operations officer for his squadron gave him responsibility for preparing pilots for combat in Korea. That was the first of many aviation leadership roles he would hold during his career. He monitored the flights of his squadron members. At times, he went on flights with the pilots. Part of the training included measuring bombing target hits. Carey had to make sure that each of his pilots reached "combat ready" status before going to Korea. While Captain Carey prepared pilots, other officers worked with the enlisted men who served as the maintenance team of mechanics. When the mechanics advanced to training other mechanics, they also were ready for their overseas assignments. The General responded to a question asking if he had concerns about sending fellow Marines into combat. Carey's reply: "You're always concerned about sending people into combat. That always bothers you. But, on the other hand, they're all anxious to go."[9]

While Carey trained aircrews for Korea, a truce ended the fighting in South Korea on July 27, 1953, 37 months after the North Koreans came south of the

38th parallel. Thirty-seven months earlier, Second Lieutenant Richard E. Carey had made a quick decision. He tore up his papers preparing to leave active duty. Sixty-eight years after the fighting in Korea stopped, the retired General offered his perspective on the war. He said that he did not think the United States won the war. The General believes it resulted from "a compromise," that had politics involved. In his view, the Marines could have successfully pushed through the 38th parallel that divided communist-held North Korea and South Korea.

While on his second tour of duty in Korea in 1954, Captain Carey went quail hunting while off duty in South Korea. (Carey family collection, 1954)

Although the fighting in Korea stopped, the United States continued to have a strong military presence in South Korea. In 1954, Captain Carey headed back to Korea for a different kind of duty. He was a pilot this time. Two friends from Pensacola, E.E Smith and Hank Commiskey, were in the same attack squadron—VMA-212. In Korea, Carey was part of a 400-man squadron of aircrew members and enlisted troops. The three former "grunts" went to an airbase at Pyeongtaek, just an hour south of Seoul. While at Pyeongtaek, Captain Carey flew daily nighttime reconnaissance sorties over the demilitarized zone, known as the DMZ. In addition to his flight responsibilities, the captain served as the squadron's operation officer (OpsO). That assignment included training and preparation for the mission. From time to time, a North Korean propeller-driven aircraft attempted to drop bombs on the airfield with little success. One evening, Carey hosted a party at his Quonset hut. A Quonset is a rounded all steel prefabricated building that is used to house military members.[10] A pilot from another squadron got into a fight. Captain Carey attempted to break it up. He separated the fighters and began talking to the man who started the fight. That flier was not interested in talking. He swung at Carey and broke his jaw, sending the captain to the hospital. As a result, the assailant's time in the Marine Corps ended.[11]

CHAPTER 7

Mid 1950s to 1960s

Following his flight assignment in Korea, Captain Carey went to Kaneohe, Hawaii, for two months of temporary duty. He had to take the equipment from Korea to Kaneohe. As the General pointed out, "I was the guy who had to do the dirty work, so to speak." While in Hawaii, Captain Carey reformed the squadron as most of its members were already in stateside assignments. After taking care of the equipment and the squadron, he received orders to Miami, Florida, in 1955. He served as the airfield operations officer for MCAS Miami. That assignment covered two airfields located side-by-side called Masters and Opa Locka. The Opa Locka airfield had more than 100 jet aircraft and supported transient military aircraft that flew into the Miami area. The airfield handled as many as 200 flights per day, including some civilian aircraft. Carey took charge of maintenance, fueling, and servicing the aircraft. In addition, the base handled temporary housing for visiting aircrews. Carey led a team that coordinated flights going to the Caribbean and South America. In that role, Captain Carey worked with both the Federal Aviation Administration (FAA) and the International Civil Air Organization (ICAO). The captain had 400 people under his command. In addition, Captain Carey tested the F7U Cutlass. He flew the Cutlass for the first time in January 1956 and flew it several more times between 1957 and 1958, according to his flight logbook. The Cutlass was a fighter-bomber flown in the mid-1950s. The aircraft faced challenges as one-fourth of the F7U Cutlass fighters were involved in accidents.[1]

Always looking for any opportunity to get back into the fighter pilot business, Carey called and wrote Headquarters Marine Corps seeking a move back to fighter aircraft. Finally, a slot opened up in Miami and Carey went to VMF-251. There, he flew the FJ-3 Fury, an offshoot of the F-86 flown by the U.S. Air Force. Explaining why he pushed to make the assignment change, General Carey again spoke of his long-term desire to be a fighter pilot when he said, "I like to be where the action is and there is more action in the tactical units potentially."[2]

While flying with VMF-251, Carey's squadron flew training sorties out of Guantanamo Bay in Cuba and Roosevelt Roads in Puerto Rico. Following the Spanish-American War in 1898, the United States signed an agreement with Cuba to lease Guantanamo as a naval installation. Roosevelt Roads also served as a naval installation. In the pre-Castro era, Guantanamo provided a tactical training area with limited commercial air traffic. Aircrew members did role-play training. One FJ-3 served as an enemy aircraft about to attack Guantanamo and the other engaged to defend the base. Air-to-air combat effectiveness was determined via the cameras on the FJ-3s. At Roosevelt Roads, the FJ-3s trained against Air Force B-47 bombers. As part of the training exercise, the FJ-3s crews attacked the B-47s. Apparently, the VMF-251 crews enjoyed some down time in the evening. At a local bar, Captain Carey, the squadron's executive officer (XO), and the commanding officer (CO) met some young women. The three Marines invited the women to see their hotel suite. The hotel's house detective believed that bringing female guests to their suite violated the law and had the three Marines arrested. After several hours in a San Juan jail cell, the trio loudly protested their arrest, consistently pointing out that their "intentions were quite honorable." The authorities released them. The General acknowledged, in 2021, that he never mentioned his jail time when he returned home. Nor did the incident appear in any of his background checks.

While in Florida, Carey took college courses for the first time. He enrolled as a part-time student from 1956–1957 at Barry College (now Barry University), a private college.

The Marines' Miami facility closed in 1957 and the assets moved to MCAS El Toro. While many from Miami went to California, Captain Carey did not make a third trip to California. He received orders to Beaufort, South Carolina.

MCAS Beaufort and NASA Opportunity

By 1958, Carey's career advanced with his promotion to major after 10 years of service as an officer. The one-time private reached the rank of a field grade officer. The move from Florida to MCAS Beaufort, South Carolina, located about 70 miles southwest of Charleston, put him with a fighter unit. During World War II, the Beaufort facility had served as Naval Air Station with a mission of training anti-submarine aircrew members. In his first year in Beaufort, Carey commanded the Headquarters and Maintenance Squadron

(H&MS) of Marine Air Group 32, known as MAG-32. There were 100 fighter attack aircraft in the MAG including FJ-3 and F-8 aircraft. His responsibilities included programming and supervising all maintenance along with minor overhaul. He also had support responsibilities for supply, electronics, engine repairs, rebuilding of airframes, ordnance, deployment support, administration, logistics, and training support. Major Carey led 600 officers and enlisted Marines. While in the headquarters squadron of MAG-32, Carey said. "I managed to wrangle my way into VMF-122." In the Operations Officer (OpsO) role with VMF-122, Carey led 350 people with 28 aircraft in his squadron. Carey never lost his desire to be a fighter pilot.

At Beaufort, Carey and fellow pilots began the process of transitioning into the F-8 (Crusader), a single-seat aircraft. For Captain Carey, "The F-8, everything was up to you (the pilot)."He also pointed out two weapons' features on the F-8. The aircraft had the sparrow missile that used radar to track enemy airplanes. During their training flights, the aviators used drones as targets. In addition, the F-8 had infrared (IR) missiles known as heat-seeking missiles. Also called the sidewinder missile, the IRs used the heat from an enemy aircraft's tail pipe. General Carey pointed out that in the 1950s, Russian pilots might have had more combat experience from World War II than American pilots might, but he said, "Technology gave us an edge. That's the secret to our success and it must be in the future."[3] While at Beaufort, he also took college classes between 1959 and 1960 through the University of South Carolina Extension program. He took classes without having to be on campus. Carey continued to have long-term plan to earn a college degree.

On October 4, 1957, the Soviet Union launched Sputnik, the world's first satellite. For the first time, the United States had to play catchup in the world of technology. The nation that developed the cotton gin, the steamboat engine, the telephone, and the automobile, was not first in space. For those outside of the scientific community, Sputnik became a wakeup call. Emphasis on science education and space exploration accelerated in schools across the United States.[4]

Following the launch of Sputnik, the United States called for volunteers to join the space exploration drive. Up stepped Major Carey, while he served at Beaufort. He applied. By January 28, 1959, Dr. T. Keith Glennan, who led the space program, announced 110 candidates selected to move forward in the application process. Applicants had to be under 5' 11", below the age of 40, in superb physical condition, and needed a minimum of 1,500 hours of flying time. In addition, the future astronauts required a college degree in either physical science or engineering. The applicants also needed to have completed test pilot training.[5] While the General did not have a college degree at that time and was not a test pilot, his record made him a candidate. He explained that he received "E" for excellence in multiple flight categories. While at Beaufort, Major Carey's competitive spirit gained notice. He won recognition for flight excellence when he received three "Es" on his record. The three areas of "E" flying included the following: successfully hitting the target in camera gunnery from an altitude of 40,000 feet; Competition Exercise (Compex) with 20 mm guns; and ground control intercept/fighter weapons.[6]

General Carey said that he and a fellow Ohio Marine assigned to another squadron at Beaufort were in the running for the Mercury 7 program. A review of Major Carey's medical records revealed the ruptured kidney that he suffered in a high-school wrestling match. That medical report eliminated the major from the space program. The other candidate, Lieutenant Colonel John H. Glenn, who served in World War II and Korea, went on to become the first American to orbit the earth. Later Glenn won election to the United States Senate, briefly ran for president, and went back into space at

While at Marine Corps Aviation Station Beaufort, South Carolina, Major Carey learned that a high school sports injury kept him out of the Mercury 7 program. Carey, seated in the center, handles administrative duties. (Carey family collection, 1958)

the age of 78. According to General Carey, he and Colonel Glenn worked in the same building while serving in different squadrons at Beaufort. Asked if he had any regrets about not winning a slot in the Mercury 7 program, the General said no. He pointed out that other astronauts did not make the rank of general. He did.[7]

While Carey was in South Carolina, his old friend E.E. "E-Square" Smith contacted him with an opportunity for his personal life. Smith knew that Carey had recently divorced his first wife, Marie Eller Buckner Carey, a Navy veteran. The couple had two sons, Paul and Michael. Smith suggested that his old friend come up to Cherry Point, North Carolina, for dinner. He also invited Maudine Adcock Norton. In other words, Smith set up a blind date for his old friend. Maudine's husband, Marine First Lieutenant James C. Norton, died in a training accident at Cherry Point in 1960. Major Carey and Maudine married, and the couple had a blended family that eventually included five boys and two girls. The General said that his commander at Beaufort, Colonel Douglas A. Bangert, played a role in changing the new Mrs. Carey's name.[8] He told Carey that he could not remember Maudine, so he suggested that everyone call her Dena. For the rest of her life, Maudine went by Dena.

Command and Staff and on to Japan

Carey's assignment to Beaufort ended in September 1961. The major had a new assignment: the Marines selected him for the U.S. Navy's Command and Staff School in Newport, Rhode Island. Senior officers attending represented all military branches and included military students from other countries. Working with foreign officers, said Carey, aided him in later career assignments. General Carey said the curriculum emphasized history and writing. To graduate from the nine-month program, class members completed a research paper. The major's topic developed proof that Fidel Castro was a communist. He selected that topic for this reason: "It was my interest in that part of the world. Of course, you are getting close to home. And, the Union of Soviet Socialist Republic [USSR] placed the missiles in Cuba and were taking the missiles to Cuba. So it was pretty easy to prove, really." Admitting his paper "was not spectacular," the General pointed out that he did not have the same level of education as other members of the class who graduated in June 1962. He, at that point, had only completed a few college courses.[9] However, while in Rhode Island, he did manage to maintain flying status by taking hops out of a nearby Quonset Point Air National Guard Base in North Kingston.

Following his graduation from the Command and Staff School, Major Carey received orders to report to Iwakuni, Japan for a yearlong tour. He arrived in Japan in October 1962 as assistant operations officer for the 1st Marine Aircraft Wing (1st MAW). Prior to going to Japan for his third overseas assignment, Carey said that he had expected orders to serve in Laos as an advisor to the Laotian military. That did not happen.

Iwakuni is about 800 miles west of Tokyo and 40 miles from Hiroshima where an American B-29 bomber crew dropped the first atomic bomb that helped hasten the end of World War II. Major Carey's primary assignments at Iwakuni covered scheduling, coordinating deployments, operations, and training for 11,000 Marines. The base housed 250 aircraft including the F-8. While his aviation assignments to date primarily put Carey on the operational side, he added a new discipline to his resume. Carey also had a career-broadening assignment dealing with global politics. Here his exposure to foreign military officers at Command and Staff School proved useful. China's expanding role in the world gave other countries concern. As a result, he coordinated political and military needs with the governments of Japan, Taiwan, Philippines, Korea, Singapore, Hong Kong, Australia, New Zealand, and Vietnam.[10]

While at Iwakuni, Major Carey drew on his previous experience in Korea as he led Marine aviation support for the Marine ground forces. In addition, he coordinated air support for the MAW's far-flung Japanese operations. He had responsibility for attack aircraft units at Atsugi Airbase near Tokyo. At Okinawa, he worked with the helicopter base there called MCAS Futema (later named Futenma) in Ginowan and had responsibility for the wing headquarters squadron at Iwakuni.

While at Iwakuni, Major Carey also participated in joint training exercises with Taiwan, South Korea, and the Philippine Islands. In some cases, the training flights out of Taiwan took the aircrews close to China. The deployment team in Taiwan consisted of a Marine Amphibious Unit (MAU) along with air support. Taiwanese troops participated in amphibious landings. Korea landed in Major Carey's portfolio as a result of his two previous assignments there as a ground Marine and a pilot during the early 1950s. South Korean Marines, the General said, patterned themselves after the U.S. Marines. He added that they were "highly thought of."

The assignment to Iwakuni was a one-year tour for Major Carey. He offered this observation about that role: "It was very beneficial to me from a career standpoint because I got to know the Far East very well." He picked up the heavy travel schedule since he was the junior officer in his organization.

On the downside of the assignment, his family remained in Texas living in Dena's hometown of Bonham. Families could not go with Marines assigned to Iwakuni. Military members refer to that as an unaccompanied tour of duty.

During his deployments around the Far East, Major Carey commented about the people he met in those countries. He said the Japanese while he was there were "very good to us." Okinawa residents, in part due to their differences with Japan, were less so. He also praised South Koreans. On the other hand, the General said that people in the Philippine Islands "resented us." He explained that he believed the people in the Philippines saw the American military presence in the Philippines as an occupation force.[11] Part of that feeling resulted from the 47-year control that the United States had over the country. Following the Spanish-American War, Spain gave up its control of the Philippines to the United States. A three-year war with the United States ensued. The United States eventually permitted more self-government. In 1946, the United States granted independence to the Philippines.[12]

Vietnam

Vietnam was America's longest war between the 18th century and the 20th century. The conflict in Vietnam took five more years than America's Revolutionary War that lasted eight years. No war fought by Americans generated as much negative response on the home front. Carey went to Vietnam three times between 1963 and 1975. The first time he arrived as a major. The next time he went to Vietnam, he was a lieutenant colonel. In his third time in Vietnam, he came as a brigadier general. Fifty-eight thousand Americans died in the Vietnam War. That number exceeded the nearly 54,000-combined total of lives lost in the American Revolutionary War, the War of 1812, and the Mexican-American War.[13] As in the Korean War, the United States did not leave Vietnam with a victory. During Vietnam, more than 1,000 Americans became POWS.

As part of his Iwakuni assignment, the major spent two weeks traveling in South Vietnam to make site evaluations for future airfields for Marine aviators in South Vietnam. Major Carey planned and coordinated the South Vietnam trip. He flew from Iwakuni in a C-117 transport airplane built by Douglas Aircraft Company. The Air Force called that aircraft a C-47; military pilots referred to it as the "gooney bird." Joining him on the flight were two other majors. The trio began and ended their evaluation in the South Vietnamese capital city of Saigon. According to the General, his tasks included determination of where to place Marine Corps assets to support wing level operations. He acknowledged that he saw a larger role in Vietnam for the United States. At that point, the United States military had "advisors" in country. The General explained that Marines had a helicopter squadron based in South Vietnam in support of Special Forces, made up of Army advisors and Marine helicopter crews. The Marines stationed in Vietnam at that time flew the single-engine HUS-1 (Helicopter Utility Sikorsky), later known as the UH-34, which carried between 12 and 14 people.

Another aspect of his two-week mission in Vietnam focused on gathering intelligence. His role as an S-2 officer in Korea provided Major Carey with his initial experience in that area. Intelligence helped determine places to deploy aircraft. Part of his intelligence gathering included what he termed "a political thing." To aid that effort, he met with Madame Nhu, sister of South Vietnam President Ngo Dinh Diem. Since President Diem was not married, Madame Nhu took on the role of South Vietnam's first lady. Madame Nhu served as good source of intelligence for Carey. The General pointed out that "she knew everybody in the government." If Carey and his team ran into any problems in dealing with local officials, Madame Nhu would be available to assist. According to Carey, his meeting with Madame Nhu proved to her that he "was for real." Madame Nhu offered her opinion on a number of issues that helped Carey prepare his briefings to the senior Marine officers in Japan. That information included both strong and weak points about Vietnam's situation. The General described Madame Nhu as courteous and nice during their meeting. He also added that she "was in love with herself." Her brother, President Diem, later lost his life due to an assassination on November 2, 1963.

In addition to Saigon, Major Carey's team went to Da Nang, Nha Tran, Bien Hoa, Cam Ranh Bay, Khe Sanh, Hue, Phu-Bai, and the area later named Chu Lai. They needed to find potential airfields that met the following requirements: secure, reasonable ability to resupply the facility, accessible, and defensible. While flying into Hue, the crew radioed the tower, but received no response. They made the decision to land anyway. The airfield was not located right in the city of Hue. The General said they did not see any people around the airfield and concluded that the Viet Cong (the communist forces in South Vietnam) had better intelligence than the Americans did at that time. The locals left the area in anticipation of the arrival of Americans. As he toured Vietnam, the one-time "grunt" offered his initial assessment of what a war in Vietnam would look like when he said, "This is going to be a tough fight." The General based that on the jungle, snakes, rice paddies, heavy thunderstorms (called monsoons) in the summer months, and mountains. He concluded that the varied terrain and weather conditions would require different equipment and it would not be an easy place to resupply. In addition, existing paved airfields needed to double in length from 4,000 to 8,000 feet. Khe Sanh only had a dirt airfield. Khe Sanh, General Carey said, played an important role for Marine ground forces during the war years. In addition to his own observations, Carey gathered information from the Marines already on the ground in Vietnam. Based on Major Carey's report, the Marines selected Da Nang and the area eventually known as Chu Lai, as bases.[14] Marine Lieutenant General Victor H. Krulak later named that area Chu Lai after himself by using Chinese Mandarin characters to come up with the name.[15]

Both sites offered a better location for tactical air operations and were in a good location for resupply. Those locations met the criteria in Carey's view. In addition, the area later known as Chu Lai also had two runways with one serving small aircraft and the other built to accommodate larger airplanes.

Being away from Dena as their second anniversary approached was difficult for Carey. In a May 20, 1963, letter to Dena, Carey talked about their anniversary. He closed his letter with these words, "I'll close for now, precious, thanking you again for being my wife, and saying without reservation—I'm the luckiest man in the world—and I know it."

Following his Iwakuni assignment, Major Carey returned to the United States and headed to Naval Air Station (NAS) Dallas where he served with a Marine Air Reserve Detachment as an OpsO and Training Officer. That assignment brought him within 70 miles of his wife Dena's hometown of Bonham, in northeast Texas. Dena and the children were already in Bonham when Carey arrived in Texas. He took leave in October to spend time with his family before beginning his assignment at NAS Dallas. Although the Careys appreciated being in Texas, the General said that he did not request assignment as the OpsO for MAG-41 at NAS Dallas, in Grand Prairie. The Carey family moved from Dena's family home in Bonham to Arlington, a suburb of Dallas located about 10 miles from the base.

During his tour of duty at NAS Dallas, Major Carey's primary responsibility involved the training of reserve pilots in the F-8 Crusader. Carey flew that aircraft during assignments in Beaufort and Iwakuni. The reserve unit at NAS Dallas began transitioning into flying the F-8s jet aircraft. The training included ground school, gunnery, bombing, flight familiarization, and standard operating procedures. The F-8 was a single-seat aircraft. Therefore, Carey flew alongside the reserve pilots in a separate aircraft. He described his Dallas assignment as "hard working time." At one stretch, the General mentioned that he did not have a day off for six months. Navy and Marine pilots flew the F-8 Crusader and both services used it in Vietnam. Major Carey trained

50 members of two reserve squadrons at NAS Dallas. Again, his leadership received recognition when the Marine Corps also tasked Carey to train additional reserve pilots on the F-8 from Andrews Air Force Base, Maryland, just outside of Washington, D.C., and Dobbins Air Reserve Base in Marietta, north of Atlanta, Georgia.

In training reservists on the F-8, General Carey had to determine if the pilots were capable of flying the aircraft safely. Training took six months, and according to the General, all of the pilots he helped train earned their F-8 qualification. Carey said the key to successful training came from applying his "personal knowledge of the problems they (pilots) would encounter." That included recognition of emergencies and hazards. The training assignment required Carey to prepare officers and enlisted ground and aircrews. He led the development of a course syllabus, directives, lectures, programs of instruction, and manuals. More than anything else, General Carey took great pride in the fact that all of the pilots completed the program without the loss of life, an aircraft accident, or a major incident with any member of the three reserve units.[16] He said, "That was the hardest assignment I ever had." In that role, Carey trained four squadrons.

Carey's flying time on the F-8 gained civilian recognition. Ling-Temco-Vought, manufacturer of the F-8 Crusader, honored Major Carey for flying 1,000 hours in that aircraft while at NAS Dallas. Ling-Temco-Vought, known as LTV, began operations in Dallas and headquartered there in the 1960s. Major Carey received a certificate from the company. The flight distance flown by Major Carey in the F-8 equaled the number of miles for a trip from earth to the moon and back. He picked up a number of flight hours as he flew on the wing of each reservist's first five flights. During those flights, he also flew near them as they landed the aircraft back at the base. For many weeks, he also worked seven days a week to accomplish all of the training objectives and requirements. Carey earned the Aviation Safety Trophy for fiscal year 1965 for attaining the highest degree of efficiency in a selected reserve squadron operation. Despite the heavy workload, Major Carey continued taking college courses. Between 1965 and 1966, he did course work at the University of Texas Arlington.

Assassination

The major reported to NAS Dallas on November 14, 1963. Due to the timing of this assignment, Major Carey ended up on the edge of American history. In the early afternoon of Friday November 22, 1963, Major Carey flew a test flight on the AF-1E. The Air Force called that aircraft the F-86 Sabre. Carey knew that President John F. Kennedy's motorcade plans called for his motorcade to drive through downtown Dallas, at noon, a few minutes from the base by air. Carey said that he flew over the Texas Book Depository. Authorities determined the shots that killed the president came from the Book Depository's sixth floor. Carey said that he flew above that area in downtown Dallas just as the President Kennedy's car began racing toward Parkland Hospital. Major Carey's flight logbook for the day confirmed he that he flew the AF-1E for about an hour and a half.

When he returned to NAS Dallas, the tower would not let him land. Years later, he said that he felt as if the staff in the tower treated him as a suspect. Explaining that he had limited fuel, Major Carey went ahead and landed his aircraft. Then, after deplaning, he learned the president had died. Carey, along with all of the military members on base, drew weapons on orders from the detachment's commanding officer. If base personnel needed to provide security in light of the assassination of the president, they had weapons. There were many unknowns and concerns that day. Although President Kennedy died in the early afternoon and newly sworn-in President Lyndon B. Johnson had already flown back to Washington, military members at the NAS Dallas remained at the base until late in that evening. The General remembered that he did not return home until around midnight.[17]

On January 22, 1996, General Carey recorded a 90-minute interview for The Sixth Floor Museum at Dealey Plaza Oral History Project.[18] In his interview with Bob Porter who worked with the Sixth Floor Museum (relating to Kennedy's assassination), the General shared his memories of the events surrounding President Kennedy's assassination. He said that the political climate in the Dallas area concerned military people with regard to the president's visit. People at NAS Dallas understood that there was potential for a problem. Prior to the president's arrival, Washington officials urged military members assigned to the area to "be prepared," said General Carey. He added that, "We kept our fingers crossed that nothing would happen." As a result, NAS Dallas was on what the General described as "quasi-alert." The nearly 200 Marines at the base formed in a unit similar to a rifle company. The Marines were prepared to react.[19]

In addition, the General elaborated about his time after returning to base. The detachment commander put the base on full alert. General Carey said among personnel on the base there was, "great concern about what's going to happen." He urged his people to keep calm as they sat and waited. Part of the reason for the full alert revolved around the unknown. General Carey said some thought there could be a coup. The nation was on edge. For the fourth time in 98 years, an American president had died at the hand of an assassin.

(Murderers also killed Presidents Lincoln, Garfield, and McKinley.) During the alert, base personnel could not make outgoing telephone calls. Carey did not speak to his family until arriving home.

Like most people around the country, the Careys spent the weekend watching post-assassination coverage on television. Early on Sunday afternoon law enforcement officials took the then-alleged assassin, Lee Harvey Oswald, to the basement of Dallas police headquarters. Authorities planned to transport him to the Dallas County jail, considered a more secure facility. As local and national media gathered in the basement, a lone gunman stepped out of the crowd and fired a shot that killed Oswald. During that weekend, the Careys watched the event in their temporary residence in an Arlington apartment. They were preparing to close on the purchase of their first home that they were buying in Arlington. As the gunman came into view, Dena Carey said, "That looks like Jack Ruby." She was right.

Just a few weeks before the assassination, the Careys twice interacted with Ruby. In October, while Carey was on leave in Bonham, before reporting to his NAS Dallas assignment, the Careys attended the annual Texas State Fair at Fair Park in Dallas. Jack Ruby set up a stage at the fairgrounds that featured entertainers. As the Carey family walked by the stage, Ruby spotted 14-month-old Tamara Carey. Ruby asked Tamara if she would like to come on stage. She stepped up on the stage, the General said. As she briefly moved around on the stage, Ruby told the family that Tamara could have a job at his club when she got older.[20]

When the Careys spoke with Ruby at the fair, he asked Carey what kind of work he did. Carey told Ruby that he was a Marine. Ruby asked him to stop in at his club called the Carousel Club. In November, Major Carey and Dena went to downtown Dallas. They went to Ruby's club. Ruby, a World War II Army Air Force veteran, stopped by their table and bought the Careys a drink.[21] The major and Dena had no idea that the club owner would end up in the American history book of infamous characters.

Reflecting on President Kennedy, General Carey said the military respected the president as a wounded war-hero. Kennedy served as a PT boat commander in the Pacific during World War II. The General added that military members appreciated his strong stance during the Cuban missile crisis.[22]

In 1992, the General watched the filming of Oliver Stone's movie titled *JFK*. He watched the Dealey Plaza portion of the film in Dallas. Carey had another reason for being there. As an extra in the film, he played the role of the commandant of the Marine Corps, General David M. Shoup.[23] The General had a non-speaking part in the movie.[24]

Promoted to Lieutenant Colonel

As his assignment at NAS Dallas wound down, Carey earned a promotion to lieutenant colonel. His dedication and successful execution of a wide range of assignments helped advance his career. He replaced the gold leaves of a major with the silver leaves of his new rank before leaving Dallas for his next assignment at Camp Lejeune with 2nd Marine Division. This was his second time at Camp Lejeune after serving there as a second lieutenant before the Korean War. This time, the newly minted lieutenant colonel had an assignment in G-4—logistics. His served as liaison for aviation units assigned to the 2nd Marine Division. The General explained his role. Primarily he coordinated the support requirements for aviation units at Camp Lejeune. For example, if the division deployed anywhere, they came to Carey. He had to answer the question, "What do we need to do in the division to support attached aviation units?"[25]

While Carey served at Camp Lejeune, a rebellious uprising began in the Dominican Republic. Rebel forces attempted to bring ousted President Juan Bosch back into power. President Lyndon B. Johnson sent in troops from two bases in North Carolina—Camp Lejeune and Fort Bragg, the home of the 82nd Airborne. The U.S. forces had two objectives. First, the military needed to protect the lives and property of Americans in the Dominican Republic. Second, they had to protect the country from a possible communist takeover.[26] As the Marines from Camp Lejeune headed to the Caribbean, a larger force of Marines already faced communist forces in Vietnam. Marine Corps Commandant General Wallace M. Greene, Jr. received a reporter's question about the possibility of two missions stretching the Corps too thin. General Greene replied, "We're in in pretty good shape." He added that the Marines had plenty of manpower.[27] Marines in Santo Domingo in the Dominican Republic killed snipers near the U.S. Embassy. They also aided in getting Americans airlifted out of the Dominican Republic onto the USS *Boxer*, the same ship that Carey served on during his first assignment out of boot camp. There was concern in the media about the commitment of the Marines in the Dominican Republic. In an April 30, 1965, editorial, Louisville's *The Courier Journal* warned, "And unless the Marines are used discreetly and withdrawn at the earliest possible moment, we must expect to hear the cry of 'Yankee Imperialism'."

Within a month, the Marines began to withdraw from the Dominican Republic.

Lieutenant Colonel Carey's assignment in this operation involved planning of the movement of Marine ground and air forces to and from North Carolina.

While his role at Camp Lejeune was a staff position versus an operational assignment, Carey maintained flight proficiency on fixed-wing aircraft at nearby Cherry Point. He also flew helicopters at New River, next to Camp Lejeune.[28] As his time with this assignment ended, the division commander, Major General Orman D. Simpson, asked him to stay on—obviously a compliment to Carey. Carey wanted to return to full-time aviation. He then received his orders to report to Cherry Point, about 60 miles from Camp Lejeune.[29]

MCAS Cherry Point, NC—Fighter Squadron

While Cherry Point may have brought back memories of the death of her husband six years earlier, General Carey said that Dena never said anything about that to him. At Cherry Point, he took command of the Marine Fighter Attack Squadron 513 (VMFA-513) in September 1966 as part of the 2nd Marine Air Wing (MAW). VMFA- 513 had a nickname—"The Flying Nightmares."

VMFA-513, in existence since 1944, had a rich history. In World War II, the squadron flew close air support in Okinawa. During the Korean War, they averaged 585 monthly combat sorties between March and October 1951. They destroyed or damaged more than 4,500 enemy trucks, tanks, freight cars, and locomotives.[30]

In the Vietnam War, Lieutenant General Lewis W. Walt, who commanded I Corps in Vietnam, said this about VMFA-513:

> The overall air mission that have [*sic*] been provided by your squadron during day and night, whether fair or foul weather, were contributing factors to the successful combat operations of the joint efforts conducted in Vietnam.[31]

Members of VMFA-513 Squadron, known as the Flying Nightmares, wore this patch on their flight suits. (Carey family collection, 1967)

Although he had only recently pinned on the silver leaf of a lieutenant colonel, Carey quickly raised the performance bar and set records compared to other 2nd MAW squadrons. He wanted to continue the successful record of the squadron. Carey knew the squadron's history. He decided it was time to make some of his own history. During the period between September 1966 and May 1967, the Flying Nightmares logged more F-4B Phantom flight hours in seven of the nine months than other units at Cherry Point. They lost the title in only January and March.[32]

While Carey's competitive spirit, dating back to his high-school sports career, came through in challenging his team to beat the competition, the effort had a practical purpose. His aircrew and maintenance members readied for their next assignment—Vietnam. Lieutenant Colonel Carey focused on maximizing training. He said, "I'm kind of a tough taskmaster when it came to that. So, we worked a lot of long hours. We made a couple of deployments to Yuma." Carey focused on getting in as many training flights as possible.

The Flying Nightmares deployed to the MCAS Yuma, Arizona, about 180 miles southwest of Phoenix. With access to more than one million acres of bombing and aviation-training ranges and superb flying weather, MCAS

As squadron commander of VMFA-513 at Cherry Point, North Carolina, Lieutenant Colonel Carey led his squadron to a record-setting 816 training sorties at Marine Corps Air Station Yuma, Arizona. Carey is in the center front row behind the sign reading 800. (Carey family collection, 1967)

Yuma supports 80 percent of the Marine Corps' air-to-ground aviation training.[33] The 13 F-4s and their aircrew members flew for 23 days during their deployment that concluded on May 19, 1967. The Flying Nightmares flew 816 sorties during 1,641.7 flight hours. According to Carey, that was the most ever flown by a Marine Corps F-4 squadron anywhere. Thirty-five pilots in the squadron averaged 56 flight hours each while the 21 radar intercept officers (RIOs) each averaged 72 hours in the air.

In answer to the question of how the squadron achieved their record-setting performance, Carey explained that he learned lessons from previous deployments. As a result, he planned in anticipation of potential problems. Major Charles Zangas, maintenance officer for 513 added, "We didn't have to change one engine." Since crews flew from 6:15 a.m. to 3:30 a.m. the following morning, the maintenance section kept at least 10 aircraft ready at all times. Lieutenant Colonel Carey led from the front. He flew 82 hours—more than anyone else in 513 did. In addition, he flew another 35 hours in the C-117. Carey explained that the Yuma training helped to prepare the pilots for duty with the 1st Marine Air Wing (1stMaw) in WESTPAC (the Western Pacific) when they served in Vietnam. Carey said, "The major emphasis was on night work." Training ranged from bombing runs to air combat maneuvers. He added, "It was strictly a team effort by everybody. I am considerably pleased with the way the squadron performed."

Maintaining the F-4s kept the aircraft in the air and out of the shop. On occasion, the maintenance section required parts to maintain the aircraft. Rather than wait for shipments of parts to Yuma, Colonel Carey took the C-117 to California to pick up the required parts. Due to Carey's initiative, parts went to the maintenance team without waiting. That allowed the pilots to fly more training sorties. Carey flew both day and night during the Yuma deployment.

Carey organized training in Yuma. In each flight, the aircrew first handled radar intercept followed by air-to-air combat. During the final 30 minutes, crews devoted their time to air-to-ground bombing runs. That gave the pilots and RIOs practice in close air support as they prepared for combat. That part of the training covered low- and medium-range bombing. The crews also performed low-level navigation exercises to increase their map-reading skills. The aircrews conducted three to four missions most every time they flew. The maintenance team played a key role in the Yuma deployment. As fliers operated around the clock, so did the maintenance team. The maintenance crew divided their members into two 12-hour shifts. After the flyers and maintenance folks completed Yuma training, they were ready for Vietnam. General Carey modestly added, "I might say they were well trained."[34]

To celebrate the completion of the deployment, the squadron held what Marines call an open mess night. Carey pointed out that an open mess night "was the first mess night for some of our younger officers and part of the job is to teach the Marine Corps' history and traditions as well as how to fly."[35] He added that along with Marine Corps history and traditions, the young fliers learned how to party. The purpose of the event was to celebrate the squadron's completion of training in Yuma, General Carey explained. The event, held in a hotel near the base, was not a formal activity. By design, the event took place off base, Carey said. The Flying Nightmares partied in civilian clothes and toasts continued throughout the evening.[36]

CHAPTER 8

Fighter Pilot in Vietnam

Carey's time at Cherry Point was about to end. In the summer of 1967, he received his orders to Vietnam. Shortly before Lieutenant Colonel Carey left Cherry Point for Vietnam, he received on an opportunity for civilian employment in the airline industry. Eligible for retirement from the Marine Corps with more than 20 years of service, Carey received a call from United Airlines. The Chicago-based airline needed a training officer. His skill as a trainer of pilots had earned him recognition in both military and civilian circles. Was he interested in coming to work for United Airlines, the caller wanted to know? Carey declined the opportunity, despite the fact that he could have increased his compensation. He explained his reason for turning down the opportunity with United Airlines. Looking back, the retired General said that he could not send "all my boys to Vietnam and then me get out." The nation was at war. The General added, "I was trained. So, it was not the time to abandon my basic purpose in life."[1] That rationale was similar to Carey's decision in June 1950 when he stayed on active duty for the Korean War. He continued to serve his country.

On his way to Vietnam, Carey had an overnight stop in San Francisco. While in uniform, he went to a restaurant for dinner where he ate his last stateside meal for 13 months. A middle-aged woman in the restaurant followed him shouting the words "baby-killer" at the lieutenant colonel.

After flying out of California the next day, he arrived in Chu Lai. By the time Lieutenant Colonel Richard E. Carey arrived in Vietnam for a full tour of duty, Americans had been in the fight for five years. The American military was fighting to stop the spread of communism. Both China and the Union of Soviet Socialist Republics (USSR) supported the North Vietnamese as they pushed for control of all of Vietnam. American service members fought and died in Vietnam during a 13-year period between 1962 and 1975.

Four U.S. presidents dealt with issues relating to the war in Vietnam. It came into the homes of Americans as the first televised war.

During the war years, protestors took to the street. Young men burned their draft cards, college students protested against college ROTC units, and politicians divided over the issue. The media covered the battlefront and anti-war protests in the same newscasts. College men who maintained passing grades received draft deferments. Non-college men either faced the draft or volunteered to avoid the draft. Some dodged the draft and military service by fleeing to Canada. Young men assigned to Vietnam had yearlong tours of duty, except Marines. Marine planners figured early in the war that the Corps would travel by ship, instead of flying Marines into Vietnam. As a result, all Marines had 13-month tours to account for the anticipated two-week one-way ship ride over at the beginning and then two weeks back at the end of each tour.

Unlike the returning veterans from World War I and World War II, Vietnam veterans did not receive parades and welcome-home ceremonies. In some cases, those returning veterans who wore their uniforms while traveling faced protestors who called them "baby-killers" and spat at them.

College students were not the only opponents to the war. Retired Marine Corps Commandant General David M. Shoup offered his opposition to the war. In May 1966, Shoup made this comment in a speech he gave at Pierce College, in Woodland Hills, California: "If we had and would keep our dirty, bloody, crooked fingers out of the business, they will arrive on a solution on their own."[2]

Despite all of the home front challenges, then Lieutenant Colonel Carey had a job to do in Vietnam. In June 1967 he arrived at Chu Lai where four and a half years earlier, he had scouted potential Marine airbase sites.

Carey initially served as a member of the Marine Aircraft Group-13 (MAG-13), co-located with MAG-12 at Chu Lai. MAG-13 pilots flew F-4 fighter jets; MAG-12 had A-4s used for close air support (CAS) and TA-4s, used by forward air controllers (FASTFACs). Marine pilots also flew C-117 transports out of Chu Lai.[3]

Although he hoped to continue serving as a fighter squadron commander, Carey's assignment called for him to lead Marine Airbase Squadron-13 (MABS-13). One major aspect of that assignment included security. His experience in Korea made him the right person for the job. Chu Lai had two airfields that were not located together. In addition to security, he commanded all base support activities. He ensured adequate staffing of all positions in his unit. He also oversaw aircraft maintenance and managed the status of all aircraft.

Lieutenant Colonel Carey's MAG-13 commanding officer, Colonel Edward N. Le Faivre, let Carey fly combat sorties in addition to his other duties. He flew F-4s and C-117 transports. Those flights included sorties over Laos to strike enemy resupply lines on the Ho Chi Minh Trail. Carey took command of Marine Attack Fighter Squadron 115 (VMFA-115) in November.

Just prior to taking over the squadron, Carey responded to a call for air support. On October 20, 1967, an Army of the Republic of South Vietnam (ARVN) unit faced serious opposition from the North Vietnamese Army (NVA) near the Demilitarized Zone (DMZ) located south of North Vietnam. The unit of South Vietnamese soldiers thought they were about to be over-run by the enemy. Marine pilots at Chu Lai, about 10 minutes away from the ARVN by air, responded to the call for close air support. Carey and his Radar Intercept Operator (RIO) joined another two-man F-4 crew for a pre-flight briefing prior to flying the mission. The two aircrews received information on the battle conditions, the overall enemy situation, and weather. They would face weather with broken clouds and small arms fire when the F-4 flew low. The mission required the pilots to fly low to provide close air support (CAS). Once over the battle site, Carey focused on the impact area and the RIO concentrated on everything else. The airborne tactical air controller (FAC(A)) told him where to target the ordnance. According to the General, his F-4 took enemy fire from small arms and .50 caliber (12.75mm) automatic weapons. Carey and his wingman broke up the attack and turned the battle around for the South Vietnamese ground troops. The pilots dropped 500-pound Mark 82 Snake Eye (retarded) bombs. They also used napalm and strafed the area with 20mm cannon fire. Carey made a combined seven bombing and strafing runs. According to General Carey, they continued to make runs "all over the place." The General explained that the additional runs were not required. They even strafed the enemy as they retreated from the battle site. Throughout the mission, the General related many years later, he maintained his focus on the impact area. The RIO watched for enemy aircraft and movement of ground forces. After flying for a little more than an hour, the aircrews found themselves out of ammunition and low on fuel. Carey and his wingman returned to the base at Chu Lai. Back at Chu Lai, the flyers went to a debriefing session where they outlined what happened on the mission. That debriefing included actions they took while in battle.[4] Both pilots earned Distinguished Flying Cross (DFC) Medals for the mission. Carey's citation included this statement, "He delivered all of his ordnance with devastating accuracy."

Those Who Served with Carey in Vietnam

One Marine aviator in Vietnam had a close-up view of Carey in action. One of Carey's RIOs, Ray Cushman (today a retired Marine lieutenant colonel) flew 29 of his 356 F-4B combat sorties in Southeast Asia with Carey. Carey flew one out of every four of his F-4B combat flights with Cushman as his RIO. Cushman said that his flight logbooks showed that he flew with more than 200 pilots in his career. He said this about the General: "[Carey] is the greatest aviator I ever flew with. Only a back-seater like myself can attest to greatness." He described Carey as "a steady leader."[5] In the F-4B, the RIO sat directly behind the pilot. Often aviators refer to RIOs as "backseaters or GIB—guy in the back." Twenty-nine times, then Captain Cushman sat within 2 feet of Carey as they flew in combat out of Chu Lai. Cushman commented, "I just have to say I have over 200 pilots' names in my log book and he was the best of the best."

While flying with Carey, Cushman described him as steady and unshakeable. The 20-year Marine Corps veteran added, "After all, he [Carey] felt the cockpit was his office and it was business as usual." When aircrew members prepared for a combat sortie, Carey, as commanding officer, conducted briefings for flights of two or more aircraft, Cushman explained. During the briefings Carey "was very thorough, covered all phases of the mission plus contingencies and emergency procedures. He wanted sharp, crisp radio discipline, and compliance with all aircraft standard procedures."

During flights with Carey, Cushman recalled returning to base with bullet holes in the wings and external fuel tanks of their F-4 after flying low-altitude sorties.

Not only did Carey win the respect of fellow officers, but enlisted Marines also thought highly of the future three-star general. Cushman said the enlisted men "genuinely loved and looked up to him." He described Carey's working relationship with ordnance and maintenance personnel as genuine, complimentary, and cheerful.[6]

Two enlisted men who served with Carey at Chu Lai offered their take on Carey. Gerald Ruud, a staff sergeant who arrived at Chu Lai in November 1967, worked the night shift in the aircraft electric shop. The former NCO described Carey this way, "can do attitude, semper fi." He also added the operation was "by the book."[7]

Retired Master Sergeant Dave Horne served as a radar technician with VMFA-115 when Lieutenant Colonel Carey commanded the squadron. He said this about his one-time boss, "Colonel Carey was a strong leader.

He pushed us to provide the maximum aircraft support possible under the conditions at the time." Horne described Carey's leadership style with one word: professional.[8]

While Carey and his team served in a war zone, there were lighter moments. An officers' club at Chu Lai offered, as Colonel Cushman put it, "a place for genuine camaraderie; you can let your hair down, and have some genuine fun." One night, Cushman sat at a table away from the bar where Carey stood. The RIO said he heard a disturbance—not, as he explained, "an unusual event in Chu Lai O Club." Apparently, an Army officer insulted the Marine Corps. Carey, then in his twenty-first year in the Corps, did not take kindly to the remarks. Cushman said Carey, who was his CO, and the Army officer exchanged angry and profane words. Carey, a one-time Columbus YMCA boxer and high school wrestler, suggested that the two of them take the argument outside of the club. "It was intense for a while, but eventually cooler heads prevailed and the Army officer left the club with tail tucked between his legs," Cushman said.[9]

Lieutenant Colonel Carey served at Chu Lai until January 16, 1968, when he received an assignment at the 1st Marine Air Wing (MAW) in Da Nang,

At a speaking engagement, General Carey (right) met with Lieutenant Colonel (Ret) Ray Cushman, his radar intercept operator in Vietnam. The pair flew 29 sorties together. Cushman said that as a pilot, Carey was "the best of the best." (Courtesy of Lieutenant Colonel Ray Cushman United States Marine Corps (Ret), circa 2017)

about 50 miles north of Chu Lai. At Da Nang, as 1st MAW assistant operations officer, Carey served under the command of Major General Norman Anderson. Da Nang was not the first time Carey and Anderson worked together. The general had been Carey's wing commander while he served as a squadron commander at Cherry Point. While in Da Nang Carey had responsibility for Marine airfields, fixed wing aircraft (non-helicopters), and helicopters in the northern portion of South Vietnam. In that role, Lieutenant Colonel Carey had a staff of 10 officers who after finding out daily air support needs, scheduled and coordinated the flights for the 1st MAW. Carey and his staff tracked weather, enemy actions, special action needs to help the squadron, and maintained records. The 1st MAW had six MAGs.[10]

As he did in his assignment at Chu Lai, Carey also flew combat sorties. At Da Nang, he flew at night and tended to his duties as assistant G-3 until March 13, when he became the G-3. In 2006, General Carey responded to questions about what he would have done if his aircraft took a hit by enemy forces along with the mental preparation for the possibility of becoming a prisoner of war. There were protocols to follow if the enemy hit the aircraft and the pilot could not return to base, he explained. If close to the coast, the pilot needed to bail out or crash over the water. There was a better chance of survival in the water versus bailing out over land.

From a personal perspective when questioned about possibly becoming a POW, the General said, "I was mentally prepared that they weren't going to take me. I do not like snakes. I didn't want to wind up in a jungle fighting snakes."[11]

Just two weeks into his Da Nang assignment, Carey's days got much longer. During the last two days in January, communist forces, made up of supporters known as the National Liberation Front (NLF), launched coordinated attacks on more than 100 locations including Hue and Saigon. Those attacks, known as the Tet Offensive, began during the lunar new-year holiday of Tet. Saigon and Hue received a barrage of attacks in the first phase. The second phase took place from May to June. The third phase began in August and lasted six weeks.[12]

Tet pushed Lieutenant Colonel Carey's team into overdrive. Requests for close air support quadrupled. The communists widened their attacks to include more than 100 hamlets and cities throughout South Vietnam. Enemy forces hit Khe Sanh, Pleiku, and Ben Hoa. Rocket fire hit Da Nang. The General said, "So we had to immediately muster our forces [fighter crews] and get them in the air." Marine aviators supported Marine ground forces, the General explained. As an example, the 26th Marines faced enemy attacks on the company-sized positions on hills surrounding Khe Sanh. The Marine pilots launched air strikes to protect the Marines on the hills.[13]

A surprise attack by communist forces hit Vietnam's ancient capital of Hue. On January 30, two Marine majors near Hue noticed what they thought was a funeral cortege. They later learned the North Vietnamese used the funeral cortege as a subterfuge. That turned out to be the way the North Vietnamese brought in weapons for the Tet offensive. By the next day, Hue, a city of more than 114,000 was under communist control. The Military Assistance Command Vietnam (MACV) compound stood just outside of Hue. Communist forces struck the facility. An Army Specialist-4, Frank Douezema, Jr., stood in the compound's tower and fired his .50 caliber machine gun. His efforts prevented the loss of the facility. Douezema, who lost both legs from enemy fire, continued to direct his fellow soldiers before losing his life. Douezema earned the Distinguished Service Cross, posthumously. Marines entered the fight, going from house to house. Within three weeks, the communists lost; but the city suffered significant damage.[14] During the battle over Hue, 129 Marines lost their lives. In addition, 810 Marines suffered wounds. An estimated 5,000 civilians died in the attack on Hue. The Citadel, a fortress built in 1805, stood in ruins.[15] An Australian newspaper story portrayed the American military's winning in Hue with a negative slant. That reporter said Americans regained Hue "at the cost of destroying it."[16]

During Hue, Lieutenant Colonel Carey ran operations from the command center at Da Nang. He sent in Cobra helicopters for CAS. He also sent in Army and Marine Corps medivac helicopters. General Carey, not always complimentary to members of the Army, acknowledged that the Army's helicopters "did a better job of evacuation than the Marine Corps." He added that he hated to make the admission, but he acknowledged that the Army helicopter pilots flew in at lower altitudes. His team at Wing Headquarters in Da Nang answered calls for fixed-wing and helicopter support. The Marine Corps, according to General Carey, dedicated their efforts to supporting Marines on the ground through artillery and air support. The communist forces lost 5,000 troops at Hue; more than 38 times the number of Marines killed in action there, General Carey said. He added that throughout the Tet offensive the 1st, 5th, and the 26th Marine Regiments fought in a "slugfest, face to face" with the communists.

For Carey, Tet meant that he had 24-hour days. He ate and said that he sometimes even slept at his desk. Carey led planning for air support and resupply for Khe Sanh during Tet.[17] At night, when things slowed down at the command center, he flew in multiple aircraft including helicopters.

He served as a co-pilot on helicopter evacuation flights. In addition to the pilot, the helicopter crew consisted of a door gunner, crew chief, and a corpsman to provide immediate medical aid to the wounded. On occasion, a flight surgeon joined Carey on the flight. The flight surgeon was a Navy captain. That decision did not go over well with Carey's wing commander. The 1st MAW commanding general, General Anderson, told Carey that, "There's more Marines that can take your place, but I only have one [1st MAW] chief flight surgeon." Anderson did not specifically tell him not to do it, but Carey understood the message. He complied.

As in Korea, Vietnam saw Carey with another near-death experience. In late January 1968, General Anderson ordered Carey to fly to Khe Sanh in a C-130. Anderson wanted Carey to coordinate air support there. However, a problem at Hue City resulted in a change of plans. Another officer went in Carey's place. Enemy fire struck the C-130 at Khe Sanh. All of the passengers, including Carey's replacement, died in the burning wreckage. Carey said, "So I think the Lord had a different mission for me."[18]

During Tet, Marine pilots averaged just over four sorties per day. During that time, 7th Air Force, under the command of General William W. "Spike" Momyer, had air management control over all flight actions in Vietnam. General Momyer, a World War II fighter ace in the European Theater of Operations (a pilot who downed five or more enemy aircraft earned recognition as an ace), established an average daily rate of 1.5 sorties for all pilots. For the second time in a second war, Carey faced a challenge from a senior officer from another branch of service. The level of Marine Corps daily sorties coming out of Da Nang caught General Momyer's attention. General Momyer went right to the source. Bypassing the chain of command, he placed a telephone call directly to Carey. General Momyer asked him, "Colonel, what are you all doing? You've exceeded our sortie rate." For the lieutenant colonel, this call was reminiscent of his contact with General MacArthur during the Korean War. Carey offered a measured, respectful, and straightforward response when he said, "General, we're answering calls for assistance, calls for air help, and will continue to do that." General Momyer answered back with this statement, "Well, you're supposed to maintain the sortie rate." Regardless of what General Momyer told him, Lieutenant Colonel Carey knew two things. First, his commander, General Anderson, would have his back. Second, he had to deal with an angry four-star general. His final comments to General Momyer were these words, "Sir, until my wing commander tells me to cut back, I'm not going to cut back. You'll have to talk to him." Nearly 40 years later, General Carey described his only interaction with General Momyer this way, "That was a tough one, but I had my boss behind me." There were no more calls from General Momyer, Carey said.[19] General Momyer returned to the United States in late 1968. He commanded the Tactical Air Command until his retirement in 1973.

While he had a run-in with an Air Force general, Lieutenant Colonel Carey said that he appreciated the support of an Air Force tanker (known as a flying gas station) pilot. He described that situation during an interview with *Allen American* (Allen, Texas) in 2012 when he said:

> I was a squadron commander and I made a night hop up to Hanoi. I was in an F-4 and we lost an engine. We were carrying rockets and all sorts of other ordnance, so we were heavy. We had to make an in-flight refueling maneuver, which was considered impossible, given all the ordnance we were carrying. When we got home, the warrant officer with me said, "Colonel, that was the hairiest hop I ever made!" When he got out he kissed the ground.[20]

While in Da Nang, Carey again served as the "go to guy" for problem solving. Two examples follow. One covered an operational issue in February 1968. General Anderson expressed concern over losses of helicopters. He told Carey, "Develop a way that we can protect our helicopters so that we can get the job done." The helicopters had a variety of roles to play including search and rescue, along with resupply of needed equipment. In addition, helicopter crews handled medivac, armed escort, and CAS with guns and rockets.

To resolve the problem relating to the helicopter and flight crew losses suffered by the Marines during the siege at Khe Sanh, Carey worked with Lieutenant Colonel Bill White, commander of helicopter squadron VMO-6. Carey and White received input from others in operations. Their objective was to build a plan that would provide protection for the helicopters.

They called the plan the "Super Gaggle." The A-4s flew into the Khe Sanh area from Chu Lai. Helicopters came out of Quang Tri. An airborne controller FASTFAC in a TA-4 coordinated the movement of the aircraft. Helicopters and A-4s arrived at the area around Khe Sanh at the same time. Due to heavy rains called monsoons, visibility became another challenge for all of the aircrew members as they conducted their sorties. The poor visibility gave the enemy's ground troops an advantage. To get around that problem, pilots used a radio beacon known as a "homer." The "homer" let pilots fly through overcast skies to avoid striking hills and mountains.

The fixed-wing aircraft carried a wide range of ordnance. Some carried 500-pound bombs. Others used 20mm rapid-fire guns. Another group of pilots carried rockets. Many of the aircraft brought low-drag 500-pound Mark 82 Snake Eye bombs. With low-drag bombs equipped with snake-eye retarders, the pilot could drop the load from an altitude as low as 50 feet above the ground while avoiding the bomb blast. Those bombs, General Carey pointed out, "have special fins on them that as soon as they depart the aircraft, the fins extend and slow the flight of the bomb." That allowed the pilot to get away from the blast unscathed. The pilots flew in at 400 knots or 460 miles per hour while dropping their bombs as they flew between 50 and 200 feet above ground. In addition, aircrews dropped napalm and CS gas. CS gas caused tearing and a burning sensation to enemy forces in the area, making it difficult for the enemy to fire weapons at the helicopters. As the pilots arrived in the area, ordnance drops began with bombs to help neutralize the area. "Then, we'd try to pinpoint them with guns and rockets," the General said. After that, the pilots dropped napalm and CS gas. Those efforts cleared a lane for the helicopters to drop supplies, evacuate the wounded, and pull out of the area without enemy fire striking them. Lieutenant Colonel Carey took charge of mission planning. He said the key person in the operation was the TA-4 (FASTFAC) coordinator who worked with the ground commanders and aircrews.[21]

In a post-operation review, Carey discussed the mechanics of Super Gaggle:

> Success of the effort was predicated on timing, coordination, and often times luck. Luck, as used, refers to the ability to guess whether the weather would hold long enough to complete an effort once it got underway. Fortunately, the tactics were so successful that during the entire period of the Super Gaggle only two CH-46s were downed enroute to the hill positions. The crews were rescued immediately by escorting Huey gunships.[22]

After successful implementation of "Super Gaggle," General Anderson complimented Carey on his planning and execution. Then, he presented him with a new challenge—the morale of the ground forces needed an uplift, in General Anderson's view. As a "grunt" in Korea Carey understood the problem from personal experience. The one-time combat rifle platoon leader recalled the positive impact of his pre-Christmas beer run in Korea. While a cold one might have been a hit with the Marines on the ground, an obstacle stood in the way. General Carey described the issue: "But at that time we had an organization back in the states of women that decided that the troops didn't have to be drinking beer." He realized bringing beer would not work. However, he knew the young Marines were miserable, hot, and dusty. Carey offered General Anderson an alternative—ice cream. He told General Anderson that ice cream "would be kind of like Christmas to them (troops)." While ice cream was a great idea, getting it to the troops offered additional challenges. For the one-time junior officer who led combat loading of a ship in advance of the Inchon landing, this became a new problem-solving activity.

Carey remembered that the Navy operated an ice cream plant on China Beach. He had a source of supply. Next, Carey had to figure out a way to keep the ice cream cold. He arranged for dry ice shipments from Japan on a C-130 transport aircraft. Carey contacted the Navy for the production and resupply of the ice cream. Now, he had to get the ice cream to the troops on a continuing basis. Colonel Carey then tapped his "Super Gaggle" team for another mission. Five-gallon containers of ice cream went into the external nets of the helicopters. The fixed-wing pilots paved the way. Years later General Carey said that he ran into Marines who never forgot the ice cream he arranged to get them.[23]

Not every rifleman who served on the critical hills overlooking Khe Sanh appreciated the ice cream delivery. A few years ago, Mike McCollum, a retired Marine reservist, said that a visitor to the Dallas Fort Worth Metroplex Marines' monthly luncheon had a different view about the ice cream delivery. When asked about the ice cream, the former Khe Sanh Marine told McCollum, "I always wondered who the idiot was that put ice cream in the mail bag." The melted ice cream ruined his mail. As it happened, General Carey did not attend that luncheon meeting, so he did not get to hear the comment first-hand. Later, friends told the General the story and he just laughed.

During his 13-month tour in Vietnam, General Carey flew 204 combat sorties including 113 in the F-4B according to his flight logbook. The remaining flights were in C-117s. Due to his command responsibilities, Carey flew the bulk of those sorties at night. While flying the C-117s out of Da Nang, he dropped flares in the enemy attack areas. The flare drops provided light that allowed the fighter aircrews to see the enemy ground action.

During each of his 204 combat sorties, General Carey said there was one commonality. He prayed prior to every takeoff. Carey's faith continued.

After Carey rotated back to the United States, that flight surgeon who previously flew with Carey, talked his way onto another helicopter flight, taking the place of a corpsman. That change paid off for one young Marine officer. First Lieutenant Lewis B. Puller, Jr, a platoon leader, tripped over an enemy land mine. The lieutenant, son of retired Lieutenant General Lewis B. "Chesty" Puller, Sr., lost his legs, and parts of his hands.[24] The flight surgeon's experience and skill enabled him to keep Puller alive until he could get to a hospital.[25]

Presidential Politics Back Home

While Carey served 13 months in Vietnam between 1967 and 1968, presidential politics began to heat up. In November 1964, President Johnson won a landslide victory over his Republican opponent, Arizona Senator Barry M. Goldwater. Just four years later, in the nation's first presidential primary held in New Hampshire on March 12, 1968, President Johnson barely defeated Minnesota Senator Eugene J. McCarthy. Senator McCarthy campaigned against the war in Vietnam. Four days after the New Hampshire primary, New York Senator Robert F. (Bobby) Kennedy, brother of the late President, entered the race for president as anti-war candidate. Fifteen days later, President Johnson announced that he would not seek reelection.

After Sunday, March 31, 1968, the parameters of the air war faced a significant change. In a 40-minute televised prime-time address to the nation that evening, President Johnson described the results of the Tet Offensive by the North Vietnamese. He explained that the attacks did not inspire uprisings in the cities and hamlets. The North Vietnamese failed to control any of the cities they attacked. In addition, the president pointed out, North Vietnam suffered heavy casualties. In an effort to push towards peace talks, President Johnson offered to stop the bombardment of North Vietnam to begin the process toward ending the war. As a first step to deescalate hostilities, he ordered the end of air attacks on North Vietnam, except in the areas surrounding the DMZ. That ended bombing of areas that included 90% of North Vietnam's population. The president concluded his speech with what many called a surprise announcement. He said:

> I do not believe that I should devote an hour or a day of my time to any personal partisan causes or to any duties other than the awesome duties of this office—the presidency of your country, accordingly, I shall not seek and I will not accept the nomination of my party for another term as your president.[26]

Prior to the president's speech, U.S. forces and the South Vietnamese took back communities attacked by the North Vietnamese. However, Tet appeared to weaken domestic support for the war. Daily television coverage of the war proclaimed that "an overall victory in Vietnam was not imminent."[27] As an example, the North Vietnamese managed to get inside the courtyard of the U.S. Embassy in Saigon. Although Marines stopped their efforts, the enemy breached the Embassy.[28] Marine Corporal James C. Marshall, a guard at the Embassy, lost his life in the attack. No other Marines died at the Embassy.[29]

Reflecting on the president's 1968 decision to limit bombing in North Vietnam, General Carey commented, "We didn't understand the rationale because we were prepared. We were pretty much winning in just about everywhere." The General added, while "Tet was a military success for us, it was a moral failure for the United States."[30]

The reduction in permissible bombing area was the 10th time President Johnson eliminated enemy territory from the target list since February 7, 1965. Both Hanoi and Haiphong were then off limits as bombing targets.[31] As the Tet Offensive wound down between April and July, post-Tet planning began. Marines returned their pre-Tet locations to defend populated areas.

Back in the United States, violence and anti-Vietnam-war protests dominated the nation during the spring and summer of 1968. Assassins' bullets struck down two major figures. On April 4, civil rights leader Dr. Martin Luther King, Jr. died after being shot in Memphis. Another assassin killed Senator Kennedy on June 5, shortly after he won the Democratic primary race in California.

Johnson's vice president, Hubert H. Humphrey, a former Minnesota senator, announced his quest for the Democratic presidential nomination in April and then won the nomination. On the Republican side, former Vice President Nixon became his party's presidential nominee for the second time in eight years. In his acceptance speech at the Republican convention Nixon said, "And I pledge to you tonight the first priority foreign policy objective of our next administration will be to bring an honorable end to the war in Vietnam." Nixon won, carrying the popular vote by just over 500,000 out of 73 million votes cast. In the Electoral College vote, Nixon received 301 votes to Humphrey's 191 votes. Third party candidate Alabama Governor George C. Wallace won 46 Electoral College votes.

Carey Working with the Air Force

Although General Carey did not like the single management system from 7th Air Force, the Marine Corps and Air Force often worked together. The Air Force flew sorties out of air bases in Thailand and Vietnam while the Marines flew out of Vietnam. In many cases, the Marine pilots were closer when ground forces needed air support. For example, the Air Force could contact the Marines with a request for a specific number of aircraft for an area. To facilitate those requests, both services operated Direct Air Support Centers (DASC). The Marines operated DASCs in Khe Sanh, Da Nang, and Quang Tri while the Air Force had one in Hue. The General explained the role of the DASCs when he said that they served as "the traffic control point for all tactical air." Requests for tactical air support went first to the DASC, then to the command center where Carey and his staff worked. Carey's team had responsibility for 500 aircraft and 20,000 Marines.[32]

When the lieutenant colonel completed his 13-month assignment in Vietnam, he had established his prowess as combat-tested fighter pilot. In addition to receiving the Distinguished Flying Cross, Carey earned one single-mission Air Medal (equivalent to a Bronze Star with combat V) and 15 Air Medals. That equaled one Air Medal for every 12.75 sorties. His next assignment would take him to Headquarters Marine Corps just outside of Washington in Northern Virginia.

Tet, 30+ Years Later

In remarks prepared for a July 4, 2004, speech to Marine veterans of Vietnam, General Carey said this about his Tet involvement. Early on, as operations officer, he scheduled "round-the-clock close air support." Carey also scheduled and coordinated C-130 resupply drops and helicopters that flew search and rescue missions. The General said this to those who served in Vietnam: "You won and came out with your head held high."[33]

Agreement with General Carey's thoughts on the war in Vietnam came from an unlikely source—a senior member of the general staff of the North Vietnamese Army (known as NVA, they were the Viet Minh in 1940s and early 1950s), Colonel Bui Tin. In 1995 Colonel Tin explained the rationale for the Tet offensive proposed by General Nguyen Chin Than. Colonel Tin led the NVA in South Vietnam as senior commander. "Tet was designed to influence American opinion," Colonel Tin said.[34]

Tin's summary of the results paralleled General Carey's view when he said:

> Our losses were staggering and a complete surprise; [North Vietnam General Vo Nguyen] Giap told me later that Tet had been a military defeat, though we had gained the planned political advantages when Johnson agreed to negotiate and did not run for re-election. The second and third waves in May and September were, in retrospect, mistakes. Our forces in the South were nearly wiped out by all the fighting in 1968.[35]

According to Colonel Tin, Giap acknowledged that Communist forces lost on the battlefield, but won the political and propaganda war.

On January 31, 2006, the Veterans Administration North Texas Veterans' Forum held a program called "What is Tet?" General Carey gave the keynote address. One major challenge in Vietnam, General Carey said:

> Unfortunately, Americans are used to quick victories and were growing weary of the war. A press that was intent upon sensationalism to sell interest and copy had a deleterious [harmful or damaging] effect on our efforts.

General Giap, who led the defeat of the French at Dien Bein Phu in 1954, had two objectives for the Tet offensive. Those objectives were the following: win over the minds and will of the South Vietnamese leading them to overthrow their government, and "inflict a humiliating defeat on U.S. forces."

In his remarks, General Carey described Tet as "the turning point of the war. It could have been the turning point to victory but instead was the turning point in the only war the United States abandoned its duty to finish [as] a victor."

General Carey pointed to the success the United States military had during Tet. Giap lost leadership of his units and "the Viet Cong . . . became ineffective." In the end, Giap's strategy worked, even though he did not achieve his original objectives. First, Americans were embarrassed. Then, the military leadership in Washington recommended against General William C. Westmoreland's request for more troops. Westmoreland, a U.S. Army officer, commanded MACV. The Congress "finally convinced President Johnson that he should unwittingly concede to Giap's original purpose—stop bombing in the North and begin peace negotiations." In Carey's opinion, had Westmoreland's request for additional forces been approved, "We could have marched to Hanoi."

Speaking to the Vietnam veterans in the audience, Carey ended his remarks with this praise: "Gentlemen, history will be kind to us. We fought hard. We did our duty, as God would have us. The heroes of that war will be elevated."[36]

CHAPTER 9

Vietnam Media Coverage

Media coverage of the war in Vietnam had an impact on the civilian community. It was the first war that came into American homes through television. General Carey blasted the media for their part in Vietnam. In his view, the media "played the bad side, never the good things." Finally, he offered his opinion about the media: "They are not our friends."[1]

From an historical standpoint, six U.S presidents including Truman, Eisenhower, Kennedy, Johnson, Nixon, and Ford played a role in Vietnam. While the term Vietnam veteran applies only to those who served in Southeast Asia between 1962 and 1975, the United States involvement started in 1950. In that year, President Truman authorized military aid to the French anti-communists. In July 1950, the United States established the Military Assistance Advisory Group (MAAG) to monitor the use of America's military aid provided to the French. During that month, a Marine second lieutenant named Richard E. Carey started his training for the Korean War. He had no way of knowing that during the next 25 years he would serve in Vietnam three times, including the final days of the war.

Five future presidents had lesser public roles in 1950. Dwight D. Eisenhower, then a retired general, served as president of Columbia University in New York. John F. Kennedy campaigned for this third term as a Massachusetts congressman. Lyndon B. Johnson served in his first term as a United States senator from Texas. Richard M. Nixon, after two terms as a congressman, began a successful run for a California U.S. Senate seat. Gerald R. Ford was finishing his first term as a congressman from Michigan. Each of the five who followed President Truman faced the issue of Vietnam while they served as president. President Eisenhower sent advisors. President Kennedy authorized putting nearly 17,000 troops in Vietnam prior to the time of his assassination.

President Johnson said in his 1964 campaign against his opponent, Arizona Republican Senator Goldwater, that Americans should not fight a war that Asians needed to fight. Despite that campaign promise, President Johnson built up troop strength in Southeast Asia to a half a million service members. Johnson's presidency floundered. President Nixon won election in 1968 by pledging to end the war. Troop withdrawals began in 1969. In 1975, President Ford closed the door on Vietnam with evacuation of more than 100,000 Vietnamese refugees in two days. Then Brigadier General Richard E. Carey led the evacuation.

Anti-Vietnam Protests in the U.S.

During the Vietnam War, the nation faced its widest division since the American Civil War, a century earlier. People saw the battles and the carnage. Many saw the war in living color as color television became a major home entertainment factor by 1965. They also heard the sound bites. Citizens became less trusting of their leaders. The term "credibility gap" entered the conversation. Young people protested the war and the draft. College campuses fueled the anti-war effort. Student protestors occupied the office of Columbia University's president. Protests pushed ROTC programs out of universities including Harvard. Young men burned their draft cards as a sign of protest.

In General Carey's native state of Ohio, the spring of 1970 campus protests culminated in the tragic killing of four young people by National Guardsmen on the campus of Kent State University in Northern Ohio. Following the shootings at Kent State, protests increased at Ohio University in the Southeast part of the state. Brick walkways lined parts of the Athens campus. Protestors allegedly threw the bricks through windows of local businesses. The campus closed early that year. In the General's hometown of Columbus, student protests accelerated during the spring quarter at Ohio State University, the state's flagship university. Three days after the shootings at Kent State, Ohio State closed for two weeks.

In July 1972, Hollywood actress Jane Fonda spent two weeks in Hanoi protesting American involvement in the war. She called the nation's leaders "war criminals." Colonel Tin said the American anti-war movement "was essential to our strategy." He added, "Through dissent and protest it [America] lost the ability to mobilize a will to win."[2]

Presidential Politics and Vietnam

While nine U.S. presidents from Truman to George H.W. Bush were World War I or World War II veterans (Truman served in France during World War I), no one who served in Vietnam (or Korea) has ever become president. Vice President Al Gore, a draftee, served as an Army Specialist 4 at Ben Hoa, Vietnam as a military journalist assigned to an engineer company for five months. Gore and fellow Vietnam veterans Senators John McCain and John Kerry all won their party's presidential nomination and lost their races in the general election. Senator McCain was a former POW. As an anti-Vietnam-war candidate, World War II veteran and South Dakota Democrat Senator George S. McGovern won his party's presidential nomination in 1972.[3] The senator lost the race to incumbent President Nixon.

U.S. Leaders on Vietnam

Even President Johnson's March 31, 1968 television speech pointed out the failure of the communist forces to take key cities that they attacked. There was no uprising in favor of the communists.

Following the evacuation from Vietnam, Secretary of State Dr. Henry A. Kissinger sent President Ford a "lessons learned memo." Regarding the media, Kissinger wrote:

> One clear lesson that can be drawn, however, is the importance of absolute honesty and objectivity in all reporting, within and from the government as well as from the press. U.S. official reports tended for a long time to be excessively optimistic, with the result that official statements did not make clear to the American people how long and how tough the conflict might turn out to be. After a while, the pessimistic reports from journalists began to gain greater credence because such positive trends as did emerge came too slowly to justify optimistic Washington assessments. In Vietnam, the situation was generally worse than some reported, and better than others reported. But the pessimistic reports, even if they were inaccurate, began to look closer to the mark until almost any government statement could be rejected as biased, not only by the opposition but by an increasingly skeptical public.[4]

Television and Newspaper Coverage of Vietnam

Tet's coverage may have been significantly impactful in the American media, and in some cases, tragically wrong. In reality, North Vietnam suffered significantly more casualties than US troops did during the Tet offensive.

The media landscape in the late 1960s consisted of three major television networks. Both CBS and NBC expanded their evening news broadcast coverage from 15 to 30 minutes in 1963. ABC went from 15 to 30 minutes in 1968. All network newscasts broadcast in the early evening. With commercials and story lead-ins, networks showed little more than 20 minutes of actual news. There were no 24-hour news channels during Vietnam. If someone missed the evening network news broadcast, there were newspapers that served as an alternative. Many markets still had more than one daily newspaper. National and international news primarily came from the Associated Press, United Press International, and *The New York Times* News Service. Cities with more than one newspaper had both a morning and afternoon newspaper in most cases. In 1970, there were close to 1,800 daily newspapers in the United States. That number declined by nearly 500 during the next 50 years.[5]

During February 1968, newspapers around the nation ran stories about the Tet offensive. In many instances, papers carried the same Associated Press story. Headlines made the difference in how the story appeared to readers. For example, *The Bridgeport Post* (Connecticut) featured this headline on February 3: "12,704 Reds, Yank Losses at 318." That headline demonstrated the success of the U.S. military, just a few days after the Tet offensive began. On the same day, the identical story in *The South Bend Tribune* ran this headline, "Reds Attack Eight Cities." *The Charleston Daily Mail's* (West Virginia) February 8, headline read "Reds Attack Marine Base at Khe Sanh." Positioning of the first three paragraphs in the Charleston paper, however, told another story. The first paragraph talked about the North Vietnamese using a combination of heavy artillery and ground attacks. In the next paragraph, the story mentioned that the "Reds" fired more than 300 rocket, mortar, and artillery rounds. Finally, in paragraph three, the story talked about the success the Marines had by describing how the Marines counterattacked with heavy artillery and air support to drive the North Vietnamese down the hill. A scan of the headline and the first two paragraphs never gave readers any inkling of Marine success at Khe Sanh.

As an example of why he had negative views about the media, General Carey talked about the coverage of Hue. The general said the Marines found a large number of civilian bodies in the Citadel. Out of respect for the dead, Marines covered the bodies with their ponchos. Media visuals left the impression that the victims were Marines, according to the General.[6]

Considering the total media coverage on Vietnam, a 2009 History.com analysis summarized it best by pointing out that the North Vietnamese achieved a strategic advantage despite taking heavy casualties during the Tet Offensive.[7]

Content Analysis of Vietnam News Stories

Post-Vietnam studies between 1979 and 2019 offered an analysis of the media's role between the military and public. Four studies are briefly summarized. Military officers wrote two of the studies and two were written by civilians.

Major Richard P. Holk, an Army public information officer, wrote his 1979 thesis while a graduate student at California State University at Fullerton. He studied the *Los Angeles Times* between 1964 and 1972. The major said, "Stories reporting U.S. forces decreased while stories reporting anti-war protests increased."[8]

In 1981, Augusta Denita Minor, an Iowa State University graduate student, wrote a thesis comparing Vietnam War editorials between *The New York Times* and *The Washington Post*. She concluded that, "Earlier research has shown that mass media, in general, supported the war in the early stages, and opposed it as the war progressed." Minor's study concluded that *The New York Times* wrote anti-war editorials. On the other hand, *The Washington Post* early positions questioned the wisdom of bombing halts.[9]

Long-time CBS News anchor Walter Cronkite went to Vietnam during the Tet offensive. In his first ever on-air editorial on February 28, 1968, Cronkite described the war as "bloody stalemate." He called for the United States to negotiate to end the war.

On July 12, 2012, Robert W. Merry, writing for nationalinterest.com called Cronkite's commentary "Cronkite's Vietnam Blunder." Merry said Tet was a "desperation move" by North Vietnam. He also pointed out that communist forces lost some 10,000 soldiers in the first days of Tet. U.S. forces, according to Merry, lost fewer than 800 service members during that same time.[10]

In 2019, Marine Major Christopher Nelson wrote an analysis of Vietnam media coverage for the Marine Corps University at Quantico (part of Carey's portfolio in the early 1980s). Nelson explained that reporters in Washington received optimistic views from senior government officials. Reporters in Vietnam had a different perspective from those who faced the enemy on the ground. According to Nelson, President Johnson turned to General William C. Westmoreland, commander Military Assistance Command Vietnam, to serve as the voice of optimism. Nelson said this about that effort,

> Their optimism campaign, combined with the deception efforts of the North Vietnamese, created a confluence of self-delusion and misunderstanding, a cognitive gap that was left wide open in the final days of January 1968.[11]

General Carey believed that General Westmoreland utilized the optimism campaign to put the Army in a positive light. In a letter to Brigadier General Edwin H. Simmons (Simmons served as director of Marine Corps History and Museums), Carey wrote,

> Westmorland was and is a stuffed shirt and I know for a fact that the down to earth combat style of the Marines rankled him. Thus if he could use the hottest area to improve the Vietnam image and concurrently give leadership credit to the Army, why not?[12]

Although General Carey did not deal with the media until he reached senior level assignments, his exposure to press coverage during Vietnam made him cautious when dealing with reporters. Later in his career, he would face negative coverage while serving as the 2nd MAW commanding general at Cherry Point, North Carolina, in 1977.

CHAPTER 10

Post-Vietnam War

Following his service in Vietnam, Lieutenant Colonel Carey went to Headquarters Marine Corps (HQMC) in the Navy Annex in Arlington, Virginia. (HMQC moved to the Pentagon in 1996.) He served as an aviation logistics officer. In that assignment, Carey led conception and consolidation of aviation logistics requirements to 1,000 aircraft and 50,000 Marines. He initiated a service-wide process for inventory control of all material as well as handling support equipment.

In this Washington-area assignment, he said, "My task was to keep resupply lines going for all (Marine) aviation." That included not only Vietnam, but also system-wide for the Marines. Since the war continued in Vietnam, keeping munitions and parts moving through to the war zone led his list of priorities. He believed that his wartime experience as a fighter pilot gave him knowledge of needed equipment in Vietnam. Although he had no trouble dealing with long workdays in the war zone, long hours in an office environment at the Headquarters Marine Corps offered a new challenge. The general described his time in headquarters environment. He left home at 6 a.m. and returned at 8 p.m. carrying two full briefcases of paperwork. He worked seven days a week. The General said, "I didn't see my family. It was kind of a bad job as far the family was concerned." That started his wife Dena's dislike for life in Washington that would become a factor in the General's career plans 14 years later. The procurement process challenged him. He described bidding as "obviously politically motivated."[1] The General explained that comment by pointing out that the Marine Corps at times competed with the Navy for aircraft parts.

In addition to the long hours, the colonel faced a career crossroads. As he approached 24 years in service, Colonel Carey had three options. Option one—retire. Option two—he could remain in the Marine Corps for a few more years with only a very slight chance of reaching the rank of full colonel. In other words, he faced a career dead end. Option three—take charge of his career and open doors for future opportunities. To execute the third option, Colonel Carey needed to earn a college degree. This had been on his horizon several times, but duties as a fighter pilot and overseas assignments limited his opportunities to pursue a degree. To advance to a senior level in the Marine Corps, Lieutenant Colonel Carey knew that he needed to obtain a college degree. The Marines had the "bootstrap" program that provided time for officers to attend college on a full-time basis. Typically, that opportunity went to rising officers early in their careers.

In any organization, people with long-term career objectives need someone in their corner. That person could help with a high-profile assignment, special training, or mentoring. In Carey's case, Lieutenant General Keith McCutcheon played that part. He served as Carey's boss as deputy chief of staff for Marine Aviation. Carey told him that he planned to retire. It was the second time in two years that Lieutenant Colonel Carey had considered retirement. General McCutcheon said no. He asked what Carey wanted. Carey told McCutcheon that he wanted to get his degree through the "bootstrap program." Carey mentioned that he had tried but failed to win a slot in the program in the past. General McCutcheon, a fellow Ohioan, told him to put in his application for the "bootstrap program" again.[2] McCutcheon told him, "This will ensure that you will make colonel." Carey added that General McCutcheon "was very considerate of me and appreciative of the hard work I put in at Headquarters Marine Corps."[3]

Carey received an approval letter to finish college in the bootstrap program on May 16, 1969 "for a period in excess of 20 weeks." He enrolled in George Washington University in Washington, D.C., between 1969 and 1971. In effect, he received a sabbatical to work on his degree. While he paid for tuition and books, Carey received his full pay and allowances as a lieutenant colonel. By applying previously earned college credits, he completed a bachelor's degree in business from the School of Government and Business in 1971 at 43 years old. The decision to complete his degree paid off for Carey. While finishing his final exams at George Washington University, he received word of his promotion to full colonel. He graduated in January 1971. It took 26 years for Colonel Carey to earn his "eagles" (rank insignia of a full colonel). Getting his college degree opened up new opportunities and aided the next nine years of his career.

Sadly, General McCutcheon did not live to see the long-term results of aiding Colonel Carey's effort to win acceptance in the "bootstrap program" and convincing him not to retire. General McCutcheon died of cancer on July 13, 1971, at the age of 55. He retired as a four-star general. McCutcheon pinned on his fourth star 12 days before his death.[4]

To Hawaii and "Hello General"

After learning of his promotion to full colonel, there was more good news for Colonel Carey as his orders for a new assignment came through. His time as a Headquarters Marine Corps desk jockey and college student ended. Carey's next assignment took him to Hawaii. With a college degree and a promotion, Colonel Carey's career had passed the dead-end position. Dena and the children were also going with him for the next 18 months. Colonel Carey took command of the Marine Air Group 24 (MAG-24) at Kaneohe, about 12 miles from Honolulu. He succeeded Colonel Kenny C. Palmer who moved to a staff position with the 1st Marine Brigade (1stMAB). According to General Carey, MAG-24 was the largest MAG in the history of the Marine Corps at that time. It was also the oldest MAG unit, having begun operations in 1942: Carey led the MAG during the celebration of its 29th anniversary. *Windward Marine*, the base newspaper, pictured him preparing a slice of cake for the MAG's youngest member. The oldest member of the MAG also participated in the ceremony.[5]

As MAG commander, Carey quickly learned that the war in Vietnam continued heating up and fighter pilots needed training. In this assignment, Colonel Carey applied lessons learned from his wartime experience in Vietnam and his training leadership role at Cherry Point. At Kaneohe, the colonel commanded three fighter/attack squadrons, an air control squadron, Marine Air Base Squadron-24 (MABS-24), Headquarters and Maintenance Squadron-24 (H&MS-24), and three helicopter squadrons. Altogether, Colonel Carey led 4,000 Marines. In that assignment, Carey said that he faced what he described as the "unprecedented" challenge of integrating helicopters into a fighter group.

The fighter pilots, who trained at Kaneohe, went to Thailand to support remaining ground Southeast Asia Treaty Organization (SEATO) forces still fighting in Vietnam. Those ground forces did not include the Marine ground units after May 7, 1971, the day the USMC ceased all ground combat in Vietnam. As the war wound down, more helicopters returned from Vietnam. With returning helicopters, Colonel Carey got himself up to speed on flying helicopters. Although he had served as a co-pilot on helicopter flights in Vietnam, the colonel was not a designated Marine helicopter pilot before his Kaneohe assignment. While there, MAG-24's aircraft included the following: CH-46, CH-53, Cobra, and Huey helicopters. As the MAG-24 group commander, and the man who led from the front, Colonel Carey became a qualified helicopter pilot.

Newly named Colonel Carey (left) took command of Marine Air Group 24 from Colonel Kenny C. Palmer at Kaneohe, Hawaii. (Carey family collection, 1971)

Just as he did with his squadron at Cherry Point, Colonel Carey challenged his pilots in Hawaii to achieve more. The objective set by the always-competitive Carey was to win the Hanson Trophy as the Marine Corps' top fighter squadron. A MAG-24 squadron met that challenge. The trophy honored Captain Robert M. Hanson, a World War II Marine pilot who served in the Pacific. A fighter ace, Captain Hanson shot down 25 Japanese aircraft (five times the number of enemy aircraft to qualify for the designation of ace). Killed in action in 1944, the captain was a posthumous recipient of the Medal of Honor.

Not only did Carey's MAG win the Marine Corps' top fighter squadron honors, one of his MAG's helicopter squadrons won the McCutcheon Trophy. That award honored the memory of General Keith B. McCutcheon. As previously noted, McCutcheon played a key role in Colonel Carey's career advancement when the General supported Carey's efforts to enter the "bootstrap program." During his career, General McCutcheon led helicopter squadrons at Quantico and in Korea.

If winning a top fighter squadron and top helicopter squadron award was not enough, Carey's team also won the Commandant's Efficiency Trophy. The MAG Carey led had the highest overall efficiency rating in the Marine Corps. Because of those major achievements, Colonel Carey received the Legion of Merit. His citation read in part:

> The President of the United States of America takes pleasure in presenting the Legion of Merit to Colonel Richard Edward Carey, United States Marine Corps, for exceptionally meritorious conduct in the performance of outstanding services to the Government of the United States as Commanding Officer, Marine Aircraft Group 24, First Marine Brigade, Marine Corps Air Station, Kaneohe, Hawaii from 10 February 1971 to 5 May 1972. Throughout this period, Colonel Carey demonstrated exceptional professionalism, executive and organization abilities and sound judgment in the performance of his challenging and demanding duties. Assuming command during the Vietnam retrograde, he exhibited superior knowledge of Marine Corps managerial concepts as he expertly reorganized personnel and material assets to facilitate the joining of five new aviation units. The two helicopter squadrons and helicopter detachment established a problematic precedent … when augmented to the historically fixed wing Group. Applying imaginative and innovative concepts, he aggressively engendered a synergetic spirit within Marine Aircraft Group 24, which promoted a unity of purpose, resulting in exceptional unit and personnel accomplishments.

After serving as commander of MAG-24, Carey moved to Fleet Marine Forces, Pacific (FMFPAC). FMFPAC, located at Camp H. M. Smith on Oahu, HI, 15 miles southwest of Kaneohe Bay, home of MAG-24. In that role, he served as operations officer (G-3) responsible for planning operational deployments and helped in leading 80,000 Marines. As part of his assignment, Carey had a rotating watch as a battle staff chief reporting to the CINCPAC (Commander in Chief Pacific Forces), Admiral John S. McCain, Jr., father of Senator John S. McCain III. CINCPAC requested that in Hawaii all branches of service provide a battle staff chief to report directly to Admiral McCain. The battle staff chiefs primarily monitored operations in Vietnam. Carey provided detailed briefings to Admiral McCain. According to the General, "I briefed the CINCPAC every time I had the watch. I was [the] one Battle Staff Chief not relieved from the Battle Staff by the CINCPAC. I was kind of proud of that."[6]

While Carey had battle staff chief duty on July 9, 1972, Typhoon Rita struck in the Pacific. The typhoon forced the crew of a B-52 to eject from the Air Force bomber about 300 miles from their base in Guam. Colonel Carey coordinated the B-52 crew rescue from the ocean with CINCPAC. One of the six crew members died before their return to Andersen Air Force Base located at Yigo, Guam.[7] That was the first B-52 rescue during a typhoon.

POWs Return from North Vietnam

On February 12, 1973, the first American POWs held in North Vietnam's notorious "Hanoi Hilton" began their return to the United States. Carey was on duty as battle staff chief that day, reporting to McCain's successor, Admiral

Noel Gayler. Including POWs held in Vietnam, Cambodia, Laos, and China, more than 1,000 American service members returned to the U.S. according to the Defense POW Accounting Agency (DPAA).[8] Carey had to assure returning Marine POWs were "appropriately handled" and that Marines would assist their colleagues as they came back to the United States. Carey contacted the returning POWs, asked if they had any problems and how the Marine Corps could help. Those he spoke with mainly expressed appreciation for the call. All of them said they were okay and would call if they needed anything. Carey said none of them called for assistance.[9]

Twenty-four Marines were among the American POWs released by the North Vietnamese.[10] Two Marine officers survived captivity in Hanoi for more than seven years. The North Vietnamese captured Captain Harlan Page Chapman on November 5, 1965. Thirty-two days later the North Vietnamese took Major John Howard "Howie" Dunn as a POW on December 7, 1965.[11]

Chapman, a fighter pilot, flew the F-8E Crusader. He was held captive in North Vietnam longer than any other member of the Marine Corps. For his time in the POW camp, Chapman received the Silver Star.

After his time as a POW, Lieutenant Colonel Chapman retired in 1976 after 20 years of service.

(Then) Major Dunn received the Silver Star for courage following his ejection from his F-4 Phantom II in 1965. Dunn retired from the Marine Corps in 1974 as a full colonel. He died in 1998 at the age of 67.[12] The General and Howie Dunn served in the same squadron at MCAS Beaufort in South Carolina. Carey said, "He was an outstanding Marine in all respects."

Promotion to Brigadier General

In 1969, Carey thought his path to promotion had passed him by. In the five years that followed, his career accelerated. Promoted to colonel in early 1971, he held that rank for less than four years when he learned of his promotion to brigadier general. The squad leader in a recruit training platoon at Parris Island in 1946 pinned on his first star in August 1974. He learned of his promotion from Lieutenant General Louis H. Wilson, Jr. Commanding General, FMFPAC. General Carey said that he received the news in a telephone call from General Wilson that began with two words—"Hello, General."[13] General Wilson told him, "You've got a choice assignment. You're being assigned out to WESTPAC as the assistant wing commander of the 1st Marine Aircraft Wing (1st MAW) stationed at Iwakuni, Japan."[14] After speaking with General

Wilson, the newly named brigadier general called Dena with these words, "This is General Carey." She excitedly and proudly responded, "You made it!"[15]

General Carey described General Wilson as both a friend and a mentor: "the type of Marine you want to be—hard-nosed, very understanding, and caring." He added that General Wilson was the "ultimate Marine who was a true hero on and off the battlefield." General Wilson earned respect for his Marine Corps leadership.[16] A World War II Medal of Honor recipient for actions as a company commander in Guam, he was nominated by President Ford to serve as the commandant of the Marine Corps in 1975, a post he held until his retirement in 1979.[17]

General Wilson suggested two reasons for calling Carey's new assignment "choice." First, Carey reported to an aviator, and second, he would have opportunities to continue flying. When General Carey returned to Iwakuni in August 1974, Marines were already planning for the eventual evacuation from Cambodia and Vietnam. Helicopters from the 1st Marine Air Wing (MAW) prepared for the evacuation. Those helicopters were on Okinawa. As the General said, "We were going to be the primary people to conduct the operations."

Back to Iwakuni

Upon his return to Iwakuni, Carey held dual assignments as both assistant wing commander, 1st MAW, and commanding general of Ninth Marine Amphibious Brigade (9th MAB). The 9th MAB consisted of an infantry regiment with attached supporting arms, a battery of artillery, tanks, and a helicopter squadron. For what Marines term "dual-hatted" roles the new brigadier general reported to Major General Norman W. Gourley, who commanded 1st MAW, was a Marine aviator who flew combat sorties during World War II, Korea, and Vietnam.[18] General Gourley retired in 1978 after 36 years in the Marine Corps.

The 1st MAW served as "the aviation combat element of III Marine Expeditionary Force." The mission of 1st MAW included offensive air support, anti-air support along with aerial reconnaissance. Reconnaissance covered electronic countermeasures. In addition, 1st MAW served as part of Naval Aviation at the direction of the Fleet Commander.[19]

CHAPTER II

Evacuation from Vietnam

During the Christmas and New Year holidays of 1974, Brigadier General Carey spent 12 days' leave with his family in his wife's hometown of Bonham, Texas. Carey arrived on December 23 and stayed until January 4. The General had his last bit of rest before what would become a very busy 1975. The local newspaper even covered his visit.[1]

Evacuation from Southeast Asia

Bringing Vietnamese refugees to the United States along with American service members and Embassy staff would mark the end of the war in Vietnam after 13 years. For General Carey, who headed the effort to bring people out, it was a bittersweet moment. Thousands of Vietnamese who aided the American effort in Vietnam would get a fresh start in the United States. Sadly, not everyone who wanted to leave Vietnam could do that. The words that follow were part of General Carey's after-action report to Admiral Gayler, CINCPAC.

> My desire to succeed in the evacuation was driven by empathy-compassion for the people and to overcome/block out the shame I felt as an American abandoning the people of a nation that had endured immense suffering who believed in us. Now here we were leaving them without hope. Of course, they had no way of knowing our reasons for leaving. In fact, why did we leave? Yes, our government pointed to a budget deficit and Vietnam was too costly so it was time to cut the cord. But you and I know we operate most of the time with a budget deficit. I think we were simply out strategized. Vietnam was a classic Mao-ist protracted warfare and the way to win was pursued by North Vietnam.

General Carey had a long-term perspective on Vietnam. Early in the war, he spent two weeks identifying potential Marine airbases while gathering intelligence from Marine advisors. In 1967 and 1968, he flew 204 combat sorties out of Chu Lai and Da Nang. In early March 1975, General Carey took over as commanding general of Ninth Marine Amphibious Brigade

(9th MAB). Now, seven years after flying combat sorties in Vietnam, he had the responsibility of bringing out of that country as many people as possible.

Prior to getting deeply involved with the evacuation, Carey received a new task that would eventually aid his efforts when it came time to bring people out of Vietnam. On October 5, 1974, General Gourley identified a challenge—reduce aircraft risk from anti-aircraft weapons and surface to air missiles (SAMs). He tasked Carey to lead a group called 1st MAW Tactical Evaluation Board. After the board met three weeks later, the members determined that night flights would reduce the risks. By December, the wing helicopters reoriented the training schedule to include night combat missions.[2]

During the planning and execution of the evacuation of Saigon, called Operation *Frequent Wind*, the General's team of Marines worked across service lines in a joint effort with the Navy, Army, Air Force, and to a lesser degree, the United States ambassador to Vietnam. Operational planning began just a few weeks before the evacuation that occurred on April 29, 1975. Leading the overall mission as commander of Task Force 76 was Navy Rear Admiral Donald B. Whitmire. A rear admiral holds the equivalent rank of a Marine major general. Carey worked on evacuation planning out of the command center on the Navy's ship, the *Blue Ridge*.

The *Blue Ridge* served as Carey's headquarters in preparation for the evacuation of Saigon. The General ran the planning meeting from the end of the right corner of the conference table. Carey's ground commander, Colonel Al Gray, future Marine Corps commandant, sits to Carey's immediate right. (Official United States Navy photograph, 1975)

An earlier effort did not go well. In the spring of 1975, President Ford approved funding to bring 2,000 orphaned children to the United States as part of a mission called "Operation *Baby Lift*". In an April 3, 1975, statement from the Office of the White House Press Secretary, President Ford said,

> I have directed that money from a $2 million special foreign aid children's fund be made available to fly 2,000 South Vietnamese orphans to the United States as soon as possible. … I have also directed American officials in Saigon to cut red tape and bureaucratic obstacles preventing these children from coming to the United States. … These 2,000 Vietnamese orphans are all in the process of being adopted by American families.[3]

The first flight of Operation *Baby Lift*, leaving Vietnam on April 4, ended in tragedy. A U.S. Air Force C-5A Galaxy transport airplane malfunctioned shortly after takeoff from Ton Son Nhut Air Base with more than 300 passengers and crew members. The cargo doors blew off along with part of the tail. Decompression in the cabin followed. Air Force Captain Dennis "Bud" Traynor stabilized the C-5. He crash-landed the giant transport in rice paddies. Sadly, 128 people died in the crash including 78 children and 50 adults. Among the adults killed were members of the Defense Attaché Office (DAO) and the Air Force.

Captain Traynor received the Air Force Cross (the nation's second highest award for heroism in combat) following that flight. His citation read, in part, "With no aircraft controls except one aileron and the engines, he guided the crippled aircraft to a crash landing in a rice paddy, thereby saving the lives of 176 of the people aboard." He completed a 28-year Air Force career and retired as a full colonel.[4]

General Carey made this observation about the crash, "Of course, my reaction to it is obviously horror that it happened and how could it happen?" He also said that the crash influenced his thinking on using helicopters for rescue instead of fixed-wing aircraft.[5]

Operation *Eagle Pull*—Cambodia

On April 13, nine days after first orphan evacuation flight, rescue efforts in Cambodia began. The code name for the mission was Operation *Eagle Pull.* Helicopters launched from ships to Phnom Penh, Cambodia's capital. Evacuations from Cambodia had unique challenges. First, the distance of 130 miles required the addition of internal fuel tanks on the helicopters to ensure that the pilots could make the round trip. Second came a navigation problem. Helicopter pilots had to navigate over land they had not been over before and get to the U.S. Embassy. When asked about navigational aids, General Carey provided a one-word response—"maps." The pilots placed maps on their knees as they flew into Phnom Penh. Another obstacle in the evacuation facing the planners was the number of potential evacuees kept increasing.[6] That would become a greater problem in Vietnam at the end of April.

On the ground, Marines kept the helicopter landing zones clear and established the perimeter to aid in the evacuation. That day, April 13, 440 Cambodians and 146 Americans including the United States ambassador to Cambodia, John Gunther Dean, boarded helicopters. As the evacuation in Cambodia wound down, General Carey and his team accelerated their efforts to prepare for Vietnam. His staff included G-1 for administration, G-2 for intelligence, G-3 for operations, and G-4 for logistics. He described that team as "pretty solid."[7] In a debriefing following the evacuation from Saigon, General Carey said, "We cut our teeth (for the Saigon evacuation) on *Eagle Pull*."

While operational planning continued, the code name changed. Originally called Operation *Talon Vise*, planners determined that people had compromised that code name. As a result, the new code name became Operation *Frequent Wind*.[8]

Prior to the start of the evacuation of Saigon, Brigadier General Carey reviews final details of the plan known as Operation *Frequent Wind*. (Carey family collection, 1975)

Having previously butted heads with a senior Army and an Air Force officer, General Carey clashed this time with a Naval officer, Admiral Whitmire, who outranked him, during both the planning and execution of *Frequent Wind*. Admiral Whitmire expressed his concern with the combat readiness of Marine helicopter pilots coming from Hawaii. To satisfy the admiral, and in a way, to prevent Whitmire from being blamed if the Marines failed, General Carey sent him a written message. He said the Marines were "fully combat ready." General Carey had prior experience with the helicopter squadrons when he commanded MAG-24 in the early 1970s. In the end, those pilots did their job during the evacuation. In his post-evacuation briefing, General Carey mentioned that he faced that challenge from Admiral Whitmire.

His combined experience with both the Marines' ground forces and aviation made Carey the ideal candidate to serve as commanding general of Operation *Frequent Wind*. He said that some in the Marine Corps referred to him as "the flying grunt." Reflecting on the assignment 30 years later, General Carey described it as a "plum" assignment.[9] While a significant amount of time went into planning the evacuation, the General understood the adage, "when the bullets start flying, plans change." General Carey added, "War is chaos and it [the evacuation] was chaotic."[10]

To accomplish the mission of bringing out as many people as possible, General Carey worked with a team of experienced Marine and Air Force pilots along with Air America. Air America, a civilian airline operated by the Central Intelligence Agency (CIA), flew refugees from around South Vietnam into Ton Son Nhut, a civilian airport located about 5 miles from Saigon. All of the military pilots had what the General termed "heavy combat experience." He added, "They did a helluva job." The North Vietnamese forces did not make the evacuation easy for the Marines as they were in the process of taking over Saigon.

In his post-evacuation debriefing, the General talked about the details that went into the planning. While the aircraft and ships made a decided difference, evacuees had to get to a designated spot for pickup. That meant ground transportation—buses. In addition, the plan called for lining up volunteer bus drivers. To establish landing zones for the helicopters, General Carey explained during the debriefing, "Safety of 'helos' [helicopters] was of paramount importance." He added, "It would have been a disaster if we didn't prepare." To make sure the landing zones were safe for the helicopter pilots, General Carey's team removed flag poles, trees, lights, power lines, and debris from the area.

During the debriefing, General Carey pointed out that "We never take anything for granted." Part of the planning incorporated night flying and instrument flying rules (IFR). Despite all of the planning, the evacuation team faced a challenge with communications. The forces on the ground could not directly communicate with the *Blue Ridge*.[11]

For the most part, the multi-service planning worked well. Unfortunately, there was one major challenge—the U.S. ambassador to South Vietnam, Graham Martin. Ambassador Martin, a career diplomat, previously held ambassadorships in Thailand and Italy. Despite the fact that the decision to leave Vietnam had been made in Washington, Ambassador Martin continued to push contacts in the nation's capital for additional support for South Vietnam. He did not participate in the evacuation planning. In fact, General Carey explained, the military had to work out their planning without him. The General described planning around Ambassador Martin this way, "It was kind of a sneaky operation." In addition, the ambassador told military members who came to the Embassy that they had to wear civilian clothes even though they flew from ships by Marine Corps helicopters. General Carey's theory on Ambassador Martin's reluctance to aid the planning of an evacuation seemed to relate to his support of the South Vietnamese. The General said, "He did not want to let it out that we were planning anything like that."

There was also conjecture that the ambassador had a personal reason for wanting to continue the fight. That personal connection involved Marine First Lieutenant Glenn Dill Mann, a UH-1 Huey helicopter pilot killed near Chu Lai in 1965. Some sources said the lieutenant was an adopted nephew of the ambassador. Another source referred to Lieutenant Mann as his foster son. The lieutenant served with VMO-6 Squadron (Marine Observation) as part of Marine Air Group 36 (MAG-36) in 1st MAW.

General Carey also offered another reason for the ambassador's reluctance to leave. The General said that Ambassador Martin simply loved the people of South Vietnam and was dedicated to them. Still, he should not have taken the approach that he did, in Carey's view.[12] In his post-evacuation comments, General Carey described the ambassador as "irritable."

While much of the planning took place on the *Blue Ridge*, General Carey often went to Vietnam by helicopter. As uncooperative as the ambassador was, the Defense Attaché Office (DAO), led by the Army's Major General Homer Smith, continually aided Carey's team. General Smith and Marine Colonel Eugene R. "Pat" Howard initially started planning for the Saigon evacuation in February. According to General Carey, "Those guys were invaluable." General Smith had experience in a major logistical military effort having served on the logistics planning staff for the invasion of Normandy in World War II as a junior officer; he later would go on to lead the U.S. Army Logistics Center prior to retiring from the Army in 1979 after nearly 36 years of service.

Support for the ground effort came from Marine Colonel Alfred M. (Al) Gray, who served as regimental commander for the 4th Marines. Colonel Gray's regiment included the ground forces and DAO security. Medal of Honor recipient and future Major General James E. Livingston, then a major, served as Colonel Gray's operations officer (S-3). That team's responsibilities included explosive ordnance disposal (EOD), radio operators, and site preparation. General Carey offered praise for Colonel Gray's performance as ground commander during the operation. He also signed off on a personal award recommendation form calling for Gray to receive a Legion of Merit Medal. Twelve years later, Colonel Gray rose to be commandant of the Marine Corps as a four-star general.

The Air Force leadership of Operation *Frequent Wind* came under the direction of Lieutenant General John J. Burns, who commanded USSAG—United States Support Activities Group/Seventh Air Force at Nakhon Phanom Thailand, usually called NKP, as it was easier to pronounce. General Burns, a fighter pilot, flew a combined 340 combat sorties in World War II, Korea, and Vietnam.[13]

General Carey sent members of the 9th MAB on a site reconnaissance mission in South Vietnam to determine possible evacuation locations. The DAO compound was on the original list. The Marines visited Ambassador Martin. He told MAB members that he "would not tolerate any outward sign of intent to depart the country to avoid it becoming a self-fulfilling prophecy." On April 13, General Carey and Colonel Gray went to Vietnam for their own reconnaissance visit. The General, as did his team, found Ambassador Martin uncooperative. Carey described the meeting with Ambassador Martin this way, "That visit was cold, non-productive, and appeared to be an irritant to the ambassador." In addition to meeting with the ambassador, General Carey and Colonel Gray held discussions with General Smith at DAO and the CINCPAC representative, Rear Admiral Hugh G. Benton. To aid in communication and to help alleviate problems with jargon and procedures unique to the Marines, General Carey assigned Major Richard K. Young, a plans officer who worked out of NKP, to General Burns' team.[14]

On April 20, 1975, 9th MAB published Operation Order 2-75, the plan for Operation *Frequent Wind*.[15] Three days later, President Ford spoke at Tulane University in New Orleans. In his speech, before an audience of 9,000,

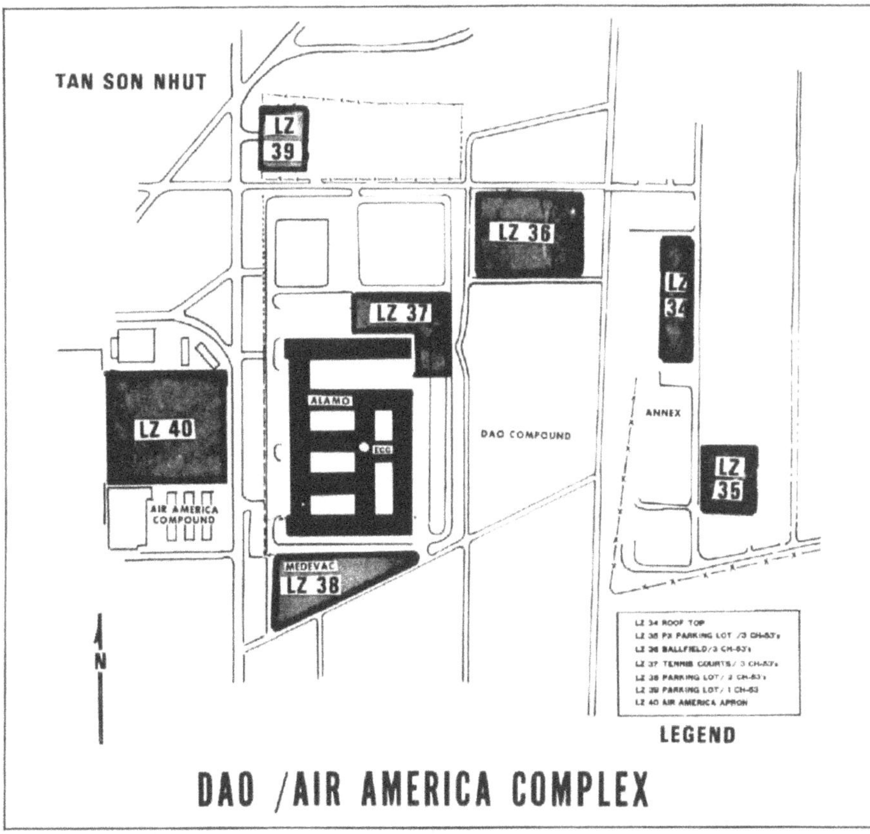

Secretary of State Dr. Henry A. Kissinger directed the use of helicopters for evacuation from the Defense Attaché Office (DAO) and Embassy compound on April 29. This diagram shows the helicopter landing zones at the DAO. (United States Marine Corps, produced by 9th Marine Amphibious Brigade)

the president said, "We can't refight a war that is finished as far America is concerned."

On April 29, U.S. Secretary of State Dr. Henry A. Kissinger sent a cable to Ambassador Martin with a list of the decisions resulting from President Ford's meeting with the National Security Council (NSC). Secretary Kissinger summarized the following three points: point one—evacuate "high risk Vietnamese" and American personnel by fixed-wing aircraft from Tan Son Nhut; point two—last day (April 29) for fixed-wing evacuation; and point three—if Tan Son Nhut is unusable for fixed-wing aircraft, then "immediately resort to helicopter evacuation from the DAO and Embassy compounds."[16]

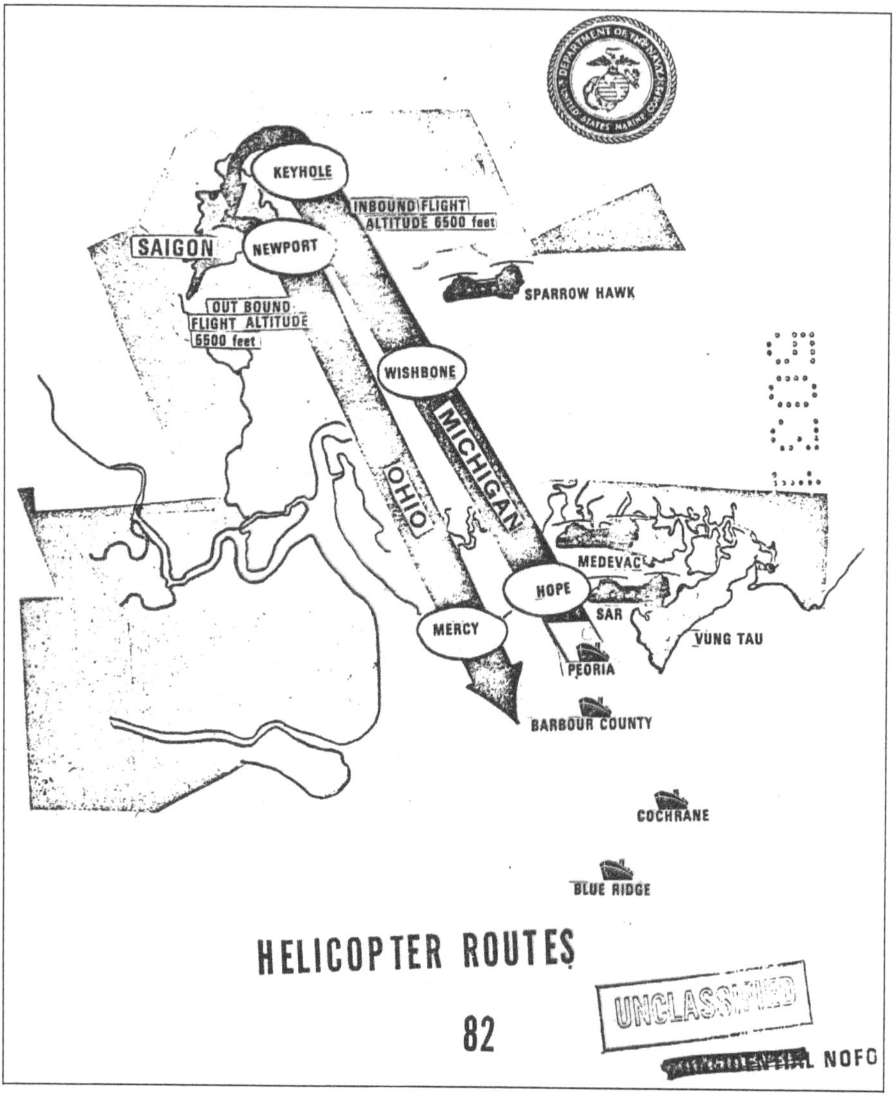

The helicopter force, under Brigadier General Carey's command, followed these routes to rescue Vietnamese refugees from Saigon. (Courtesy of the Department of the Navy, United States Marine Corps, 1975)

The operation took place on the 29th. It involved 6,000 Marines, 30,000 members of the United States Navy, and 40 ships.[17] Evacuations would take place at the DAO compound. Although the U.S. Embassy would not be the primary evacuation site, there was a contingency plan to pull up to 100 people from the rooftop. Weather could challenge the mission: reports indicated inclement weather and ceilings of less than 1,000 feet. General Carey expressed confidence in the Marine pilots. He recommended the use of tactical air. CINCPAC, led by Admiral Noel A. Gayler, authorized use of aircraft from Seventh Air Force and Navy carrier wings.

Supporting the operation on the ground were members of the Amphibious Evacuation Security Force (AESF). AESF included military

This is an overhead view of the DAO helicopter landing sites in Saigon. (From the 9th MAB Frequent Wind post-operational summary, 1975)

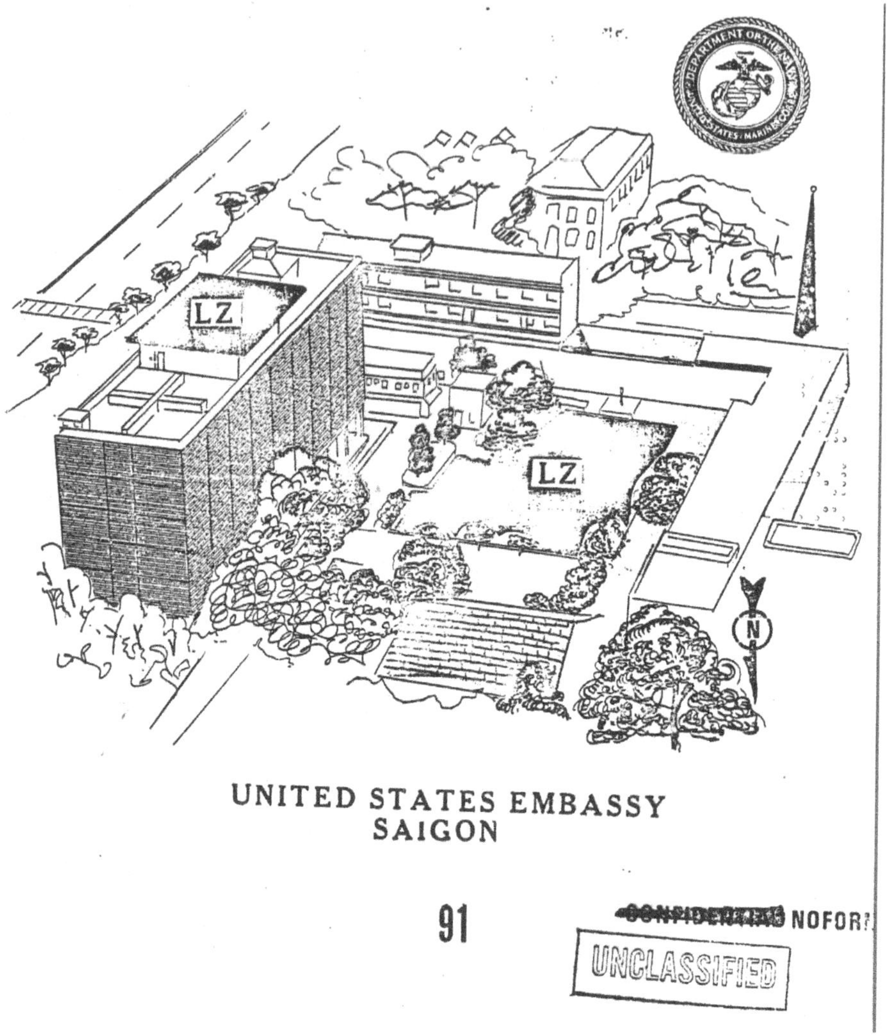

The United States Embassy ended up serving as a refugee recuse location. The rooftop served as a helicopter landing zone. (Courtesy of the Department of the Navy, United States Marine Corps, 1975)

police, interrogator-translators, and counterintelligence experts. Translators played a key role in communication between evacuees and Americans. In addition, General Carey directed Marines to use minimum force, although all commanders received authorization to increase force as necessary.[18]

Unclear communications delayed the execution of *Frequent Wind*. L-Hour to the Marines meant "landing" time. To the Air Force, the term meant "launch" time. Ultimately, that confusion caused a four-hour delay. The order to begin the operation went out at 10:51 a.m. Saigon time. Between 10:52 a.m. and 12:15 p.m., the message was lost. Evacuations began at 3 p.m. Prior to the launch, ground efforts to bring evacuees to the DAO began. Forty buses took people to the DAO, in a surface evacuation operation led by then Marine Captain Anthony A. "Tony" Wood. The buses covered six routes. To protect the buses, Wood said that he arranged to paint cars replicating National Police vehicles.[19] Those cars provided security for the buses. Captain Wood faced two major obstacles. First, he received a request to pick up Ambassador Martin's dog. The captain, now a retired colonel, said in 2021 that he sent a bus to pick up the ambassador's dog.[20] Second, as the final bus approached the gate to the DAO, Army of the Republic of Vietnam (ARVN) troops, the allies of the United States, would not let the bus pass. General Carey, who arrived at the DAO with Colonel Gray at 1:50 p.m., had to get involved. He made it simple. Cobra helicopters were making passes over the compound. If the ARVN would not cooperate, General Carey told Captain Wood, he would authorize the Cobra helicopters pilots to fire. In the end, Cobra pilots did not have to fire. The bus went into the compound.[21]

Protecting the U.S. Embassy During the Evacuation

General Carey remained at the DAO for command and control purposes. He learned that the ambassador would not be coming to the DAO as originally planned. With that surprising change of plans, General Carey reallocated assets. He sent 130 Marines to the Embassy for additional security.

Lance Corporal Anthony D. Lyons helped provide Embassy security between April 29 and 30 as a member of Charlie Company 1/4.[22] Lyons described that experience as "a tense situation" and he "got shot at" while handling security. Lyons described one tender moment. The Marines found a small child wearing only his underwear. Nicknaming the boy Charlie (in honor of their company), the Marines fixed a uniform shirt for the boy to wear.

In addition to his Embassy security assignment, Lyons had two other April assignments. He participated in the evacuation of Cambodia in Operation *Eagle Pull* and also worked security on the *American Challenger*, a Merchant Marine ship. On the ship, Lyons and his squad helped provide food and water to "over 8,000 starving and frightened refugees, some who were armed and desperate."[23]

While the evacuation was underway, General Carey had another run-in with Admiral Whitmire. The General learned that evacuation flights by the Air Force and Marines had ended. When he returned to the *Blue Ridge* command center, General Carey angrily asked, "Who the hell stopped my helicopters?" The admiral responded, "I did." The general snapped back, "Why?" Admiral Whitmire explained that he did it for safety purposes as pilots had been flying too long. Replied General Carey, "Marines don't get tired when it comes to something like this." General Carey's immediate direction put the Marine aviators back in the air. The General also made this comment, "I was damned angry at his stopping my helos, and I made that point in no uncertain terms."[24]

Admiral Whitmire should have understood the thinking of Marines. After all, the admiral started his military career when he enlisted in the Marine Corps in 1942. He was an All-American lineman at the University of Alabama when he left college. Whitmire had a year of college football eligibility left. He ended up at the U.S. Naval Academy in Annapolis, Maryland. Again, he won All-American honors and earned his commission as an officer in the U.S. Navy.[25]

As General Carey ordered helicopter pilots to continue flying, the ambassador resisted leaving Vietnam. Meanwhile, evacuations from the Embassy took out staff members and Vietnamese refugees. People desperate to leave Vietnam climbed the Embassy walls. By 2:15 a.m. on April 30, helicopters landed on the roof of the Embassy every 10 minutes. Marine Captain "Gerry" Berry flew one of those helicopters. Captain Berry received one order from General Carey. The order stated that if the ambassador refused to come out, he was to carry him out of the Embassy to the helicopter. Ambassador Martin cooperated and boarded a helicopter.[26] A copy of a radio message from the helicopter pilot sent at 5:01 a.m. (Saigon time) confirmed that the ambassador was onboard.[27]

Lance Corporal Ismael (Junior) Ortiz flew with Captain Berry as a gunner on the CH-46 flight that carried Ambassador Martin out of the Embassy. Ortiz said Berry flew nearly 18 hours in the evacuation. Captain Berry and his crew, including Ortiz, made an estimated 18 trips to the Embassy that day with an expectation that the ambassador would be coming aboard. Refugees boarded each of the flights that went back to the *Blue Ridge*. This time when they landed on the rooftop, Captain Berry was not leaving without the ambassador. Ortiz remembered hearing this about the ambassador over the radio, "The president wants him." When the ambassador boarded the helicopter and took his seat Ortiz said that he looked "relieved." As Captain Berry landed on the deck of the *Blue Ridge* Ortiz saw General Carey give the captain a thumbs up signal.[28]

Following his Vietnam service, Ortiz earned a place in the United States Naval Academy, graduated with a commission, and became an officer in the Marine Corps. He rose to the rank of lieutenant colonel before he retired.

Before receiving refugees, the USS *Hancock* left the Philippine Islands. (PHI W. L. Cook, United States Navy photograph, 1975)

While Ortiz went through TBS at Quantico, Berry was there as executive officer. Berry retired from the Marine Corps as a full colonel.[29]

While General Carey and his team led thousands of refugees out of Vietnam to the United States, four Marines under the age of 30 lost their lives on April 29. Two lance corporals and two CH-46 helicopter pilots died nearly 18 hours apart. On only their seventh day of duty in South Vietnam, Lance Corporal Darwin L. Judge and Lance Corporal Charles McMahon died when struck by an enemy rocket at about 4 a.m. while guarding a checkpoint at Ton Son Nhut Airbase. Judge and McMahon were the last American service members to die in Vietnam. Judge came from Marshalltown, Iowa, and McMahon was from Woburn, Massachusetts. The Fall of Saigon Marines Association established scholarships to honor the memories of Corporals Judge and McMahon.[30]

At approximately 10:30 p.m. on April 29, Captain William C. Nytsul and First Lieutenant Michael J. Shea continued flying search and rescue missions in their CH-46 helicopter near the USS *Hancock*. The *Hancock* received refugees from Vietnam. The helicopter pilots noticed that they were running low on fuel. They asked for permission to land on the ship. The ship's crew waved them off, meaning the sailors told Captain Nytsul and Lieutenant Shea

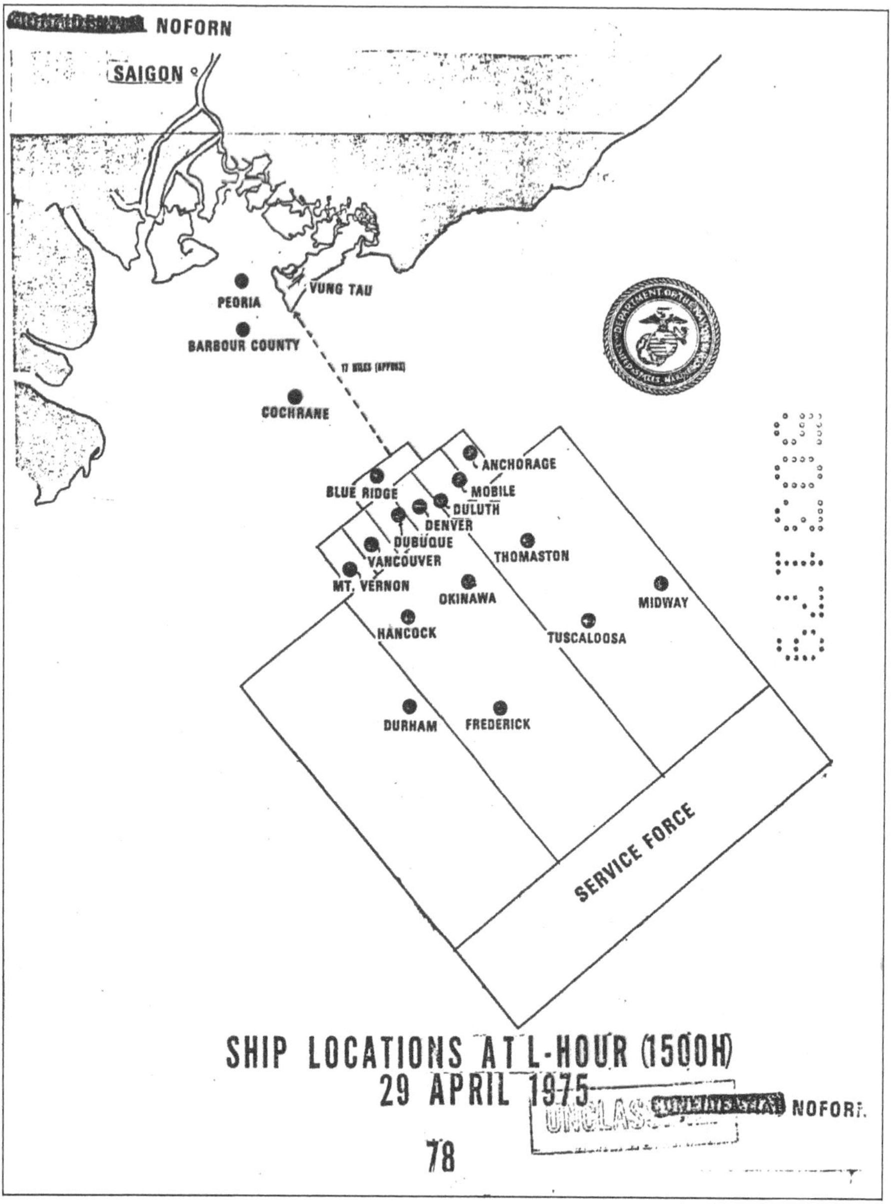

Prior to the launch of helicopters, ships of the United States Navy were in position of off the coast of South Vietnam. (Courtesy of the Department of the Navy, United States Marine Corps, 1975)

that they could not land then, as the flight deck was crowded at that time of evening. Shortly after that, their CH 46 helicopter crashed into the South

China Sea. Two enlisted crew members survived. The bodies of Captain Nytsul and Lieutenant Shea remain missing.[31]

A positive human-interest story that came out of the Saigon evacuation demonstrated great personal courage on all levels. A former South Vietnamese Air Force pilot, who in his desperate attempt to reach freedom landed a private airplane on the USS *Midway*, a Navy aircraft carrier. On April 30, 1975, Major Bung Ly (Lee) put his wife and five children in a small airplane. He spotted the carrier. Major Ly managed to drop a note that landed on the ship's deck. The note explained that he had an hour's worth of fuel. Major Ly needed helicopters on the deck moved out of the way so could land. Captain Lawrence Chambers ordered $10 million worth of helicopters tossed overboard and Major Ly landed his aircraft on the carrier's deck. No one was injured. The entire Ly family came to the United States and all of them earned their American citizenship.

Captain Chambers was certain that his decision to dump the helicopters would result in disciplinary action against him. It did not. In fact, he received two more promotions and rose to the rank of rear admiral. Captain Chambers made two historic personal accomplishments. He was the first African American to command an aircraft carrier. When he reached the rank of rear admiral, he became the first African American Naval Academy graduate to achieve that rank.[32]

In 1989, Admiral Chambers and the Ly family met for the first time since they saw each other on the *Midway* 14 years earlier. They reunited at the Naval Aviation Museum in Pensacola, Florida. The museum displays the plane that Major Ly flew on to the *Midway* in 1975.[33]

As the last refugees and Americans left Saigon, NVA Colonel Bui Tin accepted the unconditional surrender of South Vietnam ending the war.[34] Tin left Vietnam in 1991 and lived in exile in Paris until his death in 2018 at the age of 91.

Brigadier General Carey briefs pilots and platoon leaders on the USS *Hancock* prior to the evacuation of Saigon. (Gunnery Sergeant Donald L. Shearer, United States Marine Corps photo, 1975)

South Vietnamese Vice President Nguyen Cao Ky (second from the left wearing a cap) was among the refugees landing on the USS *Midway.* (Official United States Navy photograph, 1975)

A week after the evacuation, an Ohio newspaper carried a brief observation from a first cousin of the General's. Mildred Carey Marshall "is awfully proud of Brigadier General Richard E. Carey who directed the mass helicopter evacuation of Saigon."[35]

Most telling about Carey's thoughts about his evacuation involvement were his hand-written notes preparing for his after-action report. Those thoughts not only made up his report, but Carey later incorporated them into his commentary over the next 40 years. This statement summed up his thoughts about the attitudes of civilians stationed in Saigon:

> For Americans without Vietnamese families, it was a matter of convincing them that the time had come. The reality of it all was indeed a bitter pill for many Americans. Most significant of which was the Ambassador. To some, Vietnam was their lover, as it offered the pleasures of adventure, the exhilaration of relief from the horrors of war, and the pleasures of Saigon, the tangible and intangible fruits of their labors, and finally, the fulfillment of just being a part of the action in the false glamour attributed to war.

In his notes, Carey pointed out the original plan called for the evacuation of one million refugees. In the end, the total was only around 100,000. He also believed that the Army of the Republic of Vietnam (ARVN) "lost its sense of purpose."[36]

Shortly after Operation *Frequent Wind*, General Carey faced an investigation. Washington officials questioned the delay in communicating the directive to launch the helicopter rescue mission. General Carey described the investigation process this way: they "hammered at me and my staff." Regarding the investigation into General Carey, Major General Livingston, in 2021, described the continued success of both Carey and Colonel Gray. Livingston said that Colonel Gray became commandant of the Marine Corps with four stars and then Brigadier General Carey added two more stars. According to General Carey, he never heard anything else about the investigation.

While Ambassador Martin did not fully cooperate with the evacuation, he praised the execution of the operation in a May 6, 1975, letter to Marine Corps Commandant General Robert E. Cushman. The ambassador mentioned "heroic and meritorious achievement in connection with the final evacuation from the Republic of Vietnam." He pointed out that, "The Marines remained in their posts until all non-combatants in the evacuation sites were removed ..." Ambassador Martin recommended General Carey for what he termed "an

A United States Marine Corps CH-53 landing in Saigon to pick up refugees. (Gunnery Sergeant Donald L. Shearer Department of Defense photo Marine Corps pd A150942)

appropriate award."[37] Had the ambassador cooperated with evacuation planning, more Vietnamese would have been able to leave Vietnam for the United States.

General Carey's actions during the evacuation did earn him an award when he received his second Legion of Merit. The citation read:

> Brigadier General Richard Edward Carey, United States Marine Corps, was awarded a Gold Star in lieu of a Second Award of the Legion of Merit for exceptionally meritorious conduct in the performance of outstanding services to the Government of the United States.

Carey used his experience with Ambassador Martin to develop recommendations for future evacuations. To prevent similar situations from occurring, Carey's August 5, 1975, report on *Frequent Wind* covered the evacuation from the Embassy. In that document, he did not discuss any issues with the ambassador. Carey diplomatically recommended joint State Department and military planning for future evacuations in foreign lands. The General said in his report, "Transfer of responsibility from the State Department to the military will be necessary in the future."[38]

Coming to the United States

General Carey and his team helped some 100,000 people flee the incoming communist regime in Vietnam. Many of the evacuees had worked with American service members. Others had held leadership positions in South Vietnam. All of those people and their families faced retaliation by the communists. Getting safely out of Vietnam was one thing. They brought little or nothing with them, most did not speak English, and few knew anyone in America. While willing to work, the refugees often had to take menial jobs to provide for their families. The refugees from Southeast Asia needed sponsors in their new land. Church groups and private citizens stepped up and aided them. The children of refugees went to American schools, learned a new language and customs, and found opportunities.

From Vietnam, refugees went to Subic Bay in the Philippine Islands before going to a tent city on Guam. From Guam, they flew to the United States. Some went to MCAS El Toro, California, and others went to either Fort Chaffee, Arkansas, in the western part of the state or Eglin Air Force Base in North Florida's panhandle.

Arkansas Governor David Pryor spoke to the first arrivals at Fort Chaffee through a translator. The governor said, "This is your first day in America. We hope you realize that our people in Arkansas and America share at this moment in the agony, pain, and sorrow you have experienced."

In Florida, the Cuban community in the state welcomed the refugees. In the early 1960s, Cuban families came to the United States following the Bay of Pigs incident. They remembered and understood what the Vietnamese were going through.

One refugee received sponsorship from a fellow Vietnam war veteran. Captain William Cowan, a Marine, volunteered to help one refugee. He sponsored a South Vietnamese Army veteran. From Captain Cowan's perspective, the two men shared war. Now they would share peace.[39]

Not everyone was so welcoming. At Eglin Air Force Base in the Florida panhandle, Air Force personnel set up a tent city to house up to 1,500 refugees. Members of the Florida Congressional delegation expressed concern over sanitation and the lack of permanent housing.[40] Congressman Robert L. F. Sikes, whose district included Eglin, visited Fort Chaffee after refugees arrived in Florida. He said, "I think the military is doing an extraordinarily good job with this." Congressman Sikes learned more about the situation in his district. Local leaders in Florida found that Eglin would be a staging area for the refugees. Refugees no longer stayed at Eglin after December 1975.[41]

"The evacuation was the biggest challenge [of my career]," General Carey said in 2021. "That determined the fate of a country," he explained.

General Livingston worked with General Carey and Colonel Gray on the Vietnam evacuation project. Livingston, now retired, served three tours of duty in Vietnam. The general is a Medal of Honor recipient for his actions at Dai Do, Vietnam between April 28 and May 3, 1968. A few months after the evacuation, Livingston likened the operation to a football team. He said, "The helicopters landed, and they ran out to pre-assigned positions. I could only relate it to a well-rehearsed football play."[42] General Livingston described General Carey's demeanor as that of a typical Marine commander doing his job. According to General Livingston, General Carey faced a quickly moving situation. Waiting for Ambassador Graham Martin to agree to close the Embassy delayed the mission, General Livingston explained. The Marines faced "intense pressure" to pull Americans out of Saigon. He also said that General Carey adjusted the plan "on the fly."

Livingston served aboard the USN *Blue Ridge*, assisting Task Force 76 as an advisor on the operational side. On April 29, 1975, General Carey directed the flow of helicopters, U.S. Embassy security, and monitored details of the operation.

Recognizing individual accomplishments of the 9th MAB, Carey signed off on 26 personal award recommendations in June 1975. There were two Legion of Merit recipients including Colonel Gray. While most of the recipients

Vietnamese refugees on the USS *Hancock* after flying in helicopters flown by Marine Corps pilots. (Gunnery Sergeant Donald L. Shearer Department of Defense photo Marine Corps pd A150963)

received the Navy Commendation Medal or Navy Achievement Medal, the remaining awards included one Distinguished Flying Cross, one Bronze Star, and two Meritorious Service Medals.

Success Stories of Evacuees

Retired Marine Corps Lieutenant Colonel Richard Meydag served as a helicopter pilot during Operation *Frequent Wind.* He was one of the many experienced pilots who aided General Carey.

During Operation *Frequent Wind*, Meydag (then a major) primarily served as a helicopter maintenance officer and flew as a co-pilot bringing refugees out of Saigon. He said that helicopter pilots tried to bring as many people as possible out of Vietnam on to the USS *Hancock*, a ship used to transport refugees to Subic Bay on April 29, 1975. Meydag acknowledged that many of the flights carried more people than authorized for the aircraft.

Before his involvement with the evacuation, Meydag said that he served with Marine Air Group 36 (MAG-36), based on Okinawa, Japan. With his

500-plus hours in twin-rotor, twin-engine helicopters while earlier serving in Vietnam, Meydag knew that he could help and volunteered for the assignment. He flew to the *Blue Ridge*, the ship serving as General Carey's headquarters. From Meydag's perspective, General Carey "knew exactly what had to be done." He added that the General could "adapt" as the situation changed. Meydag said that General Carey handled the changing situation "in stride," and in his opinion, the General did "an outstanding job."

After his retirement from the Marine Corps, Meydag's military service earned him a spot in his high school's Hall of Fame. His alma mater, Will Rogers High School in Tulsa, Oklahoma, honored the retired helicopter pilot. A fellow Will Rogers High School alumnus from the early 1980s reached out to Meydag. "Were you the Marine helicopter pilot who took my family and me from Vietnam to the *Hancock*?" asked Hung (HT) Tan. After their discussion, they realized Meydag had not flown the Tan family. However, the two men, bound by their ties to Vietnam, Tulsa, and Will Rogers High School, became friends.

Just 12 years old when evacuated from Vietnam on April 29, 1975, Mr. Tan talked about the time leading up to the evacuation of his family, his journey to the United States, and his life in new country. His immediate family and his uncle's family learned the American government wanted to help all of them get out of Vietnam as Saigon was about to fall. Mr. Tan's father had fought against communist forces as a combat officer in the Vietnamese Army and his older brother served in the Army at that time.

On April 28, 1975, an unmarked van brought the Tan family to Ton Son Nhut Air Base in the village of Ton Son Nhat, just outside of Saigon. North Vietnamese forces began shelling the base and the Tans went to a hangar guarded by members of the Marine Corps for safety. The family did not know what was going to happen. Mr. Tan said that his father recognized the sounds of American weapons from his Army experience. At one point, Mr. Tan said, "We thought we were done for and really thought the worst would happen." The Tans spent approximately 24 hours in the hangar. At one point, they tried to leave the hangar, but could not. Then, helicopters arrived. "Marines jumped out, grabbed us, and put us on the choppers." He added that during that time, he and his siblings ended up separated from their parents. The twin-propeller helicopters took the evacuees to the USS *Hancock*. At one point, he thought that the backwash would toss him into the ocean. Sailors formed a perimeter and he said, "One caught me." Soon, Mr. Tan and his family reunited on the ship that took them to Subic Bay.

After getting off there, the evacuees went to Guam, a United States territory island located in the Western Pacific Ocean about 4,000 miles from Hawaii.

Refugees boarded a helicopter that took them to the USS *Midway*. (Official United States Marine Corps photo, 1975)

The evacuees spent about a month in a tent city. From Guam, Mr. Tan said, they boarded a Boeing 747 that brought them to Fort Chaffee, Arkansas. While there, College Hill Presbyterian Church in Tulsa, Oklahoma, agreed to sponsor the Tans. They arrived in Tulsa in July, just a few weeks before 12-year-old HT would start school. With little command of the English language, Mr. Tan's father worked menial jobs as dishwasher in a Tulsa cafeteria, and later was a janitor in a warehouse and then worked in a dry cleaner's shop in Houston, Texas. Mr. Tan said that his father made "a lot of sacrifices for us." Young HT did well in school. He won a full scholarship to Boston University and earned a bachelor's degree in mechanical engineering. While a student at Boston University, he earned his American citizenship in 1982. In Boston, Mr. Tan met a young woman from Oklahoma City. The Marines had evacuated her family from Vietnam several hours before the Tans left the country. The couple eventually married. With another scholarship, he received a master's degree in mechanical engineering from Rice University in Houston.

A Vietnamese woman (right) arrived on the USS *Midway* before going to Guam and then the United States. (Official United States Navy photograph, 1975)

Mr. Tan then took a job with Exxon U.S. In that position, based out of New Orleans, Louisiana, Mr. Tan helped drill oil wells. Then, he made a career change when he returned to Boston University and earned a law degree. He became a patent attorney with a New York City law firm. The firm sent him to Washington, D.C. In 2000, he opened his own practice. Mr. Tan and his wife have three children. One works in accounting and the other two were in college as of 2021.

Although Mr. Tan never met General Carey, he is grateful for his efforts that brought his family to the United States. He said, "I believe in America. It is an awesome place. People are so warm." Of Lieutenant Colonel Meydag, his fellow Will Rogers High School alumnus, he said, "He's a helluva guy." Mr. Tan mentioned his medals and combat missions. Meydag earned the Silver Star during his service in Vietnam where he flew more than 1,000 combat missions. He also twice served in the Presidential Helicopter Squadron, HMX-1. As part of that squadron, he piloted Marine-One during the administrations of Presidents Richard Nixon and Jimmy Carter.[43]

A Dallas-area Vietnamese refugee, DT Nguyen, then 12 years old, left Vietnam on April 30, 1975, with three generations of his family on a boat manned by South Vietnamese Marines. Mr. Nguyen's father served in a variety of senior government and military positions in South Vietnam. He held the position of province chief of Da Nang and was the incoming mayor of Saigon. On the military side, he served as High Command Chief of Staff for the South Vietnamese Army's Airborne and Special Forces. Mr. Nguyen said his father also attended military courses in the United States.

The Nguyens went to Saigon to the U.S. Embassy. Seeking to pick up documents at the U.S. Embassy, they learned that their paperwork was not there. The family left to go to a coastal city to attempt to board a boat. After the family reached the coast, they discovered that North Vietnamese forces had closed all of the roads to Saigon. They went aboard the Vietnamese Marine ship designed to hold 29 people. Mr. Nguyen said there were actually around 200 people on the ship. By April 30, nine members of the Nguyen family that were part of three generations reached a cargo ship. They went on board by using the climbing nets. The ship, escorted by the U.S. Navy's Seventh Fleet, sailed to Subic Bay in the Philippines. The Nguyen family later went to Fort Chaffee and then moved to Houston. Mr. Nguyen graduated from the University of Houston with a degree in computer science. Today, Mr. Nguyen is a successful entrepreneur. He created Koan Health, a leading company in the health care industry. He met General Carey in Dallas where he joined forces with the General to work with returning Gulf War and post 9/11 service members suffering from PTSD.

Ian Bui, a Dallas resident, had a brief opportunity to meet General Carey a few years ago. The General's efforts on the evacuation of Vietnamese refugees not only helped Mr. Bui on his journey to the United States, but eventually impacted five generations of his family. On April 29, 1975, 16 members of the Bui family waited several hours in the United States Embassy in Saigon for a rescue helicopter. His grandmother, parents, an aunt, siblings, and cousins were part of the group. Half of his family went by helicopter to the USS *Hancock*. From the *Hancock*, they went to Subic Bay before arriving in Guam. Mr. Bui, then 13, and 7 other family members eventually went to another ship by helicopter. It would be weeks before the teenager saw the rest of his family. Around the tent city established for refugees on Guam, family members posted names of missing relatives on paper plates. Mr. Bui's relatives, who arrived on Guam before him, received permission to wait for the remaining family. However, there was a deadline. On the last day before that group of the Bui family had to leave Guam, Ian spotted a younger brother outside of a bathroom. The reunited family took a Trans World Airways (TWA) flight that went from Andersen Air Force Base to MCAS El Toro. From there the three generations of the Bui family went to Fort Chaffee and awaited a sponsor.

While at Fort Chaffee, his sisters met four high-school classmates who did not have any other family members with them. Mr. Bui's parents took them in. A Catholic Church group from Shreveport, Louisiana, agreed to sponsor the 16 members of the Bui family, but did not offer to sponsor the other four teenagers. Bui's mother, who spoke a few English words, pushed the issue. In the end, St. John's Parish in Shreveport agreed to sponsor all 20 of the refugees. Mr. Bui attended a Jesuit school In Shreveport. He, in his own description, "sucked at English, but did well in French [a language he learned in Vietnam] and math." To develop his English language skills, the young man put a dictionary beside his bed and studied it every night. The effort paid off. He won spelling bee contests in school. During his career, he wrote articles for a magazine serving the Asian market and today has his own business translating Vietnamese into English. In his family, two new generations were born in the United States.

Following retirement after 33 years in the Marine Corps, General Livingston said that for a time he lived in New Orleans where many Vietnamese refugees settled and opened markets and restaurants. He said that he often spoke with the former refugees and attended their events. He described the Vietnamese people who came to the United States as "hard working people, real contributors to their [new] country."

An Unplanned Post-War Vietnam Stop

After the evacuation of Saigon, Dena visited the General in Japan. The military allowed service members and their families to fly on a military aircraft at no cost when space was available, and the Careys found an Air Force transport with "space available." That flight took the General to his fourth stop in Vietnam, but this stop was unplanned. The Careys' flight left Japan. Getting low on fuel, the Air Force pilot radioed the tower near Ho Chi Minh City (formerly Saigon). The tower granted the pilot permission to land. Dena, who had never been to Vietnam, left the aircraft to go to the terminal and walk around the airport. The General could not leave the aircraft. He was not supposed to be there. After refueling, the pilot continued on to the Philippines before going back to Japan.[44]

Looking Back at the Evacuation Years Later

Over the years, General Carey spoke and wrote about the evacuation experience. His views formed during and just after those challenging days in 1975 stayed with him.

On the 10th anniversary of the evacuation, the General wrote a column for *The Columbus* (Ohio) *Dispatch* when he commented:

> The failure of leadership, which led to our defeat in Vietnam, was political, not military. In fact, in Vietnam we did not lose a single major conflict. Television brought the horrors of war into our living rooms.[45]

Twenty years after the evacuation, on April 28, 1995, The Discovery Channel ran a two-hour special called "The Fall of Saigon." In an April 10, 1995, news release announcing the program former President Ford was quoted as saying, "It was a terrible defeat for the United States and a drastic condemnation of our policy—not our objective. We made a lot of mistakes and they were culminated with the evacuation from the Embassy." In addition, the news release tied in with General Carey's observations in his notes with this statement from the Discovery Channel:

> Although some Vietnamese successfully fled Saigon, many who had been promised evacuation by their American friends and employers were left behind. Betrayed by what they perceived as American broken promises, many South Vietnamese suffered years of excruciating work and inhumane treatment in Vietnamese labor camps. At the same time, many Americans who tried and failed to rescue their South Vietnamese comrades have been burdened with guilt ever since.[46]

The Discovery Channel invited General Carey to participate in an April 25, 1995, symposium panel discussion on Saigon Remembered and Vietnam's Current Realities.[47] Both General Carey and General Homer Smith (DAO) participated.[48] In addition, General Carey provided photographs relating to the evacuation. Discovery Communications, Inc. thanked the General for "sharing your memories, your talent, and your time with us."[49]

Garrick Utley narrated the program. As a correspondent for NBC News, Utley reported from Vietnam in 1964, during the Tet offensive in 1968, and again in 1975, just prior to the evacuation.[50]

On the 30th anniversary of the evacuation media coverage again reviewed that day. Two examples follow. One story covered the life of a Reno, Nevada, area resident who Marines evacuated from the U.S. Embassy in Saigon. Another story included an interview with the last Marine to leave the U.S. Embassy. Reporters for both newspapers interviewed General Carey for their stories.

Hong Le Thi Nguyen, then 24, and members of her family awaited rescue on the rooftop of the Embassy in 1975. Three other family members joined her on a Marine CH-46 helicopter. Thirty other evacuees flew on that helicopter designed to hold 18 people. General Carey said pilots flew through rain, darkened skies, thunderstorms, and smoke from burning buildings. Pilots kept returning to pick up more people. "Every time they did, they were risking their lives," the General said. Again, going back to his hand-written notes of 1975, General Carey said:

> I had a job to do—it was to get as many people out as possible. It was a humanitarian act, because we know those who worked with Americans, they were going to retraining camps and many of them would have perished. We owed it to them.[51]

As for Hong Le Thi Nguyen, she worked, saved her money, and eventually bought her own home—getting her share of the American Dream.

In a Fort Worth newspaper article that ran the same day, Marine Master Gunnery Sergeant John Valdez shared his story about being the last Marine to leave the U.S. Embassy in Saigon. For an hour, Valdez and 10 other Marines waited. They wondered whether fellow Marines would rescue them. Finally, a CH-46 helicopter arrived. Valdez, the senior NCO, climbed aboard following his Marines at 7:53 a.m. on April 30.

For the Fort Worth newspaper story, General Carey talked about the evacuation. On April 29, 1975, he said, "Things were going pretty well until 9 o'clock [p.m.]. I got a call from the ambassador at the Embassy." Ambassador Martin told the General that he and the staff would evacuate from the Embassy. "That was a whole new ball game," General Carey said, and he added, "That screwed us up."[52]

On April 29, 2021, in a speech honoring Vietnam veterans in Frisco, Texas, General Livingston said, "Vietnam is the most misunderstood and misinterpreted war apart from the Korean War, which fell into total obscurity." His speech marked the 46th anniversary of the evacuation of U.S. forces and Vietnamese refugees from Saigon. General Carey attended the event along with more than 100 other veterans who served during the war in Vietnam. General Livingston praised General Carey for his role in the evacuation. According to General Livingston, General Carey never received enough credit for his efforts in the evacuation of Saigon. General Livingston reiterated that praise in an August 11, 2021, telephone conversation with General Carey.

Colonel Wood said this about General Carey's handling of the evacuation of Saigon, "He got us out. He inspired confidence. I didn't love him. I respected him."[53]

As he reviewed the evacuation in 2010, General Carey said, "We abandoned the South Vietnamese people. All I can say is the evacuation time to me was the saddest part of my life. To me it was a black eye on the United States government." He also pointed out that the United States trained the Vietnamese, built them up, and walked out when we stopped supplying them.[54]

In August 2021, the United States withdrew from Afghanistan. The military evacuated Afghanistan citizens who aided the United States and American citizens. Veterans of *Frequent Wind*, public officials, and the media drew comparisons to the 1975 Vietnam evacuation. Jim Webb, a Marine Corps Vietnam veteran, Navy Cross recipient, Secretary of the Navy in President Ronald W. Reagan's administration, and a former Democratic U.S. senator from Virginia, wrote a critique of the Afghanistan evacuation. In part, he compared it to the evacuation from Vietnam. Webb said:

> Contrary to the prevailing media rhetoric, assisting our Vietnamese friends after the fall of Saigon in 1975 does not provide a mirror of the unexplainable incompetence that we have witnessed in Afghanistan.[55]

As the evacuation from Afghanistan began, General Carey pointed out the evacuation from Vietnam took planning, coordination, and execution to bring thousands of people out of Vietnam.[56] General Carey concluded that the overall results of the Afghanistan evacuation demonstrated the effort "should have been better planned and executed."[57]

CHAPTER 12

General Carey's Supplement to the Command Chronology on *Frequent Wind*

On August 5, 1975, Carey wrote a "Command Chronology on Frequent Wind." In the foreword, the General wrote:

> If one point can be made on why this operation was a success, it is that by meticulous planning of an integrated Marine air ground team, 'Any Challenge Can be Met.'

In the foreword, General Carey also said he prepared the report "as seen through the eyes of the commanders and staff within the 9th Marine Amphibious Brigade." Carey's 119-page report covered topics ranging from planning to execution to lessons learned from *Frequent Wind.* It included organization tables, statistics, and diagrams.

Especially significant were a list of what Carey called lessons learned. From Carey's perspective, those lessons would aid future joint-service operations. Recalling the different understanding of the term "L-hour" by the Air Force and Marine Corps, Carey recommended "common definition of terms." Future operations need early liaison among key commanders, especially when force location is widespread.[1]

Successful night operations proved to be an important part of the evacuation from Saigon. Approximately one-half of the evacuation flights took place in the dark with reduced visibility. Carey recommended that future planning include darkness as a factor. In addition, evacuation forces needed training for what Carey termed "the worst possible situation."[2]

To meet *Frequent Wind* mission requirements, helicopter crews flew 689 missions, logging nearly 1,200 flight hours between April 29 and 30, 1975. The average crew flew 13 hours. One crew flew 18.3 hours. Helicopter crew members flew the following aircraft during *Frequent Wind*: CH-46, CH-53, AH-1J (Cobra), and UH-1E (Huey). Helicopter crews flew 530 evacuation missions. The CH-46 helicopters not only went on evacuation flights, but their pilots also used their aircraft for search and rescue and medical missions. The Huey crews had command and control responsibility. Carey explained command and control. Senior people in the Hueys were the commanding officers in the air, the General said. Those commanders coordinated the efforts of the CH-46 and CH-53 crews and provided evacuation instructions.[3] The Cobra crews flew escort for the helicopters.[4] While the number of hours and missions were impressive, there was a toll. General Carey explained:

> This operation was tiring for aircrews and taxing on the machines. All were pressed to the limit. In situations such as this, men make mistakes and aircraft malfunction, therefore losses can be expected.[5]

The General referred to the deaths of CH-46 pilots Nytsul and Shea. In another similar aircraft loss, crew members on a Cobra survived a crash 4 miles from their destination, the USS *Kirk*, when their Cobra lost fuel. A post-crash analysis pointed out that the fuel gauge was faulty. Carey offered his take on aircraft losses when he wrote:

> Although the goal of any operation is to lose no aircraft, the taxing nature of operation "Frequent Wind", and the adverse conditions under which aircraft were flown lent itself to accidents. Only through professional conduct of all personnel associated with the air operations were more mishaps averted.[6]

Carey attributed the fact that there were few casualties during *Frequent Wind* to what he called: "a stroke of extremely good fortune, not to mention, planning, surprise and mass." He recommended continuing to address the possibility of casualties by planning for medical support to save lives.[7]

In addition, Carey pointed out two other challenges faced by helicopter crews. At the Embassy, the pilots faced space limitations on both the rooftop and in the parking lot as they picked up 2,000 refugees and American citizens.[8] Communication interference with controllers and aircrews also presented a challenge. Messages came through in both Vietnamese and English. The English-speaking messages were vulgarities directed at the helicopter crews and the controllers.[9] Those messages appeared to be a futile attempt to harass or intimidate the Americans. If that was the plan, it did not work.

CHAPTER 13

Mayaguez Rescue

On May 12, 1975, Cambodia's communist Khmer Rouge seized the SS *Mayaguez*, a U.S. container ship. Captain Charles T. Miller and his 39-member crew on their way to Thailand from Hong Kong faced Khmer Rouge forces sailing in a gunboat. The Khmer Rouge accused Captain Miller of sailing into Cambodian waters.[1]

Originally named SS *White Falcon* when commissioned in 1944 as a freighter during World War II, the ship went to private hands in 1947. Renamed *SS Mayaguez* after the city in Puerto Rico, the ship sailed for Sea-Land-Services, Inc. Between 1965 and 1973, the *Mayaguez* brought supplies to the U.S. military in Southeast Asia.[2] At the time of capture, the ship carried 274 truck-sized containers including 77 holding government and military materials from the U.S. Embassy in Saigon.[3]

At the initial *Mayaguez* National Security Council (NSC) meeting, President Ford asked his advisors if the incident was an act of piracy. The response back to the president—yes. After the Khmer Rouge boarded the ship, it sailed toward the Cambodian island of Koh Tang. The NSC outlined three actions. First, the USS *Henry Holt* would move alongside the *Mayaguez*. Service members were to board the ship. At the same time, Marine forces would take Koh Tang while the Air Force would bomb the port of Kom Pong Som. That day, tragedy struck. An Air Force helicopter carrying 23 service members, including 18 members of an Air Force Security Police (SP) squadron, crashed in Thailand, killing all aboard.[4]

The next day, May 13, Khmer Rouge forces ordered the captain and his 39 *Mayaguez* crew members to move off the ship. The *Mayaguez* crew then boarded a fishing-boat sailing toward the Cambodian mainland. On the 14th, Marines boarded the *Mayaguez* only to find there was no one on the ship.

Three major events happened on May 15. First, 100 Marines landed on East Beach of Koh Tang via helicopters. Second, Cambodians fired at the helicopters resulting in the loss three helicopters and the deaths of eight Marines and two Navy corpsmen.[5] Third came the news that the USS *Henry B. Wilson* had rescued the entire *Mayaguez* crew. None of the crew suffered injuries during their capture. Captain Miller sent President Ford a telegram shortly after the rescue. He said, in part, "Thank you and all the brave military forces who are fighting and dying to save our lives."[6] Later that day, additional Marines arrived to rescue their fellow Marines who landed at Koh Tang and faced enemy fire.

Three Marines remain missing to this day: Private First Class Gary L. Hall, Private First Class Joseph Hargrove, and Private Danny G. Marshall. In total, 38 other American service members lost their lives in the *Mayaguez* rescue operation.[7]

A December 9, 1975, after-action report prepared by 2nd Battalion, 9th Marines (2/9) stated, "Reconnaissance of the island [Koh Tang] was insufficient to allow evaluation of enemy positions, strengths, etc." That contributed to members of 2/9 led by Lieutenant Colonel Randall W. Austin landing away from the beach. They were approximately one fifth of a mile away from the landing zone.[8]

In the middle of the investigation about his role in *Frequent Wind*, General Carey learned about the *Mayaguez* situation. Even though his efforts in the Vietnamese evacuation came under additional scrutiny, the General's overall results from *Frequent Wind* caught the attention of Pentagon leaders. He received a directive—reconstitute (reorganize) the brigade that handled the *Frequent Wind* mission. The directive ordered Carey to go rescue the ship. In addition, the order to General Carey charged him to aid the Marines on Koh Tang.[9] As he was getting his troops ready to support the rescue effort, the Marines faced a delay due to a mechanical issue on the *Hancock*.

The Marines at Koh Tang needed the rescue helicopters to get on the island. Air Force OV-10s had a mission to support the ground forces but faced a communication issue: OV-10 pilots said they could not speak to the Marines on the ground via radio. Said General Carey, "Well you've got high frequency (HF), talk to them that way. The Marines have HF radios." That communication problem cost a few hours of valuable time, the General said. He also pointed out that, "They should have waited on the Marines to do it. That's our expertise." Asked if there was a concern by those putting the operation together that the Marines could not get there in time, General Carey acknowledged that it was an issue. He then added, "They put it together too quickly." The General described the operation as "a disaster." General Carey

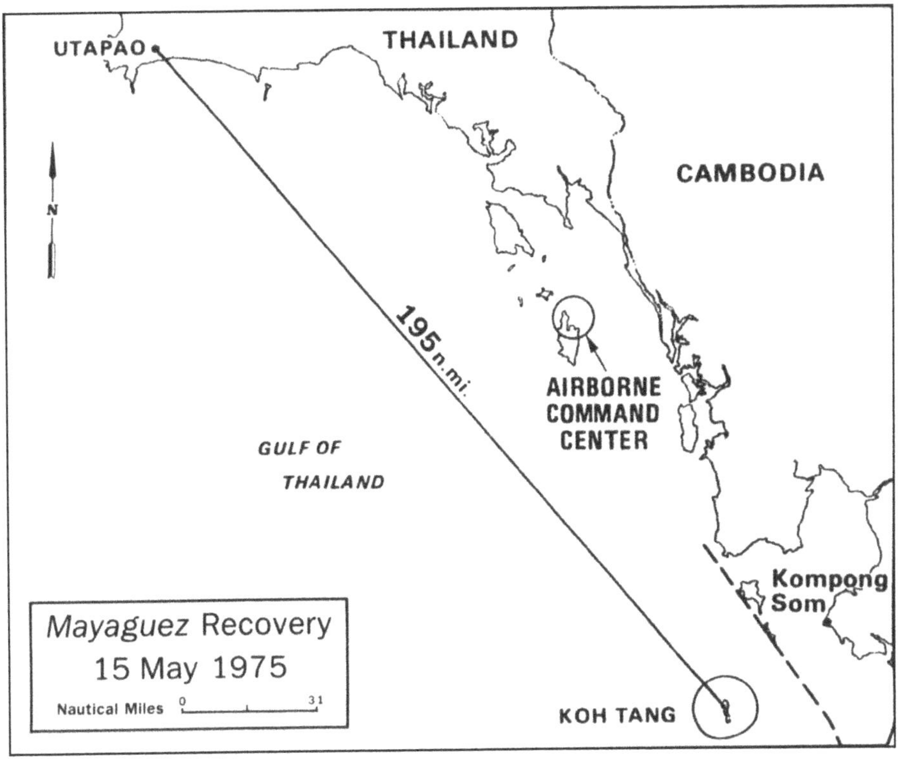

Map of the *Mayaguez* rescue. Regarding the Mayaguez rescue, General Carey said, "They should have waited on the Marines to do it. That's our expertise." (United States Marine Corps)

believes that if the Marines were handling the rescue, "it wouldn't have happened that way."[10]

In 1990, the General said that he believed that those in the field should have made the decisions. Carey said this about the *Mayaguez* operation:

> Modern communications are wonderful, but they are also deadly. The capability to talk over thousands of miles from the highest levels [National Security Council] to the front line foxholes takes many of the decisions out of the hands of the responsible commander, the man on the scene. Decisions were driven by the desire to do something and do it as quickly as possible. To undertake a mission of this type from 195 miles away and with inadequate resources is naïve and foolhardy. The results only reinforce my statements.[11]

General Carey explained those comments. Regarding the 195 miles, he pointed out that was the distance from Thailand to Koh Tang. He also explained that Air Force helicopter pilots handled search and rescue. That was different from the way Marine pilots operate. The Air Force pilots dropped the Marines onto Koh Tang and flew out. General Carey said Marine pilots would have landed on the island.

CHAPTER 14

Headquarters Marine Corps and Senior Leadership

Following the evacuation of Saigon and the *Mayaguez* crisis where the General led the rescue of Marines on Koh Tang, General Carey's next assignment returned him to Headquarters Marine Corps. There, he reported to the deputy chief of staff of Marine Aviation (DCSA), Lieutenant General Thomas H. Miller, Jr. This was Carey's second tour of duty at HQMC. His responsibilities included requirements and acquisition of all Marine Corps aviation needs along with the training and the assignment of 60,000 Marines. The General described that assignment as staff work. General Carey oversaw a staff of more than 100 Marines with experience and expertise in aviation. The staff included colonels, lieutenant colonels, and senior enlisted personnel. Problem solving highlighted the work of the General's team. Carey described his involvement as working with a team when aviation issues or problems arose. In that position, he brought together people who provided recommended solutions.[1]

Along with those leadership roles, General Carey and his staff worked on the development of three aircraft. One aircraft was a helicopter—the ECHO model of the CH-46 (CH-46E) transport helicopter. In addition, he oversaw development of the AV-8, better known as the Harrier, designed as a vertical/short takeoff and landing aircraft (VSTOL). He also aided the development of the FA-18 Hornet, a fighter attack jet. He worked with his staff and the aircraft manufacturers. Work on both the CH-46E and the Harrier led to upgrades that aided the Marine Corps for more than 40 years.

The CH-46E was an updated version of what Marines called the Sea Knight, a medium assault transport helicopter manufactured by Boeing and first flown by Marines in 1962. The Sea Knight transported Marines and needed cargo to Vietnam from Navy ships in the China Sea. Between 1964 and 1968, Marine pilots flew 180,000 missions in 75,000 hours on the CH-46. With modifications and upgrades, Marines flew the CH-46 for 48 years until the

V-22 Osprey replaced it in 2014. In addition to service in Vietnam, the CH-46 supported action in *Desert Storm*, Iraq, and Afghanistan.[2]

General Carey and his staff also coordinated improvements to the Harrier by working with the McDonnell-Douglas factory on maintenance and aircraft development issues.

The Marines started flying the Harrier, initially developed by British Aerospace, in 1971. Flown by a single pilot, the vertical/short takeoff landing aircraft could fly up to 662 miles per hour, carried up to seven 500-pound bombs and had a range of nearly 700 miles. The Harrier went through upgrades and changes through a joint effort with the Marines, McDonnell Douglas, and British Aerospace. The aircraft served in *Desert Storm*, Iraq, and Afghanistan. The Marine Corps expects to use the Harrier until 2025.[3]

The Harrier had the interest of Carey's boss, General Miller. Many called General Miller "the father of short takeoff and vertical landing in the United States Marine Corps." General Miller, a fighter pilot, flew combat sorties in World War II, Korea, and Vietnam. At General Carey's next assignment in the late 1970s, Harriers and the General would come under media scrutiny.

The FA-18, also known as the Hornet, carried out both air-to-air and air-to-ground missions. In other words, it could take out a MIG, then transition for ground support operations. Both Marine and Navy pilots flew the aircraft starting in 1983. Produced by McDonnell-Douglas, the Hornet flies at speeds up to nearly 1,400 miles per hour. The aircraft carries a 20mm cannon with 570 rounds, along with up to 17,000 pounds of ordnance including bombs, rockets, and missiles. Pilots flew the Hornet in *Desert Storm* and Afghanistan.[4] While McDonnell-Douglas had the Hornet in development, General Carey flew one of the early models. With more than 20 years of aviation experience including his time in combat during the Vietnam War, the General offered a special expertise when he flew the aircraft for the first time. He said that he understood the needs of the Marines when it came to a fighter attack aircraft. The General wanted to make certain the airplane met Marine Corps aviation requirements. After taking the aircraft up, he concluded the FA-18 exceeded expectations. "I was impressed," he said.[5] He flew the FA-18 nearly eight-years before it became part of the Marine Corps' fighter aircraft inventory.

While most of this assignment had the General dealing with operational related issues, Carey also handled responses to Congressional inquiries relating to Marine aviation issues. His efforts working for the DCAS Marine Aviation earned the General a promotion to major general and assignment as commanding general to the 2nd MAW at Cherry Point, North Carolina.

Wing Commander at Cherry Point

Out of a staff position and back in operations, Major General Carey returned to Cherry Point for his second tour of duty. In his first assignment there, he led a fighter squadron as a lieutenant colonel. While on his Headquarters Marine Corps assignment, he worked on the CH-46E and Harrier projects. At Cherry Point, he commanded squadrons of those two aircraft.

The General took a measure of pride in coming back to Cherry Point as the wing commander. At that time, the base served as Marine aviation's largest command with 500 aircraft and 14,000 people. He hoped that his rise from squadron commander in 1967 to wing commander in 1976 would be an example for the young aviators serving in the 2nd MAW. Carey shared his story with up-and-coming officers.

In his assignment at Headquarters Marine Corps, the General worked on Harrier development. At Cherry Point, he flew the Harrier and commanded the base's Harrier squadrons. Before this assignment, General Carey had only received media attention relating to the evacuation of refugees and Americans from Vietnam and Cambodia. His personal take on media coverage in Vietnam made him wary of the press. Now, however, Harrier crashes drew media coverage that involved the General. In July 1977, two Cherry Point Harrier captains, both in their early 30s, died in separate crashes on July 13 and July 27. Between late July and August, Richard Whittle, a staff writer for *The News and Observer* in Raleigh, covered the Harrier story in multiple by-lined stories. On July 28, Whittle wrote a story about two of the three Cherry Point Harrier squadrons that "stood down" (held from flying) on the 27th for what Carey called "an unscheduled safety inspection." The third Harrier squadron already had an inspection on its schedule that also included maintenance. Whittle quoted General Carey: "I don't have any plans to stop operating the Harrier program."[6] *The News and Observer* editorial headline read, "Harrier Jet Is Death Machine." The editorial, written on July 28, the day after the loss of the second Cherry Point Harrier pilot, cited the recent accidents and the difficulty of flying the aircraft.[7] Over the next 16 days, the paper published two more editorials questioning the Harrier program.

Also on July 28, 1977, Bruce Hall from CBS News television's Atlanta Bureau came to Cherry Point to cover the Harrier story. He did a brief interview with General Carey. Following the interview, Mr. Hall and his camera crew went to Harrier Squadron VMA-231's ready room. The camera crew went with three Harrier pilots to observe their flight equipment. Then,

Major General Carey prepares to fly the Harrier at Cherry Point Marine Corps Aviation Station in North Carolina. The Harrier faced negative media coverage in 1977 while Carey served as Commanding General of 2nd Marine Air Wing at Cherry Point. (Carey family collection, 1976/1977)

they went with the flyers to pre-flight and taxi. CBS filmed the pilots flying vertical takeoffs and landings. Following lunch, the CBS team boarded helicopters. The pilots again flew the Harriers as CBS took aerial film. After the pilots returned to Cherry Point, Mr. Hall interviewed them. All three pilots received a question about possible deficiencies with the Harriers. The pilots all said there were none. The CBS crew spent approximately seven hours covering the Harrier story.[8]

WITN, an NBC television station affiliate in Greenville, North Carolina, spent three hours at Cherry Point on July 28. WITN's time at Cherry Point overlapped with CBS. Chuck McClendon, WITN's reporter, conducted interviews with the MAG-32 and VMA-231 commanders. In addition, WITN filmed Harrier takeoffs and landings. On the station's 6 p.m. newscast, WITN ended the Harrier story with an editorial comment that said, "Maybe it's time for the Marine Corps to open up its accident investigation and find the problem before there are any more Harrier accidents." Captain James M. Pendergast, from the Cherry Point Public Information Office, expressed surprise about the comment. He said the reporter told him that he wanted to tell the true story and "refute some of the speculation about the airplane which has been rampant." The captain added, "Obviously, that was not his intent." He called the station's news director and let him know that there was "discontent with the editorial statement."[9]

On July 31, 1977, *The Charlotte* (North Carolina) *Observer's* front-page headline said, "The Harrier: does it need elite pilots?" The article pointed out that 15 of 24 Harrier crashes resulted from pilot error. In addition, the story explained that the first group of Harrier pilots had lower crash rates due to the fact more experienced pilots flew the aircraft. It quoted General Carey who said, "Initially, we selected pilots we needed to make the program work." The General also explained the need to train newer pilots. His former boss at Headquarters Marine Corps (HQMC), Lieutenant General Thomas H. Miller, deputy chief of staff for Marine Aviation, acknowledged the challenge of using less experienced pilots. In a letter to Wisconsin Representative Les Aspin, a member of the House Armed Services Committee, General Miller said the Marine Corps moved "too rapidly in assigning new pilots of varied training and operational experience into the [Harrier] program."[10]

Commenting on the Harrier pilots' inexperience, the *News and Observer* said the crash rate with inexperienced pilots was six times the 1974 rate when more experienced fliers flew the Harrier.[11]

Along with coverage of the deaths of the two pilots, Whittle wrote about the crash rates and General Carey's defense of the Harrier's safety record during an August 2 news conference. At the news conference, General Carey said the Harriers had a crash rate of 3.59 per 10,000 flight hours in six years. The F-8's crash rate was 5.9 per 10,000 flight hours and the F-4's rate was 3.46, according to General Carey's comments. The General told media members, "There is no discernable pattern to them [the crashes] or any evidence which might lead us to believe that there is any inherent problem with the airframe, its systems or the pilot-aircraft combination." Carey explained the term pilot-aircraft combination. He said that was part of the process used to select Harrier pilots. He also said, "I would question the inference that it's a difficult plane to fly."[12] General Carey spoke from experience when he made that comment. The General's flight logs between October 1976 and January 1977 showed that he flew the Harrier four times. Carey's Harrier flights totaled seven hours while he was at Cherry Point.

As part of the Harrier pilot selection process, commanders looked at a candidate's potential, capabilities, and flying experience. A pilot's squadron commander provided the initial recommendation for a Harrier pilot candidate. A positive recommendation from the squadron commander led to an extended interview process and analysis of the candidate's performance. Carey explained that the process "narrowed down" the candidates. Finally, commanders considered the pilot's potential for success. In addition, the General said, they wanted to make sure that a candidate understood what they were going to be doing as Harrier pilots. The Marine Corps "had to be careful about who was selected for Harrier training," General Carey said. He explained that candidates first had to be fixed-wing pilots. As part of their training, they had to acquire helicopter pilot skills. The Harrier combined capabilities of a fighter jet and a helicopter. Although General Carey flew both fixed wing and helicopters during his career, he said that he knew "it was not easy for a fixed-wing pilot to fly helicopters. It was a significant transition."[13]

On August 5, 1977, the Raleigh paper printed a second editorial calling for grounding of the Harrier. That editorial stated, "As a matter of both lives and money, it should be grounded, and further purchases postponed, until it is made operationally safe and effective."[14] In an August 13 *News and Observer* editorial, the paper questioned General Carey's crash rate figures that he used in his August 2 news conference. The general pointed to a 3.59 per 10,000 hours of Harrier flying time since the aircraft had been in use. In questioning the General's numbers, the editorial said, "What General Carey didn't say was that the Harrier loss rate for the year prior (1976) is 5.59 per 10,000 hours prior to the latest crash. The latest crash raises that figure to an alarming 6.0." The editorial concluded that the Harrier needed to be grounded "until it is made as flightworthy as Marine officials asserted it to be."[15] That was the third *News and Observer* editorial on the Harrier issue over 17 days. Three days earlier, Whittle wrote a story about the crash rates. He pointed out that 3.59 rate was average for the entire Harrier program. Whittle used an *Aviation Week & Space Technology* article as his source for the higher rate numbers. Whittle also said the magazine claimed, "Marines tightened pilot selection procedures and changed the training syllabus."[16]

On August 23, General Carey said the Harrier would not fly a demonstration flight at Cherry Point's annual air show set for September 10. Captain Pendergast made the announcement. The captain said:

> The Harrier is still operating in aerial demonstrations, but at the Wing level, it is the commanding general's (Carey) desire that we reduce demos in the interest of training aircrews and more efficient use of the airplane.

The captain added that Harriers would participate in an Atlanta area show that weekend.[17] In 2021, General Carey said, he wanted to work on the aircraft's capabilities and at the same time provide an opportunity to demonstrate the aircraft outside of the base. As a result, he sent the most experienced Harrier pilots to NAS Dobbins Air Reserve Base in Georgia for the demonstration flights. Less experienced fliers needed additional training before they could be part of an air show, the General said.[18]

On September 12, 1977, General Carey went to Washington for a review of the Harrier situation.[19] General Miller led the review meeting. He announced changes in the Harrier program on September 13. General Miller said that the Marine Corps changed the Harrier pilots' low-altitude flight minimum from 100 feet above ground to 200 feet. In addition, better pilots would be going into the Harrier program. General Miller admitted that Marine Corps "made some wrong moves," related to training. The Marine Corps enhanced its Harrier pilot training program.[20]

On September 16, Carey's former commander at FMFPAC, General Louis H. Wilson, Jr., then the Marine Corps commandant, came to North Carolina for a review of Marine facilities located in Eastern North Carolina. The Naval Air Rework Facility (NARF) provided General Carey's team the opportunity to demonstrate their conversion to the E model CH-46 helicopter. The updated CH-46 featured larger engines allowing for a greater load lift. At Camp Lejeune, 60 miles from Cherry Point, VMA-542 Harrier unit demonstrated their use of the updated training program. The Harrier pilots trained to operate their aircraft "from minimally improved sites in a forward zone close to battlefronts." The pilots trained on a grass-strip training site at Camp Lejeune called LZ (landing zone) Lark. Even the *Windsock*, the weekly base newspaper at Cherry Point, referred to the Harrier, called AV-8A, as "controversial," after three months of civilian media coverage.[21] General Carey said he believed that the commandant's visit resulted from the issues with the Harrier and General Wilson wanted to see the changes in the program first hand.[22]

Pendergast, in a March 2, 2022, email, outlined General Carey's involvement in dealing with the media during the Harrier issue. In preparing for the news conference, Pendergast described General Carey's approach:

> He was quite competitive by nature, and embraced the opportunity to articulate his beliefs regarding the value and performance capabilities of the aircraft to the Corps. To this very day, I still believe that General Carey's personal background as an enlisted Marine and subsequently as a Marine rifle platoon commander during the Korean War was central to his conviction of how important that particular aircraft was to providing ground combat Marines the timely close [and accurate] air support they needed, and deserved. I think that prior experience

made him more qualified and credible to successfully deal with this extremely critical issue, perhaps better than any other Marine general officer serving at the time.

During the Harrier situation, Pendergast and General Carey initiated many of the media events. Pendergast said that the General "understood that we needed to deal with the media by taking the initiative." Pendergast helped prepare potential media questions for the General and helped advise Marine pilots and maintenance staff scheduled to meet with reporters.

Pendergast described Carey's demeanor with the media as "engaging and positive, yet firm." He said the General "almost always wore a smile." Pendergast added, "We [he and Carey] knew that without our input the story would continue to play out negatively."

Regarding specific coverage of the Harrier situation, Pendergast offered several observations. He pointed out that *News and Observer's* Richard Whittle "singularly focused on accidents and deaths, and never the plane's value to Marines in combat." With that, Pendergast said the paper's negative editorials that summer did not surprise him. Concerning the *Charlotte Observer's* story, Pendergast said, "I was somewhat surprised with the Charlotte paper's tone on the topic, since that paper never once sent a reporter to actually visit, or even call and inquire."[23]

The General kept a three-inch binder of media coverage on the Harrier issue from May to September 1977. Included were newspaper clippings, synopses of interviews that he did, and timelines of media visits about the Harrier issue. The binder also included a 23-page transcript of the General's August 2, 1977, news conference.

Following the media coverage of the Harrier at Cherry Point, Carey received a December 16, 1977 letter from the Marine Corps Director of Information, Brigadier General V.T. Blaz. Blaz's letter offered an opportunity. He invited the General and/or colonels and up, to attend a two-day seminar on public affairs. The list of speakers included the assistant secretary of defense for public affairs, an advertising agency executive, and an ABC News reporter. One of the topics on the agenda would have been most helpful during the Harrier issue at Cherry Point. A speaker from Allied Chemical's topic—"Management of the Crisis Situation."

Despite dealing with the Harrier challenges, in 1977, General Carey's only full calendar year at Cherry Point, the 2nd MAW won the Hanson Trophy. That was the second time in five years that Carey led a team to achieve top fighter unit status. Carey led two different organizations that earned the Hanson Trophy.

Norway

The 2nd MAW, under Carey's leadership, participated in a joint cold-weather training exercise in Norway. Members of the wing provided close air support for Camp Lejeune's 4th Marine Amphibious Brigade (MAB). The Soviet Union (since the 1990s, called Russia) borders Norway's most northern tip. However, the Russian port of Murmansk is less than 100 miles from the Norwegian border. Since the United States had no military bases in Norway, the exercise allowed forces from both nations to train in case of an attack by the Russians.

As commanding general of the 2nd MAW, Carey attended the exercise for 10 days. It was the first time he was in Europe since his pre-Korean War Mediterranean cruise duty in 1950. While there, Carey met with Norway's King Olaf V. The King led Norway's defense organization. Carey said that

As Commanding General of 2nd Marine Air Wing, Carey (front, left) reviewed a joint exercise in Norway at Orland Air Base with Marines from Cherry Point and Camp Lejeune, North Carolina, and Norwegian military members. The exercise took place approximately 300 miles from the Arctic Circle. (Carey family collection, 1977)

King Olaf hosted him for lunch. The General recalled that they ate steak, sweet potato, and salad. During their meeting, Carey said that the King told him, "If and when you have to deploy, you will have my full support."

Coincidentally the General's daughter, Tamara, married a native Norwegian named Jan Solum. Solum recalled his first meeting with his future father-in-law at which General Carey told him he knew someone from Norway—King Olaf. The General asked Solum if he knew the king. Solum said that he did not.

The Solums held two wedding ceremonies. The first ceremony took place in the United States. The second was held in Norway. Solum said the local custom in Norway called for guests to bring desserts to the wedding dinner. General Carey, Solum said, wrote hand-written thank-you notes on his letterhead to all the people who brought desserts to the dinner. According to Solum, his friends and family always appreciated the General's kind gesture.[24]

CHAPTER 15

Atlantic Command

In 1978, General Carey moved from operations to a multi-national staff assignment with the Atlantic Command in Norfolk, Virginia. There, he worked with senior military officers in other branches of service, State Department officials, and diplomats from other countries. The General held the position of Political, Planning, and Contingency Operations Officer with the Atlantic Command. He reported to the commander of the Atlantic Command (CINCLANT), Admiral Harry D. Train. Admiral Train held that post from 1978 to 1982. At the same time, the Admiral also served as NATO's Supreme Allied Commander Atlantic.[1]

The Atlantic Command defends the Atlantic Ocean, Gulf of Mexico, and the Caribbean seas. If facing war, the CINCLANT leads the Air Force, Army, Marine Corps, and Navy in those areas.[2] When General Carey served in the Atlantic Command, the organization had 250 ships, 1,800 aircraft, and a team of 225,000 men and women. Due to Admiral Train's NATO (North America Treaty Organization) responsibility, his staff included representatives of the 15 NATO countries (the number of NATO member countries in 1978). In addition, senior military officers from the Air Force, Army, Marine Corps, and Navy served as members of the Admiral's team. The Newport-News, Virginia's *Daily Press*, reporter P. J. Budhans wrote this about the Atlantic Command's senior military staff, "... by some accounts, the greatest concentration of admirals and generals south of the Pentagon."[3]

Although General Carey had worked with foreign governments in earlier assignments in the Pacific, those tasks were a smaller part of his responsibilities. At the Atlantic Command, he spent most of his time working with allies of the United States. He coordinated efforts with the State Department along with the political and military staffs of foreign governments. He worked closely with the governments of the Azores and Iceland to revise defense procedures. The Department of Defense decreased the number of troops in those locations due to Defense Department budget cuts during President Jimmy Carter's administration.

In addition, General Carey held a leadership role in formation of a Rapid Deployment Joint Task Force that responded to the Iranian hostage crisis. Iranians held 52 Americans hostage for more than 400 days beginning November 4, 1979. Nine Marines assigned to the U.S Embassy in Tehran were among the hostages. The military responded on April 24, 1980 with aircrews, but pilots aborted the mission to rescue the hostages due to a combination of mechanical problems with the helicopters and high winds resulting in poor visibility from dust. After the halt of the mission, the helicopters were on the ground for refueling before returning to the ships from where they launched. Blinding sand swirled around the refueling aircraft, a C-130 Hercules. A CH-53 helicopter, directed too close, struck the C-130 transport. Fires and explosions from bullets on the aircraft followed. Eight service members died. The hostages remained in captivity until January 20, 1981.

In August 1980, a group of six senior military officers, including three retirees and three active-duty members, issued the Iran Hostage Mission Report. Admiral James L. Holloway, III, retired Chief of Naval Operations, led the group. In addition to Admiral Holloway, the other retired officers included U.S. Army Lieutenant General Samuel V. Wilson and U.S. Air Force Lieutenant General LeRoy J. Manor. The three active-duty members of the group were Major General James C. Smith of the U.S. Army, Major General John L. Piotrowski from the U.S. Air Force, and Marine Corps Major General Alfred "Al" M. Gray.

The report found no evidence of neglect or incompetence.[4] The group called the plan adequate with the exception of not having backup for helicopters. The report also cited the need for "better provisions for weather." The report called those involved in the planning execution as "the most competent" with the "best qualified people available."[5] As a recommendation, the group felt that the mission would have benefitted from a dress rehearsal.[6] Speaking of the Iran Hostage Rescue Mission Report, General Carey said that he appreciated the fact that General Gray was the lone Marine in the group that put the report together. The two worked together during the Saigon evacuation. General Carey pointed out that he never talked to General Gray while he was involved with the report.[7]

For his contributions during his assignment with the Atlantic Command, Lieutenant General Carey earned the Defense Superior Service Medal. Assistant Commandant of the Marine Corps General Kenneth McClennan (left) made the presentation. (*Quantico Sentry*, March 6, 1981)

Three-Star General

In October 1980, 34 years after boot camp at Parris Island, Richard E. Carey earned his third star, with his promotion to lieutenant general. His work at CINCLANT earned him the Defense Superior Service medal. He assumed command of the Marine Corps Development and Education Command (MCDED) at Quantico, Virginia. His predecessors included Generals O. P. Smith and Ray Davis. General Carey earned his commission at Quantico in 1948. Now, he would train the next generation of Marine Corps leaders.

CHAPTER 16

Final Assignment Quantico

In what would be General Carey's last stop in a nearly 40-year military career, he led and directed revised training leadership programs at Quantico, Virginia. Under his command, the Marine Corps opened 23 new schools with standardized instruction programs, training aids, and equipment. General Carey also managed a $46 million budget.

Training programs, according to the General, had a basic goal of educating Marines by example. He regularly spoke to second lieutenants in TBS; he always said that TBS was so important to his own career development, and he used the opportunity to address the new lieutenants as a recruiting tool. The General shared his personal experiences and urged the lieutenants to think about the potential of being career Marine officers. In addition, he believed that TBS had an influence on whether or not the young officers stayed in the Marine Corps.[1]

As commander, General Carey aimed to design training programs to update the Marine Corps. Key changes involved the Command Staff and Amphibious Warfare Schools. Those trained at the various schools applied the training at their individual units. General Carey said the first goal of the overall training changes was "enhancement of leadership." He also emphasized the importance of being able to solve problems that did not have a precedent. General Carey pointed to his involvement with the evacuation of Saigon as an example. "There was no book," he said.[2]

Marine Corps Marathon

Part of Carey's leadership enhancement centered on physical fitness. From his personal combat experience in Korea, General Carey understood the importance of physically fit troops in battle. The Marine Corps Marathon was the public face of the physical fitness objective. The marathon, a 26.2-mile race instituted in 1976, appeared to be on the chopping block due to costs. According to Carey, the Marine Corps paid an outside firm to handle race administration. Carey received a call to attend a meeting at Marine headquarters to discuss the marathon. Marine Corps Commandant General Barrow said that that the Marine Corps could no longer afford to operate it. Then Lieutenant General Carey, while serving at Quantico, offered to "take over that duty." He said, "It was not going to die, if I can help it." As a result, General Carey took on the Marine Corps Marathon project.

Marine Corps Commandant and long-time friend of Carey's, General Robert H. Barrow (left), attended Lieutenant General Carey's change of command ceremony at MCB Quantico. Carey began his final assignment as Commanding General Marine Corps Development and Education Command. (Carey family collection, 1980)

General Carey and his staff handled administration for the race instead of using an outside vendor. The Marine Corps Marathon continues to operate, although Covid 19 forced cancellation of the race in 2020 and 2021. In 2019, just over 30,000 participants from all 50 states and 60 countries participated in the nation's fourth largest marathon.[3]

General Carey listed several reasons for pushing to retain the event. One was personal. "I loved to run," he said. The General also wanted to set an example of the importance of physical fitness for his people. In addition, he said that one of the most important parts of leadership is to set an example. "Ductus Exemplo" is the official motto of the Marine Corps OCS. It is a Latin term meaning "lead by example."[4] Finally, the General said, "I wanted to demonstrate that older guys can do lots of things not expected, physically." General Carey, 54 when he ran the Marine Corps Marathon in 1982, finished at three hours and 19 minutes, then a record for the event in his age bracket. The race began at the Iwo Jima Memorial in Arlington, Virginia, and wound through Washington where runners passed by the Lincoln and Jefferson Memorials, the Washington Monument, and the White House. According to General Carey, his 1982 time remained the record for his age group until General Joseph F. Dunford broke it.[5] General Dunford served as commandant of the Marine Corps and led the Joint Chiefs of Staff.

Not only did Lieutenant General Carey save the Marine Corps Marathon, he ran in the event. His time earned him a slot in the Boston Marathon. (Carey family collection 1982)

In 1982, 9,996 people participated in the race.[6] An Associated Press pre-race story said nearly two-thirds of the runners were first-time marathoners. The AP story referred to Carey as the "Commander in Chief of the Marathon" and quoted General Carey as saying, "This is truly a people's race." In addition, the AP said the Marine Corps Marathon was one of the better-organized races due to the support of an estimated 1,700 Marines.[7] Carey ran the Marine Corps Marathon twice. His three-hour-and-19-minute time at the Marine Corps Marathon qualified him for the Boston Marathon. Conquering the famed "heartbreak hill" at the Boston Marathon, Carey finished that race in three hours and 30 minutes. Previously, he competed in a triathlon (biking, running, and swimming) and a half-marathon. Overall, General Carey said that he appreciated the opportunity to influence the Marine Corps and help prepare future officers for command.[8]

Anti-Drug Abuse

During his time at Quantico, General Carey led a drive to battle drug abuse in the Marine Corps. In an effort to reduce drug use and prevent drugs from entering Quantico, General Carey initiated random searches of cars driving through the military checkpoint on Fuller Road. Fuller Road, a public road, runs through Quantico and is a government road. Major James M. Pendergast (who had worked with Carey at Cherry Point as a captain), who spoke on behalf of the General, said in an October 13, 1982, interview with *The Washington Post* that the searches helped reduce drug use on the base. "It's the government's road, and Lieutenant General Richard E. Carey, Quantico's commanding officer's first responsibility is to the security of the base and it is his prerogative to institute this policy to achieve that," Major Pendergast said. While the searches of cars provided a benefit to the base, local citizens stopped by Marines and asked to open their car trunks did not appreciate it. Virginia's General Assembly, the legislature's lower house, looked into the issue. There were complaints about the inconvenience. A 72-year-old lady said she had driven on Fuller Road for more than 45 years. She said that no one ever stopped her for a car search. The car searches generated petitions, calls to elected officials, and one lawsuit. General Carey admitted that the searches did not "last very long."

On the base, the General led programs that tried both to prevent drug abuse and to deal with Marines facing the problem. He made certain that instructors added drug abuse training into leadership schools. On the base, unit leaders handled drug issues. Initially, the units dealt with the problem at an individual level. Those General Carey termed "bad abusers" faced punishment that included discharges from the Marine Corps.

The General explained that boot camp recruits at San Diego and Parris Island caught using drugs received an immediate discharge. At Quantico, he initiated a program to rehabilitate drug users. Those who admitted being drug users (not many did) and those caught using drugs went into what Carey termed a "special environment." In that program, Marines received observation and supervision. Doctors and civilian advisors aided the rehabilitation project; it was designed to last six weeks, but the advisors found that long-term addicts needed additional time. According to General Carey, that was a first-of-its-kind program in the Marine Corps. Participation in the program did not become part of an individual's record. In addition to helping Marines overcome drug use, the program saved some from unsatisfactory discharges and reduced overall discharges.[9]

General Carey's efforts against drug abuse attracted the attention of the White House. President Ronald W. Reagan's Chief of Staff and Assistant to the President James A. Baker III commented on the General's program in a letter endorsing Carey's nomination for a Horatio Alger Award in 1983. Mr. Baker said, "He also established a successful drug abuse program which has served as a model for other drug abuse programs across the country."[10] Although the General did not receive the award, his efforts won recognition from a senior member of President Reagan's staff.

Along with helping fellow Marines facing drug problems, General Carey acknowledged that his son Michael Scott's issue with drug addiction entered into his rationale for the Quantico program. As a teenager, Michael Scott

Lieutenant General Carey greeted President Ronald Reagan when the president went horseback riding at Quantico. Chief of Staff James A. Baker, wearing a cowboy hat, stands behind General Carey. (Carey family collection, 1981)

experimented with drugs, the General said. His son, General Carey said, "is very bright and that was the sad part of it. It was really a shame; he was smart. He didn't use it." Michael Scott enlisted in the Army and served in a stateside infantry assignment. Drugs continued to be part of his life and the Army discharged him.[11]

There was a lighter side to Carey's job. With a new gate at Quantico under construction, General Carey looked for a way to leave his mark. He realized that one day the main gate would again need replacement, and when the construction crew takes down that gate, they will find a fifth of Johnny Walker Scotch with General Carey's name on it.[12]

Presidential Visits

At Quantico, General Carey's responsibilities included ceremonial roles. For example, when President Ronald W. Reagan went horseback riding at the base, the General greeted the president when he arrived at Quantico. The stable kept horses used for Marines' recreation on base, and the president rode a horse named Jackpot.[13] From the south lawn of the White House, Marine One, the president's helicopter, took him to the Marine Corps Air Facility at Quantico, which housed HMX-1, the helicopter squadron that included Marine One. The president's Daily Diary indicated that the trip took about 15 minutes. The president rode his horse for nearly an hour and a half before returning to the White House. President Reagan's Daily Diary showed his first horseback ride at Quantico took place on March 25, 1981—just five days before a lone gunman shot him on March 30 in Washington, D.C.

Other visitors to Quantico included Vice President George H. W. Bush (later the 41st president of the United States) and Presidential Chief of Staff (the future secretary of treasury and state) Baker, a Marine Corps veteran. In addition, Assistant for National Security Affairs William P. Clark and Nevada Republican Senator Paul Laxalt came to Quantico with the president.[14] Secret Service agents and the White House physician also accompanied the president.[15] According to General Carey, Vice President Bush and Chief of Staff Baker were the only administration members who rode with the president. General Carey shared a story about the vice president's visit. For security reasons, the president and vice president arrived separately. President Reagan was already out riding Jackpot when Vice President Bush arrived. The vice president went to a wooded area on the base and then hollered out, "Where in the hell am I?" Shortly after that, he caught up with the president.[16]

General Carey described the president as "very cordial and pleasant." He added that Mr. Reagan was the type of person that you could become friends with after meeting him. The General said that he greeted the president each time that he came to Quantico. When asked about his thoughts when meeting the president, General Carey said that he felt "honored that he [President Reagan] selected Quantico for his recreation time." The General also said that he "felt blessed and very fortunate to get to that point in life" where he could meet a president. He added that the president "was down to earth and a good officer."[17]

The base also supported the president's security team. When the president went riding, Marines hid in the woods along his route. Following the assassination attempt, General Carey said the base security efforts for the president's visits did not change. However, he noticed the president's security team was "more attentive." The General said that he received notice of the president's trips to Quantico several days in advance.

Vice President and Mrs. George H. W. Bush host a military and intelligence reception at the vice president's residence (Naval Observatory) and greet Lieutenant General and his wife Dena on September 25, 1981. (Courtesy George H. W. Bush Presidential Library and Museum)

Media coverage of the president's visits was limited to a brief photo of the president horseback riding by White House-credentialed photographers at an assigned location. The White House press staff handled the media for Reagan's trips to Quantico, Pendergast said.[18]

In addition, General Carey said that he did get to know Chief of Staff Baker. The Careys hosted Mr. Baker at dinner in their home on the base.[19] In the 1950s, Mr. Baker had served as a lieutenant in the Marine Corps.

Although HMX-1 was based at Quantico, the unit did not report to General Carey. HMX-1 reported to three entities: the deputy chief of staff for Marine Aviation at Headquarters Marine Corps; Operational, Test, and Evaluation Department (OTE) in Norfolk; and the White House Military Office. HMX-1 is the only Marine Corps unit with three chains of command. Marines first provided transportation for President Eisenhower in 1957 and continues that mission today.[20]

In addition to the president, Virginia officials came to Quantico. General Carey and his wife Dena greeted members of the Virginia General Assembly on February 1, 1981. An artist's rendering from that meeting hung over the fireplace in the General's home in Plano, Texas. Virginia Lieutenant Governor

Charles "Chuck" Robb, a former Marine major, Vietnam veteran, and Bronze Star recipient, spoke at the luncheon that day. Robb was President Johnson's son-in-law. He later served as Virginia's governor from 1981–1985 and as a two-term U.S. senator between 1989 and 2001.

In August 1981, General Carey represented the Marine Corps at an annual equipment display show in Tucson, Arizona. Each year a Marine or civilian received the "Iron Mike" award for "extraordinary contributions to the United States or the Marine Corps." "Iron Mike" is a statute at the Marine Corps Training Depot at Parris Island. Erected after World War I, "Iron Mike" honors the memory of Marines who died in World War I. The 1981 "Iron Mike" honorees suffered wounds during the assassination attempt on President Reagan. Press Secretary James Brady, Secret Service Agent Tim McCarthy, and Washington police officer Thomas Delahanty received the awards.[21]

Quantico and John Hinckley

General Carey assigned a nightly command duty officer (CDO) to serve as his representative and stand watch after normal duty hours. By chance, on March 30, 1982, then Major Pendergast, Quantico's public affairs officer had the CDO duty.[22]

The major described Quantico's tie-in with John Hinckley after his arrest for shooting the president. A call came for General Carey. Pendergast answered with these words, "Major Pendergast, Command Duty Officer." Marine Corps Commandant General Barrow was on the line. Pendergast knew Barrow from his time as Marine Corps liaison officer to the U.S. House of Representatives. Barrow said, "Jim, this is General Barrow. I'm calling for General Carey." Pendergast explained that General Carey had already headed to his quarters and offered to transfer the call. General Barrow replied, "No, there's no time for that. I'll call him there later. I need you to do something right now." General Barrow gave Pendergast his charge. Pendergast needed to let the front gate guards know that several black vehicles would soon be approaching the gate. General Barrow explained that vehicles would be traveling at high speed and should be waved through the gate without being stopped. He then told the major, "In fact, get an MP with a vehicle over there to lead them directly to the brig [jail]. Lights and sirens. They've got Hinckley." Pendergast first contacted the provost marshal to relay Barrow's instructions. Then, he briefed General Carey.[23] Authorities held John Hinckley in an isolation cell in the brig. He did not receive an opportunity for bond.[24]

Pendergast realized that Quantico faced what he called a potential media "onslaught." After he spoke with the public affairs staff at HQMC, Pendergast learned that the FBI public affairs team would handle the media. The major said, "It was clear from the outset that there would be no repeat of the Jack Ruby business following President Kennedy's assassination."

Pendergast and the FBI public affairs contact understood the need to provide a secure photo opportunity for the media in the morning. Realizing that his team had work to do that evening, Pendergast called General Carey's chief of staff who arranged for another Marine officer to take the CDO assignment. Pendergast worked with the FBI's public affairs staff to finalize plans to deal with the media. The FBI alerted the national media and Pendergast notified local reporters. The plan included stringent guidelines for the Hinckley photo opportunity the next morning. Media members came to the main gate at 9 a.m. and parked their cars. The FBI checked credentials of the media. A Marine Corps bus took the media to the brig. Hinckley could not answer questions. The media could photograph or film Hinckley from the front door of the brig at a specified distance. Following the photo opportunity, the bus returned the media to the front gate.[25] For the second time in 18 years, General Carey was on the periphery of a presidential shooting.

In August 1981, after a psychiatric evaluation at the Federal Correctional Institute in Butner, North Carolina, a Marine helicopter returned Hinckley to Quantico after four months.[26]

Embassy Guard Training

While Quantico houses many training schools, a unique school involved the training of guards for Embassy duty. Historically, Marines guarded U.S. Embassies around the world. Those carefully selected and highly trained Marines receive their Marine Security Guard (MSG) Battalion training at Quantico. MSGs protect classified documents at Embassies. Their six- to eight-week training program covers everything from marksmanship to etiquette. An MSG trainer explained why there was a need for etiquette classes. Marines, he said, know how to eat out of a can or in a mess hall. For MSG duty, they have to be able to eat at an ambassador's table.

Five times a year, 100 MSG candidates come through Quantico. Only the best earn the Embassy slots. When General Carey served as the commanding general, about 25 percent of the candidates did not make the cut. The candidates train at Marshall Hall, named for Corporal James C. Marshall, the only Embassy guard to die in the 1968 Tet Offensive in Vietnam. In Marshall

Hall, the training staff displayed the passports of the last two Marines to die in Vietnam, Lance Corporals Darwin L. Judge and Charles McMahon. Graduates of the program make a two-and-a-half-year commitment to the MSG program. Their first assignment takes them to a remote duty station followed by another position at a more desirable location.[27]

Post-Marine Corps Opportunity

A 1979 charity event in Ohio that introduced General Carey to Wendy's founder Dave Thomas resulted in a friendship. During the next three years, the pair frequently spoke. In the fall of 1982, the General and Mr. Thomas talked by telephone. Mr. Thomas wanted to know if the General could meet him at the Ohio State-Michigan football at the "horseshoe"—the nickname for Ohio Stadium—on November 21. This meeting would turn out to be more than just two friends watching a football game. Mr. Thomas had seats in a reserved section of the stadium, and he wanted the General to meet someone that day. For the General, Ohio Stadium had special memories. As a boy, he had earned money handling Coca-Cola bottles during football games. In high school, he ran state track meets there.

At the game, General Carey met Ohio's governor-elect Richard F. Celeste for the first time. The governor-elect just won the office earlier in the month. He sat next to the General and the two men spoke at length as they watched the Buckeyes defeat their archrival Michigan Wolverines by a score of 24–14. Although it was the first time the men met, Dave Thomas had recommended the General for a role in Celeste's administration. As a former Marine, Mr. Thomas told the incoming 64th Ohio governor that General Carey was a leader and to use him as he saw fit. Late that afternoon, Mr. Celeste asked the General, "How would you like to work for me?" General Carey asked, "What job?" The governor-elect told him the position—Director of Liquor Control. The General told him that he really was not interested in the assignment. He explained to

Ohio Governor Richard F. Celeste (right) appointed Carey to his cabinet as Director of Liquor Control. Carey assumed the position right after his retirement from the Marine Corps. (Carey family collection, 1983)

Mr. Celeste that as a Christian he had reservations about encouraging the sale of alcoholic beverages. The governor-elect persisted. He asked General Carey to take that job. General Carey explained that he had an interest in developing a state program for disabled veterans. Mr. Celeste told the General that he would think about it. An admirer of President Reagan, General Carey told the governor-elect, "You gotta remember, I'm a Republican." Replied Mr. Celeste, a Democrat, "Don't worry about that. You have the leadership qualities that I want."[28] In retrospect, the General realized that incoming Governor Celeste wanted Carey's stature as a Marine general in his new administration.

After two years at Quantico, the General seriously looked at retirement. This was his third tour of duty in the Washington area. Dena's view remained the same as did in the early 1970s: the job was not good for family life. General Carey left the house at 6 a.m. and often did not get home until after 8 p.m. Dena told him, "I can't stand Washington." The General said they often only had time together at social functions. Dena wanted to return to Texas,

Lieutenant General Carey (left without helmet) participated in an exercise held at 29 Palms, California. (Carey family collection, 1982)

but really wanted out of Washington. In addition, their daughter Melody, a high-school basketball player, did not see much of her father.

In December 1982, General Carey drove to Headquarters Marine Corps to meet with General. P. X. Kelly, assistant commandant of the Marine Corps (ACMC). General Carey told General Kelly that he planned to retire at the end of February. General Kelly responded, "No you're not." General Carey firmly said, "Yes I am." At that point, although it was not public, General Kelly anticipated that he would succeed General Barrow as commandant of the Marine Corps. General Kelly told General Carey that he wanted him to be his ACMC. That meant a promotion to four-star general. While taking the ACMC position did not come with a guarantee, accepting the ACMC billet would mean a shot at becoming commandant of the Marine Corps. Carey explained to Kelly that he had a civilian job opportunity in his native Columbus, Ohio. Going to Columbus would take General Carey on a detour before he went to Dena's home state, but Dena was onboard. The new job got her out of the Washington, D.C., corridor. In addition, Melody had a chance to play basketball at Ohio State University. Finally, the assignment would give the Careys the chance to spend time with his Ohio family.[29]

Just prior to the General's retirement, Quantico's base newspaper, *The Quantico Sentry*, ran a front-page story about him on February 25, 1983. Sergeant Chris Fordney interviewed Lieutenant General Carey for the article. Carey talked about new equipment and weapons coming into the system. He said, "A lot has been put into these reequipping programs at all levels. I've just been a link in the chain."

General Carey expressed his feelings about the state of the Marine Corps:

> But the most important thing we have in the Corps are its people, and with the ongoing elimination of the drug users and non-producers, we can ensure that we have a first-class outfit with first class people. Let's face it; the Marine Corps is the best in the world. It always has been and always will be. We're just making it better.

The General discussed his accomplishments during his time as commanding general at Quantico including the establishment of a separate doctrine center. That, he explained, would provide Marines with doctrine "they can rely upon as the basis for fighting and defeating any adversary in this age of modern warfare."

Regarding his retirement plans, General Carey said this about the Marine Corps: "I'm not going to sever the ties with the Marine Corps or forget about the Marine Corps. There are a lot of Marines in Ohio, where I am going, and I plan to maintain close contact with them."

In a February 23, 1983, open letter in *The Quantico Sentry* (the base newspaper), General Carey said this about his retirement:

> It has been that association with such fine, brave conscientious men and women—truly the best our great nation produces—that makes the break so difficult. I am grateful for having had the honor and privilege of sharing with you the title "Marine."

The General's last official act at Quantico was participation in the February 27 change of command ceremony. Major General David M. Twomey succeeded General Carey. The article also mentioned the General's retirement position—the director of the Ohio Liquor Control Department in March.[30]

When the General retired, he received congratulatory notes from fellow Marines, current and past, and even a Supreme Court Justice. Words of praise came his way at the change of command ceremony.

Acting secretary of the Navy James F. Goodrich, in a letter to General Carey, wrote:

> Your achievements throughout your more than 37 years of Marine Corps service attest markedly to those qualities of leadership and professionalism upon which the strength of our armed forces and our Nation are based. Men of your caliber are fully deserving of the appreciation and respect of both this Country and its Government.[31]

Shortly before he retired, General Robert H. Barrow, Marine Corps commandant, wrote to General Carey. He said:

> As an infantry officer in Korea, you showed the indomitable spirit and ability that would mark your later career as an aviator ... you led the Brigade through the incredibly complex and sensitive evacuations of Phnom Penh and Saigon. The success of these two operations is a tribute to your unique abilities.[32]

After he retired, General Carey thanked General Barrow for his letter. The commandant, who planned to retire in July, replied, "You have been a stalwart among our ranks for almost four decades, and your record of achievement commands the respect and admiration of all who had the privilege to serve with you." He added, "I salute you."[33]

Supreme Court Justice Harry A. Blackmun, who was unable to attend the General's retirement ceremony, sent a letter that said, "I hope the ceremony went off well and that you are becoming well-settled in your new duties in Columbus."[34]

The best tribute came from his youngest child, Melody, a high-school senior. She wrote a poem as a tribute to her father's long career in the Marine Corps.

"Retirement"
By Melody Carey

Retirement is the time to open your eyes,
Long since sworn, how time flies
All your life you've been brave and strong,
Now out on your own is where you belong.
There you will stand with a tear on your face,
Your hands will sweat and your heart will race,
But deep down inside there is something you've known,
Through all these years, your pride has grown.
The band will play its final tribute,
The speech will come and you will say.
I never thought that I'd see this day.
Yes! The day has come and with it the end,
Your true feelings now you must not pretend,
Those stars on your shoulders, no one will borrow.
They are here today will be tomorrow.
The only thing now you must put in your mind,
The Marines are past but not left behind,
So open your eyes and stand tall and true,
For you know there is no Marine like you,
No one will down you or put you away,
Your life is not over, it begins today,
Please don't be discouraged or don't be sad,
For always remember, I love you dad![35]

CHAPTER 17

A Brief Entry into Politics

When military people retire from service, they often find new careers and keep working. Depending upon the length of their careers, retired military people may have many years left in the work force. Channeling their skills acquired in the military into a civilian career can be a challenge. Having just turned 55, General Carey had years left to contribute. He had led and managed large organizations and succeeded at every assignment. During his career, he achieved much and had much to offer. The General offered skills in large-scale logistical operations, senior-level management, motivation, and training. Carey brought experience in operations, international relations, pressure situations, and staff leadership. He also offered a future employer the stature of a three-star general. Bringing in a retired general offered credibility to the cabinet of a newly elected governor. But the General was not a political hack. Although he was an Ohio native, General Carey was an outsider.

With the change-of-command-ceremony at Quantico over on February 27 and General Twomey installed as his replacement, the newly retired General headed out on the 450-mile drive to Columbus. Taking no time off between jobs, Carey started his first non-military opportunity since his package delivery job in Columbus in the early part of 1946. He started in his position in the Celeste Administration on March 1. Asked why he went straight to the new job, Carey replied, "I didn't need any time off."[1] He took the final drive on the beltway. Washington, D.C., was now behind him, and the General began his assignment as director of the Ohio Liquor Control Department.

The job consisted of three parts. First, he managed 300-plus state liquor stores and the warehouse operation supplying them. The retired General also had responsibility for dealing with agency stores. Private citizens operated the agency stores. Agency store operators earned a commission based on store dollar sales. The agency stores served communities with a population of less than 10,000 people. There were more than 100 agency stores around the state. In addition, the director was responsible for licensing some 25,000 bars, restaurants, and establishments that sold beer and wine. State stores only sold hard liquor. The Liquor Control Department's charge included selling more alcohol to drive revenue to the state of Ohio. Nearly 2,000 part-time and full-time people worked in the state operated stores and warehouses.

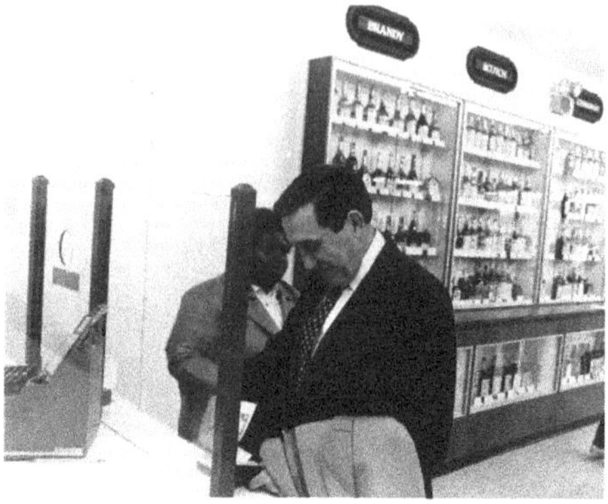

To understand the retail liquor business as Director of Liquor Control, Carey made frequent visits to individual state operated stores. (Carey family collection, 1983)

The Ohio system of packaged liquor sales came about with the end of Prohibition in 1933. Designed to stop consumption of alcoholic beverages, Prohibition just did not work in the United States. People wanted alcoholic beverages. Bootleg liquor became part of the American culture for 13 years. Before World War I, the Anti-Saloon League led the effort to stop the sale of alcohol. The group's national publishing headquarters operated out of the Columbus suburb of Westerville. The publishing division of the Anti-Saloon League turned out up to 40 tons of printed material promoting their cause each month.[2] Alcoholics Anonymous began helping those with drinking problems in the northern Ohio city of Akron in 1935, just two years after the end of Prohibition. As Carey took on his new assignment, he learned that a portion of the state's nearly $400 million in alcohol revenue ironically went to support work with people struggling with alcoholism. While Carey was responsible for increasing sales of alcohol, he faced an ongoing challenge from the neighboring states of Indiana and Kentucky. Those states had privately run liquor stores that offered lower prices than available in Ohio.

With the Liquor Control Department, Richard E. Carey came in as the new person. He had no prior experience with the liquor business. He had never worked in state government. He was not a typical political appointee. When Carey arrived, the staff was in place. As in any new assignment, he faced a learning curve. Applying the skills he learned in 38 years in the military, Carey went to where the action is in the liquor business. He drove around Ohio and met with the state store managers. From those meetings, he saw challenges and opportunities. State stores did not operate like typical retail stores. Consumers walked in the stores. They filled out a request sheet. A staff member pulled the liquor from the shelf and the customer paid for their order. There was no shopping and no in-store merchandising such as point-of-sale material. By design, that set up did nothing to encourage impulse purchases.

While in the stores, the new director had the following objectives: establish relationships with store staff, discuss the store's business, and ensure that all employees followed both the departmental rules and state laws.

During his first six months on the job, Carey visited more than 100 state-operated and agency stores. In the department's employee newsletter, Carey made these observations, "by and large our people have good appearance and decorum, but only a fair attitude. I want to work to change that." The General also said:

> As I perceive it, another reason for poor attitude is environment. We want to foster pride by improving the appearance of our stores. Working in a clean, modern, and orderly place goes a long way towards making us feel good about what we do …

Although Carey did not come into the job with any retail store experience, he quickly summarized the situation through the eyes of a customer. His suggestion was straightforward and simple. Carey told employees that greeting customers with the words, "Good morning may I help you?" would help change attitudes.

In a department newsletter was a picture of Governor Celeste during his June 30, 1983, visit to the Department of Liquor Control's central office. The governor told the staff, "Your efforts are appreciated."[3]

By November 1983, Carey's team made changes designed to help boost sales and reduce operating expenses. Part of the logistics of the state store system included warehousing inventory. The state rented the warehouse space.[4] When Carey started with the department, distillers, who manufactured and sold liquor, shipped their product to the state-operated warehouses. Distillers only received payment when store operators pulled product to the store. Seventy-five of the 306 state stores began a pilot program. In those stores, distillers could place pieces of point-of-sale material in each store. The distiller's sales team put the display advertising in the stores. State employees did not handle point of sale material. In addition, the Liquor Control Department introduced the bailment system. In that system, the distillers delivered their products to the stores rather than the warehouse. In the retail trade soft drink, bread, dairy, snack, and beer companies use that system called direct store delivery (DSD) to ship their products to retail stores. Rozanne Glass, chief of public information for the department, said the bailment system offered up to $59 million in potential annual cost savings to the state.[5]

The General explained his objectives for the department. He led efforts to make the system more profitable, reduce underage drinking, and support efforts to aid recovering alcoholics. Reducing warehousing costs with the implementation of the direct store delivery program aided profitability. To prevent sales of liquor to underage buyers, the General put the word out in a directive to the stores—enforce checking of proper identification. He met regularly with Governor Celeste. According to the General, the governor seemed pleased with the changes and improvements that Carey made in the department. In addition, Carey sought more funding to deal with alcoholism. That did not happen. The governor's response to that request was, according to the General, "I'll think about it." Carey said, "I did everything I could to help the system."

Carey came up with another idea designed to reduce the size of state government. Unlike many political appointees, General Carey did not want to expand his role. During a meeting with the governor, he recommended that Ohio get out of the retail liquor business and let private enterprise handle it. Again, the answer came down to "I'll think about it." From his first meeting with Celeste at Ohio Stadium, Carey found that response came whenever he presented new ideas that did not interest the governor.

While advocating moving the liquor business from the state to private enterprise in his conversations with the governor, Carey publicly supported the current system in a commentary in the Forum section of *The Plain Dealer* (Cleveland) on June 25, 1985. He responded to a June 6, 1985, *Plain Dealer* commentary urging Ohio to end its liquor sale monopoly. Carey pointed out two financial reasons to keep the state in the retail liquor business. Liquor generated $80 million in net profits to Ohio in fiscal 1985. In addition, Carey said that there were two additional financial benefits to Ohio. Alcohol education and treatment programs run by the state's health department received $2 million and $18 million went to help retire bonds used to make loans to small businesses. Carey also reiterated the post-Prohibition reasons for the state-run-liquor stores. First, the goal was to minimize consumption of liquor and to boost revenue for Ohio. "This is important because alcohol is not just any commodity; it is the most commonly used and abused substance in our society," Carey said. He also pointed to a 1983 Governor's Office of Recovery Services report that stated alcohol costs due to reduced job performance, additional health care costs, drunk driving, and other crimes cost the nation $116 billion.[6]

On the same day that *The Plain Dealer* ran Carey's commentary, the paper responded with an editorial calling for privatizing retail liquor sales.

The editorial described the Department of Liquor Control this way, "It is a bastion of political patronage—a place where the most inept-but-loyal political flunky can find a paycheck, if not a job to perform by currying favor with the winning political side."[7]

In line with helping the system and increasing profits, the General led the implementation of a security camera system to prevent shoplifting and employee theft. His research showed that theft was a quarter-of-a-million-dollar per year problem. The Liquor Control analysis identified the 30 stores with largest inventory shortages. Carey committed $17,450 to lease camera equipment. He said stores faced two types of theft problems. Shoplifting by customers contributed to the problem, he said. He also pointed out, "We do have quite a bit of shoplifting by employees." The Liquor Control Department committed to a five-year agreement with a private Columbus firm to set up the camera system as a theft deterrent.[8]

Jack Hicks, a newspaper columnist with the *Cincinnati Enquirer*, wrote about methods the Liquor Control Department agents used to stop out-of-state liquor purchases. Hicks pointed out that agents went to great lengths to catch people bringing liquor from Kentucky to Ohio. One Kentucky liquor store operator toyed with the agents, according to Hicks. As the Ohio agents watched, one of the liquor store employees placed liquor boxes in the car of a driver with Ohio license plates. As soon as the driver crossed into Ohio, the agents stopped the car. The agents only found empty liquor boxes.

Use of a helicopter to stop the flow of out-of-state liquor into Ohio was another example of the extreme efforts agents used against Ohioans purchasing liquor out of state.[9] The agents served under the Liquor Control Department enforcement group.

Battling lower-priced liquor in neighboring states of Kentucky and Indiana created challenges to Carey's efforts to increase liquor profits. Enforcement agents from the Liquor Control Department went into Covington, Kentucky, and followed those purchasing liquor back to Ohio. If the drivers had more than one liter of out-of-state liquor, they faced criminal charges for illegally transporting liquor across the state line. The Mayor of Covington, Tom Beehan, called the process "economic blackmail." Mayor Beehan pushed for city ordinance making it unlawful for Ohio Liquor Control agents to park outside of privately owned Covington liquor outlets. Carey's staff estimated that out-of-state liquor purchases cost Ohio a million dollars a year in revenue.[10]

Carey's involvement with enforcement led to his assignment on a state committee that prepared the 1986 Report on the Organized Crime Consulting

Committee. Governor Celeste appointed Carey as one of 20 committee members. Ohio Attorney General Anthony J. Celebrezze, Jr. led the group that, in addition to Carey, included prosecuting attorneys, county sheriffs, and police chiefs. The report noted that the Liquor Control Department seized 335 illegal electronic gambling devices from bars and restaurants between 1984 and 1985.

Politics

While Carey's Marine Corps experience included logistics, leadership, and management, nothing prepared him for the political side of the job. One example involved Carey and Senator John H. Glenn. In 1984, Senator Glenn campaigned for the Democratic nomination for president. Carey hosted a fund-raiser at his home for Glenn. The Democratic nominee that year would face incumbent President Reagan, a man Carey admired from his time at Quantico. Yet, Carey supported Glenn. They were both Marines, Korean War veterans, and they knew each other for more than 25 years. When Carey served at MCAS Beaufort in South Carolina, he and Glenn had worked in different fighter squadrons in the same building, and both sought positions in the Mercury 7 space program. Carey's fund-raiser for Glenn drew attention. Among the invited guests were liquor company leaders. In early March, Governor Celeste's chief of staff, Joseph Sommer, told Carey those invitations were inappropriate.[11] Carey said that he did tell the liquor company representatives that they did not have to contribute to the Glenn campaign, and he viewed the invitations as a social event.[12]

In this job, Carey found himself in the news. Some of the coverage was good but most was negative. *The Columbus Citizen Journal's* "Being Civil" columnist Sam Perdue made Carey the subject of four columns written in August 1985. On the 5th he wrote, "Overheard in the Statehouse, if Dagmar Celeste, Ohio's first lady is committed to combating alcoholism and other chemical dependency, and is smitten with Liquor Director Richard Carey's commitment to running a clean liquor operation, how is she privately reacting to Carey's son hustling booze for Seagram's?"[13] The General said that his son did not work for Seagram in Ohio. Seagram hired him to work in New York.[14] On August 12, Perdue mentioned the pay increase given to Patricia Holly. During an eight-month period, her pay increased by 43% from \$5.64 an hour to \$7.88. Carey acknowledged that Holly was "a distant cousin."[15] Perdue shared both sides of his take on Carey's performance in his August 19 column headlined "Politics is tough, a general finds out." On the 29th, Perdue again commented on Carey's department hiring one of his relatives (Patricia Holly). Perdue mentioned that in 1972 law enforcement officials arrested Carey's second cousin Patricia Holly on a felony theft charge, later reduced to a misdemeanor. She included that information on her application. Perdue asked Carey's spokesperson, Rozanne Glass about hiring a relative. She answered, "Is there a difference between a distant relative (second cousin) and family?" Glass also said a misdemeanor did not disqualify an applicant.[16]

While Sam Perdue, a Columbus newspaper columnist, often criticized Carey, he praised Carey's fund-raising efforts in a bike-a-thon. Carey's cycling prowess raised $1,300 for charity. (Carey family collection, 1985)

On the positive side, Perdue mentioned Carey's appearance at an Ohio State Senate budget hearing in April. Carey told the senators that the liquor department had not kept up with "modern technological advances." In addition, Carey shared his department's new guidelines for adding new items and dropping slow movers. "The absence of such criteria resulted in a bloated inventory and special treatment for liquor vendors with access to various administrations." Perdue suggested that was "a rap against past directors" (Carey's predecessors).

Perdue also said that Carey's concerns about overindulgence of alcoholic beverage drew the notice of Governor Celeste's wife Dagmar, Ohio's first lady. Mrs. Celeste worked closely with the state's employee assistance program that dealt with drinking and chemical dependency.

In addition, Perdue mentioned that Carey led and participated in a Bike-A-Thon that raised money for the Ohio Hunger Task Force. He personally raised the largest amount—more than $1,300 in pledges for miles ridden.

On the other hand, Perdue pointed out that Carey attended the May 1985 National Alcohol Beverage Association conference in Bal Harbor, Florida. According to Perdue, a trade publication included a picture of Carey with executives of Seagram's. In addition, Perdue again mentioned Seagram's hired Carey's son Paul in July.[17] Carey said that he only recalled one brief conversation with Perdue.[18]

Director Carey (far left) joined Governor Richard F. Celeste for a golf outing. (Carey family collection, 1984/1985)

Another aspect of politics focused on the agency store appointments. Over the years, agency store opportunities became political footballs. During Republican administrations, agency stores went to Republicans. When the Democrats came into office, the opposite took place. Agency operators often contributed to both political parties. One Republican agency operator acknowledged that he contributed to the Democratic Party. In 1986, the *Dayton Daily News* analyzed the agency store and politics issue during 1983 and 1984. When a new agency operator came on, they rented a different location. According to reporter Joel Rutchik's story, 10 out of 11 agency stores relocated between 1983 and 1984. All of those stores, Rutchik reported, went to Democrats. One went to a man who pledged contributions to the Democrats. Six of those 11 stores resulted in liquor volume losses after the change. One Republican who lost his agency store charged that Carey told him not to worry and the next day called to tell him that the agency store went to someone else. The man claimed Carey called him and said that he received an order to make the change. Carey denied making the call.[19] However, he acknowledged that he cooperated with Governor Celeste. In some cases, the decisions on agency appointments came from the governor's office.[20]

Port Columbus International Airport

Although the General said that he liked the governor and enjoyed working for him, he really did not like the political aspects of the job. By the end of 1985, Carey had had enough. He met with Governor Celeste and told him that he planned to take the position of administrator of the Port Columbus International Airport. Columbus Mayor Dana "Buck" Rinehart had made that appointment. The governor told him that he was sorry and disappointed to hear that he was leaving. In a statement to the media, Governor Celeste said this about Carey:

> General Carey did an excellent job. He was faced with a horrible mess when he came in. There were $50 million in unpaid liquor bills stuffed in a desk. He paid the bills and got the department back on track.

The General explained that as an aviator for 30 years, flying "is my first love."[21]

Over the next week, both of the newspapers in Columbus commented on General Carey's appointment to the airport leadership role. *The Columbus Citizen Journal* mentioned the Saigon evacuation and Carey's time at the Department of Liquor Control. It also pointed out that he "is about to take on another tough assignment." The editorial pointed out two issues that arose during Carey's time with Liquor Control with this comment:

> Early last year he was rebuked by the governor for overly zealous political fund raising. This fall, he was under fire for developing a cozy relationship with a large distillery. We hope Carey will be more circumspect in his new city job.[22]

The Columbus Dispatch also weighed in on Carey's new assignment. The first sentence of their editorial said, "Richard E. Carey is a take-charge kind of a guy in a position that clearly calls for aggressive leadership." The paper pointed to his experience at Cherry Point, Opa Locka, Chu Lai, and the Saigon evacuation. In addition, the paper closed by stating, "We wish him success in this important venture."[23]

Thirteen days before *The Columbus Citizen-Journal* went out of business, columnist Joe Dirck took a shot at both Carey and his new boss, Mayor Rinehart. Dirck offered this commentary:

> In an administration that has not demanded terribly high standards from its Cabinet officials, Carey was increasingly seen as an embarrassment. He had developed unseemly ties with the liquor distillers he was supposed to be regulating. That sort of coziness may be the norm at the Pentagon, but in civilian politics, it doesn't play well at all.

Dirck also said that Carey received the airport job appointment one day after Mayor Rinehart received an appointment as Marine Corps reserve captain. According to Dirck, the mayor sought the appointment for years, "but was only successful after appointing a retired Marine general to a cushy job." Mayor Rinehart denied that Carey helped him. Carey, on the other hand, said Rinehart asked for his assistance and he made a telephone call on the mayor's behalf.[24]

Carey kept Dirck's and Perdue's columns for nearly 40 years and highlighted some of their negative comments about him with a yellow highlighter. When asked why he kept those columns Carey said, "It's me."[25]

On the family home front, Dena liked being in Columbus. She had the chance to spend time with her husband's family and enjoyed attending Ohio State football games. She also knew that her husband did not enjoy the politics of the Liquor Control Department. Besides, she understood the fighter pilot who loved aviation. Columbus Mayor Rinehart and his Utilities and Aviation head Mike Long selected Carey for the job that paid just under $56,000 per year. The general took a $4,000 pay cut to take the new assignment However, the job came with a rent-free house at the airport.

The General's experience as a wing commander at Cherry Point, his time at Chu Lai, Vietnam, and Opa Locka, Florida, gave him a broad understanding about running an airport. He handled issues of security and safety in all of those roles. In addition, his experience at Opa Locka had acquainted him with civilian aviation. On paper, it appeared that Carey was the right selection. He faced an immediate challenge as "the new guy." His predecessor as administrator at the airport had been there for 16 years. Carey soon found that many staff members were used to one way of doing things, were not open to change, and found Carey, in his words, "too strict."

By the summer of 1986, Carey's position at the airport appeared tenuous at best. He faced challenges from his staff. Those differences bubbled up to Mike Long. He had responsibility for the airport and had the ear of the mayor. Two letters sent to Carey by a civil engineer at the airport, Ralph L. Warne, in July and August copied Mike Long. In July, Warne complained to Carey about the fact that he placed a note in his personnel file and requested that he (Carey) remove it. Warne copied Long.[26]

In August, Warne's written response to Carey again copied Long. Warne told Carey:

> I do not appreciate the implication in your letter and it is important to note that several of the details are reported inaccurately in your letter even after I have previously attempted to clarify the facts and circumstances to you.[27]

As he took charge of the airport, Carey identified two areas needing improvement—security and maintenance. He found that the employees did not like his directives about making the airport more secure. Part of that change involved the increased supervision of security and keeping the airport clean. The General also insisted on overseeing employee performance. While the airlines appreciated his direction, Carey said, the employees were not on board with the changes.

In addition, the General said that he could help Mayor Rinehart get a better understanding of airport operations. A fast tracker in Republican Party circles, Rinehart won election as mayor at the age of 37. The General and the mayor had a common bond—the Marine Corps. The mayor had joined the Marine Corps Reserves at the age of 19 in 1965 and risen to the rank of lieutenant colonel when he retired from the Marine Corps Reserve in 1995.[28] The Marine Corps connection did not help their working relationship, according to the General. He found that Mayor Rinehart was "not open for instruction or criticism."[29] A former Rinehart aide offered a different perspective than General Carey had about the mayor. The former staffer, interviewed for the mayor's 2015 obituary article said, "He learned by absorbing viewpoints."[30] However, the General found the mayor "pretty wired PR-wise." He added the mayor was "a good politician."[31]

Carey received a termination notice a week before he would have been eligible for an opportunity to appeal in the civil service system. While not going into specifics, Long said the reason for the decision to relieve the General came down to "irreconcilable management differences." The correspondence between Carey and Warne did not help the General's situation.[32] Carey said that he had already informed the Mayor and Long that he was leaving prior to receiving the termination notice. From Carey's view, he had had enough and was ready to move on. He had moved from state politics to the buzz saw of office politics.[33]

Carey for Mayor

Despite the bumpy road of his return to Columbus, Carey had one more thought in mind. Republican Mayor Rinehart planned to run for a second term. No one in either party stepped up to challenge him. Democrats reached out to the General. He hated politics. He hated politics so much that he thought about running for mayor of Columbus to take the politics out of public office. First, he consulted with Dena. In retrospect, he should have listened a little closer when she asked, "Are you sure you want to do this?" He entered the race. The initial step in running for mayor required 3,246 valid signatures on the petition. When Carey supporters turned in his petition, he had 4,359 signatures—more than 1,000 above the requirement. But there was a problem: fewer than 3,246 signatures were valid. While an appeals process existed, it did not look good for Carey's candidacy. If he ended up short of enough valid signatures, Carey said that he already ruled out a write-in challenge of Mayor Rinehart. Since no other candidate qualified, Mayor Rinehart would win reelection without opposition, unless someone else entered the race as a write-in candidate. No write-in candidate emerged.[34] The initial analysis of the petition gathered by Democrats showed that Carey was more than 400 signatures short of the number needed for qualification as a candidate.

When the General learned of the invalid signatures, he had enough. As a Marine, he lived by the principle of honor and this statement: Honor guides

Marines to exemplify the ultimate in ethical and moral behavior. Never lie, never cheat or steal.

While Democratic Party officials began an appeals process, Carey made it clear that he was no longer a candidate regardless of the results of the appeals. He said, "I would not have anything crooked. If approved [the appeal] I would not run." In addition, he said that he understood the names of dead people were on the petition.[35]

Franklin County (Columbus is in Franklin County) elections' officials reviewed the Carey petition sent in by the Democratic Party. Two of the elections' board voted in favor of the petition and two opposed Carey's petition. Since that vote ended in a tie, the issue went to Ohio's Secretary of State Sherrod Brown.[36] Secretary Brown, a Democrat, concluded that the Carey petition fell at least 243 signatures short. As a result, only Mayor Rinehart's name appeared on the November ballot, and he won reelection for a second term without opposition.

Saying it was God's will that he would not be mayor of Columbus, the General was ready to move on with his life. He said that he had two reasons for attempting to take on Mayor Rinehart. The first reason, he said, involved his plan to take politics out of city government. Second, he said that he thought about possibly running for governor of Ohio in the future. Being mayor of Columbus would have helped him launch that run.[37]

As Carey moved on from Ohio politics, he joined Sundow Corporation as its president. Unknown to General Carey, the company's owner, Louis Bethune, had a shady past that included time in federal prison. Bethune used Carey's resume as part of a scheme to gain public financing for land development projects as a minority business owner, but then left investors and vendors with unpaid bills. Sundow went bankrupt and closed after four years in business. Carey said that he received $7,500 as a consulting fee. When he resigned in August 1987, Bethune owed Carey another $12,500. He never received the money. Said Carey, "Unfortunately, he took me in. He talks a good game believe me. He's a pretty slick dude."[38] Press reports indicated Bethune had failed projects in Ohio and Alabama. Sundow turned out to be Carey's only post-Marine Corps private business involvement.

Carey said the world of Ohio politics led to his decision to leave Columbus. He said:

> I left as soon as I could. I had no desire to stay there. I was so upset over why I was leaving Columbus. I thought that I'll find something after I get there [Texas] if I decided to get a job."[39]

CHAPTER 18

Aiding the Dallas District Courts

After four years in the world of Ohio politics, the General and Dena looked southwest. For the first time in 22 years, the Careys headed back to Dena's home state. Hello, Texas; good-bye, Columbus. The Dallas area called the Metroplex became the final stop for the Careys.

With Columbus and an ill-fated attempt to run for mayor behind him, General Carey and Dena moved to Texas in 1987. The General's military career took him to 16 stateside assignments in South Carolina (three times), California (two times), North Carolina (four times), Virginia (three times), and once each in Rhode Island, Florida, Texas, and Hawaii. He also served in Korea (two times), Vietnam (three times), and Japan (two times). After multiple moves, combat service in two wars, and a return to the General's native Ohio, the forever home for the Careys would be Texas. They settled in North Texas in 1987. Seventeen years later, in 2004, the Careys purchased a home in Plano, a suburb north of Dallas. The General continues to live in that home with his two pet Bichon Frise dogs named Max and Angel.

While Carey went to the Dallas area without a job offer, an opportunity to continue in public service came to him. Dallas County Commissioner Chris Semos contacted Carey about a position.[1]

Dallas County paid a court administrator to manage the State of Texas District Courts that operated in Dallas County. Dallas County commissioners appointed Carey to the position in 1987. His long career that included leading organizations proved valuable to the leaders of Dallas County. Commissioner Semos helped convince the General to take the assignment. Carey told Semos that he would not stay in the job for a long time. He would be back in the world of politics, he acknowledged. "I was overconfident that I could handle it."[2]

In that assignment, Carey explained that his role included logistical functions, security, property management, and computer functions for the judges. His Marine Corps experience in logistics proved useful in his new job. His office was in the Purse Building, in downtown Dallas, across the street from both the State of Texas Civil and Criminal District Courts. On a typical day, Carey said that he worked with the district judges and the County Commissioners to ensure the smooth operation of the courts. With a staff of about five, Carey's team managed the budget, paid employees, and looked for efficiencies and potential cost savings. A major responsibility dealt with tracking records and managing the case flow to prevent trials and court activities from running late. Carey had to prevent clogs in the system to avoid delays.

In 1989, a shooting in a courtroom in neighboring Tarrant County that included the city of Fort Worth brought increased attention to courthouse security. On August 1, 1989 a gunman entered the courtroom of Justice of the Peace Robert Ashmore. The gunman confronted his ex-wife, who served as Judge Ashmore's clerk. The angry ex-husband held both Judge Ashmore and his clerk hostage in the judge's chambers. The gunman freed Judge Ashmore. He later killed his ex-wife and then took his own life at the end of a seven-hour siege.[3] In Dallas County, General Carey ensured installation of metal detectors used as people entered the courts. The General's Marine Corps security experience aided his efforts. More importantly, General Carey wanted to prevent a "copy-cat" shooting incident in the courts.

The General reached out to individual judges and their courtroom bailiffs to find out ways that he could help them. When visiting judges came to the courthouse, Carey arranged space for them to work and hold trials. He also handled facility management and worked with the Dallas County Commissioners and the county attorney. He led staffing, training, and managed personnel issues.[4] The General's time in working with the judges preceded the days of personal computers. As a result, his department hired administrative assistants and trained them to support the work of the judges.

Another aspect of the job required Carey to attend the weekly Dallas County Commissioners Court meetings with the commissioners. To develop a working relationship with the individual commissioners, Carey worked to set up meetings with each of the four elected commissioners and the county judge. In Texas, the county judge heads the Commissioners Court and is elected by voters, countywide. Voters in each district also elect their individual commissioners. Carey met with all of the commission members except one. He said that he never could set up a meeting with Commissioner John Wiley Price, who took office in 1985 and won his 10th four-year term in 2020.[5]

By 1991, Carey decided to keep his commitment to Commissioner Semos. He had told Semos he would not stay long, and he did not. Carey stepped down from his post at the age of 63. He said that in the end, the job simply was not challenging enough for him. He described the assignment as an "easy job that I just didn't love." Part of the reason for that was politics. The General said, "I just didn't see how politics would become important and affect decisions relating to the job." He added, "I had no obligation to any group."[6]

CHAPTER 19

General Carey Continues to Serve in Retirement

General Carey was still working as Dallas County district courts administrator in the summer of 1990 when Lieutenant Colonel George Rivers, USMC (Ret), a three-tour veteran of Vietnam, introduced him to a founding member of the Metroplex Marine Coordinating Council (MMCC or "Metroplex Marines"). The General quickly connected with two local attorneys who were members of the MMCC. The pair, Mike McCollum, a Marine reservist, and Ed Fitzmaurice, a former Marine C-130 pilot, were Vietnam veterans. McCollum and Fitzmaurice aided General Carey in finding his true passion—helping and supporting former Marines and the Metroplex veteran community.

For many years prior to Carey's arrival, the MMCC existed as a small group of former Marines meeting periodically at various venues to discuss Marine issues. Carey brought the stature of a three-star general and the desire to help veterans to the MMCC.

Sports Equipment for Marines in the Middle East

General Carey, along with retired and former active-duty veterans of all services, regularly attend the monthly MMCC luncheon events. The MMCC's first project after General Carey joined was collecting books, exercise, and sports equipment for forward-deployed Marines in Saudi Arabia during the *Desert Shield* buildup in the fall of 1990. A Dallas couple, Carolina and John Pace (a former Marine), learned that items donated by civilians for *Desert Shield* did not get to Marines in the field. The items went, instead, to rear-echelon units near major bases in Southwest Asia. The Paces reached out to General Carey. They asked the General if he could help get the books and sports equipment to Marines in northern Saudi Arabia. Carey agreed and reached out to the Metroplex Marines for help.

This was the first time Carey, a "by the book" career Marine General, worked side-by-side with a group of reserve and retired Marines. Both sides had a steep learning curve. While recognizing their "accomplish the mission priority," Carey was somewhat leery of the group's disregard for "standard operating procedures" (SOPs). The Metroplex Marines marveled at the General's leadership by example approach. The General would be the first to load or unload book and sports equipment donations. Seeing a retired three-star Marine general dive into a physical task set a quick example. No Marine wanted to be standing around while the 63-year-old General out-worked them.

As time went by, General Carey grew more comfortable with MMCC Marines' focus on mission accomplishment versus following standard operating procedures (in other words, seeking forgiveness versus asking for permission).

Over the last 32 years, local Marines grew accustomed to General Carey's lead-from-the-front philosophy. As a result, MMCC developed into a forum that includes speakers who talk about issues of interest to local veterans of all service branches. The active-duty Marine units in the Dallas Fort Worth area (often called the Metroplex) regularly send their representatives who provide updates on their activities. These units include the following: Headquarters Battery, 14th Marines, 2nd Battalion 14th Marines; Marine Air Group-41 (MAG-41); 8th Marine Corps District (MCD); and the Recruiting Commands of both Fort Worth and Dallas. Seven high-school Marine Corps Junior ROTC from counties surrounding Dallas and Fort Worth always receive invitations to attend the luncheons. Routinely, the Officer in Charge (OIC) of one or two of the units attends along with their cadets. The Metroplex Marines now serve as a forum for charitable organizations that serve all veterans. Those attending receive information about the mission of the Metroplex Marines. Metroplex Marines support the following areas of interest to the veteran community: financial assistance, government veterans' benefits, hospice and burial arrangements, career search, community service, education, legal, medical, veteran-owned business, and camaraderie.

Shortly after General Carey began meeting with the Metroplex Marines, group leaders identified a need for raising money to help many of the organizations and projects supporting veterans. That led to the creation of the Metroplex Military Charitable Trust (MMCT), an Internal Revenue Service 501 (c) (3) charitable trust, in February 1991. Colonel D. Grant Seabolt Jr., USMC (Ret), the former MAG-41 staff judge advocate and longtime attorney for the Metroplex Marines, created the Trust. General Carey, as the ranking Marine, serves as the presiding trustee of the MMCT's Board of Trustees. Major General James L. Williams, USMC (Ret) is the MMCT's assistant presiding trustee. General Williams and General Carey are also members of the North Texas Veterans Administration Advisory Board.

The Trust provides funding for many projects supporting active duty, reserve, retired, and former service members in the North Texas veteran community.

While the Metroplex Marines and MMCT serve veterans, reservists, and military retirees, those groups opened doors for General Carey's post-military career. As the area's senior Marine, the General is neither window dressing nor a figurehead for either organization. Since 1990, Carey has been personally involved in a wide range of projects supporting fellow Marines, and the entire veteran community. Carey's involvement raised the profile of the Metroplex Marines and the MMCT in North Texas. Their work includes "hands-on" assistance by Metroplex Marines and financial assistance by MMCT to major civic projects and programs. General Carey worked with both organizations on the following: leadership speaking series, North Texas VA patient volunteer shuttle program, Metroplex Toys for Tots (since 1990), Metroplex Veterans Legal services (a periodic pro-bono legal clinic), emergency grants to veterans who served honorably, and grants to high school Marine Corps Junior ROTC units.

General Carey never forgot his comrades in arms. He worked on a wide range of projects. His fundraising efforts behind the Chosin Few Memorial at Quantico helped honor those who served in that key Korean War battle. He served as a member of the Dallas Veterans Administration's Board of Directors and spoke to veterans' groups to gain support for a veterans' cemetery in the Dallas Fort Worth area. He became an in-demand speaker. More important were the simple courtesies he extended to veterans or their families. In addition, over the years, local communities and officials honored General Carey for his many years of service.

Helping in North Texas

Since 1947, the Marine Corps Reserve sponsored and delivered the Toys for Tots program, an effort that brightens the Christmas holidays for needy children. General Carey's involvement solved a major problem facing Toys for Tots in North Texas in the early 1990s, according to Fitzmaurice. Unfortunately, the locally collected toys did not always get to needy children but were stolen. General Carey led the initial effort to have churches and schools identify children in need, Fitzmaurice said. By doing that, the truly needy children received the toys, as staff at churches and schools helped prepare lists of

Presented with challenges in the Dallas Toys for Tots program, Carey recalled his wife Dena's involvement at Quantico and took a leadership role in Dallas. (Carey family collection, 1982)

deserving children. It was a more organized approach that prevented theft. In addition, Fitzmaurice recalled that the General was mindful of the need for advance planning. General Carey started each year's program in the summer. Fitzmaurice described the General's leadership style with the Toys for Tots program as "pensive, low key, and high minded."[1]

Toys for Tots was important to the General as Dena had taken a lead role in Toys for Tots during Carey's final assignment at Quantico. Major General William E. Gossell, USMC Reserve (Ret), chaired the Toys for Tots program after General Carey led the reorganized process. General Gossell headed the program for 25 years until his death in May 2020.

Veterans Cemetery

After living in the Dallas Fort Worth area for a few years, General Carey learned about a project to build a veterans' cemetery. Dallas and Fort Worth families of veterans looking for a National Cemetery had to go to San Antonio or

Houston or out of state to bury their loved ones. A local veteran, Cloyde C. Pinson, Sr., began the effort to build the cemetery in North Texas. Mr. Pinson's son, a Marine rifleman, died in combat while serving in Vietnam on May 12, 1967. Since no veterans' cemetery was located in the Dallas area, the Pinson family buried their son, Pvt. Cloyde C. Pinson, Jr., in Laurel Land Memorial Park in Dallas.[2]

In 1985, Mr. Pinson began working to get a cemetery for veterans in the Dallas Fort Worth area. In 1989, he became president of the Texas National Cemetery Committee. General Carey joined the project in 1992. Mr. Pinson, a retired Air Force captain, had entered the Army in 1941. During World War II, Mr. Pinson had assignments in the North African and Italian campaigns. He transferred to the Air Force in 1947 when it became a separate branch of the military. He took part in the Berlin Airlift between 1948 and 1949. Captain Pinson retired in 1961. In an online tribute to Mr. Pinson, his friend Bill Melton called him the "father of the DFW Veterans' Cemetery."[3]

As the ranking Marine in the Dallas area, General Carey lent both his name and his time to the cemetery project. He worked on fundraising, spoke to veterans' groups, and worked with Mr. Pinson's group to push for the cemetery.

In June 1992, Veterans Affairs published an environmental impact statement supporting the selection of property in southwest Dallas known as Mountain Creek. Cattle grazed on that land. In its report, the VA identified Dallas Fort Worth as one of the most significant regions in the nation with the greatest need for a national cemetery. At that time, 500,000 veterans lived within 100 miles of Dallas. Supporting the placement of the cemetery on that site were numerous civic and elected officials. Dallas Baptist University, located near the Mountain Creek, area also supported the location. There were no Environmental Protection Agency (EPA) issues concerning the site.

Thirty-three years after his son died from enemy fire in Vietnam, Mr. Pinson saw his goal reached when the Dallas Fort Worth National Cemetery (area residents call it DFW National Cemetery) opened on May 12, 2000.

On November 10, 2000, the 225th birthday of the Marine Corps, General Carey gave the keynote address at the dedication of the U.S. Marine Memorial at the Dallas Fort Worth National cemetery. He shared his pride in the Marine Corps when he spoke these words:

> But I would propose to you that it's not only our indisputable superiority and success in battle that makes Americans want a Marine Corps ... yes ... America needs a Marine Corps for our military capability, but more so, America wants a Marine Corps.

The General also pointed to the bond Marines have with one another and camaraderie Marines have for active duty, retired, living, dead, and reserve. He also recognized one retired Air Force officer—Captain Cloyde C. Pinson, Sr.—for leading the drive to build the cemetery.

On April 12, 2006, the casket bearing Mr. Pinson's son went from Laurel Land Memorial Park to the National Cemetery. Ken Watterson, a wounded Marine veteran who served two tours of duty in Vietnam during the 1960s, had the Marine Corps League arrange the burial. Mr. Pinson placed two American flags on his son's grave. Two days later, Mr. Pinson, 83, died. On April 18, Mr. Pinson's graveside service took place at the cemetery he was so instrumental in creating. He lies next to his beloved son.

General Carey's involvement with the cemetery project paid long-term dividends. By 2022, the Dallas Fort Worth National Cemetery became fourth busiest in the United States with an average of 21 burials per day.[4]

On Veterans Day in 1995, the General spoke at the Sam Rayburn Memorial Veterans Center in Bonham. Not only was Bonham Dena's hometown, but it was also the home of the late speaker of the house, Representative Sam Rayburn. General Carey spoke from an historical perspective. He talked about the 56 signers of the Declaration of Independence and connected them to the 41 million people who served in the military during nearly 220 years. The General focused on World War II, as 1995 marked the 50th anniversary of the end of that war. He called the end of World War II "one of the most significant events in the history of the world." He added that the end of the war "was only surpassed by the birth, life, and resurrection of Jesus Christ." In addition, Carey acknowledged the home front sacrifices families faced with rationing during World War II.

VA

Ken Watterson, president of the Homeless Veterans Service of Dallas, weighed in on the General's involvement in North Texas.[5] Watterson referred to General Carey as a "veteran's veteran." The General served on the board of the Veteran's Administration Hospital. The VA hospital in Dallas was "at the bottom of the barrel 15 to 20 years ago," Watterson said. General Carey advocated for improvements. Changes came about and improved health care resulted. As Watterson put it, the General "still takes care of his troops." During meetings, Watterson described General Carey as a "good listener."

Helping Veterans

In the spring of 2004, General Carey paid a visit to former Marine Private Raymond M. Clausen, Jr. at the Dallas VA Hospital. In 1970, Private Clausen, serving in his second tour in Vietnam, rescued Marines from a minefield. President Nixon presented him with the Congressional Medal of Honor in 1971. His citation read, in part:

> Private First Class Clausen quickly leaped from the helicopter and, in the face of enemy fire, moved across the extremely hazardous, mine-laden area to assist in carrying casualties to the waiting helicopter and in placing them aboard. Despite the ever-present threat of further mine explosions, he continued his valiant efforts, leaving the comparatively safe area of the helicopter on six separate occasions to carry out his rescue efforts. On one occasion while he was carrying one of the wounded, another mine detonated, killing a corpsman and wounding three other men. Only when he was certain that all Marines were safely aboard did he signal the pilot to lift the helicopter.

Clausen was both a tragic and a heroic figure. General Carey described him as a Marine who was unregimented. He used the term "screwup" to describe Clausen. Clausen faced a drinking problem. Yet, one day he walked through a minefield to save the lives of fellow Marines. The General pointed out that Private Clausen "wanted to rescue fellow Marines. No one told him to go into the minefield." According to General Carey, Clausen's heavy drinking resulted in liver disease. While visiting with Clausen prior to his death at age 56, General Carey told him he was "a good example of a fighting Marine." He also told Clausen that the Marine Corps wanted to help him through his problem. According to General Carey, Clausen remained in the Dallas VA Hospital for rehab for about a month. Following rehab, the Medal of Honor recipient returned home where he died of liver disease.[6]

Fisher House

In 2006, Korean War veteran and Distinguished Service Cross recipient Major Richard Agnew, U.S. Army (Ret) chaired the Dallas-area Fisher House Drive. Operating under a model similar to the Ronald McDonald House program, Fisher Houses provide free lodging for families visiting veterans receiving long-term care. Since 1990, some 70 Fisher Houses have opened to serve veterans' families in the United States and in Europe. Fisher Houses are located near either VA hospitals or military hospitals. The Fisher family donated $20 million to get the program started.

Major Agnew, a long-time friend of Carey's, contacted the General to help raise funds for a Fisher House with 21 suites located near the Dallas VA Hospital. General Carey agreed to help and contacted potential donors. Twenty-six years later the Dallas Fisher House is one of seven Texas Fisher Houses available to families needing a place to stay while a loved one is hospitalized.

Volunteer VA Patient Shuttle Service

The General understood the role of severely wounded Afghanistan and Iraq war veterans' family members. Those family members were full-time caregivers. In addition to helping Major Agnew with the Fisher House project, General Carey also helped launch a program to support those caregivers with a day for themselves. According to Mr. Watterson, General Carey aided the drive to fund vans with ramps for the handicapped veterans. In addition, he helped recruit volunteer van drivers. The drivers, mostly Korean and Vietnam War Purple Heart recipients, picked up the veterans. They drove them to the VA Hospital for their appointments. More importantly, they waited for the veterans and then returned them home. That allowed the caregivers to have time for their own needs, while the veterans received medical care.

General Carey Touches People One by One

General Carey touched the lives of many people and on occasion one at a time. Friends of the General who attended Prestonwood Baptist Church in Plano, Texas, asked General Carey to write to a young Marine corporal, Jeffrey V. Ross, serving in Iraq. In a March 4, 2003, letter, General Carey said that he was "honored to be asked" to write to the young man. In his letter to Corporal Ross, General Carey wrote, "Receiving a letter from a Marine Lieutenant General will probably surprise, even shock you; but I am pleased to write one of our forward deployed Marines!" In his letter, General Carey talked about his time in Korea. He told the young Marine, "You will have many moments of utter frustration and will be tempted to throw up your hands in protest, but you are an NCO … a leader and you set the example. If you fail as a leader your unit will fail." The General urged him to look to God. General Carey also told the corporal that following the September 11, 2001, attacks, he had reached out to the commandant of the Marine Corps offering to return to active duty. The commandant told General Carey that it was not his time now.

On March 16, Corporal Ross sent General Carey a note of appreciation. The young corporal, a Marine reservist, received call-up orders during his senior year at Texas Tech University. Corporal Ross wrote, "In your letter you wrote that you could relate to what I am going through. There is no possibility that I could ever relate to what you had experienced and endured." He also told General Carey that he shared his letter with fellow NCOs. The corporal closed with these words, "From one surprised and honored Marine to another Marine."

On Memorial Day in 2003, Carey spoke at the Dallas Fort Worth National Cemetery. Joining him that day were United States Republican Senator Kay Bailey Hutchinson from Texas and Dallas-area Congressman Martin Frost, a Democrat. In his speech, General Carey quoted from the letter he received from Corporal Ross who said,

> I know that not everyone agrees with us being here, but you put it best saying that's what we are fighting for … freedom, even the right to protest. I joined the Marine Corps because I felt I owed it to my country and to the men who gave (their) lives for my freedom."

In his comments, General Carey pointed out two occasions where America failed to win wars for freedom. Regarding Vietnam, he said that the U.S. "exhibited weakness of moral fiber and character," and the nation "gave in to protestors." The second time came during *Desert Storm.* General Carey charged, "We failed to complete the task of defeating an aggressive enemy." As a result, he explained, innocent people faced persecution and slaughter during the past 12 years (since *Desert Storm* in 1991).

Regarding *Desert Storm*, General Carey saw a news story about seven Marines killed by "friendly fire." An Air Force A-10 Thunderbolt missile struck a Marine Corps light armored vehicle (LAV-25) on January 29, 1991.[7] Only eight years removed from active duty, General Carey called his old friend from the Vietnam evacuation—Marine Corps Commandant General Al Gray. Carey said that he made the call so there would be "follow-through at a high level." He added that General Gray "was in a position to do something about it."[8]

A post-*Desert Storm* review for the Marine Corps Historical Division referred to the A-10 tragedy as "fratricide." That was one of two friendly fire incidents on the same day that resulted in the deaths of 11 Marines. The Marines reviewed several options to prevent another A-10 tragedy. One solution suggested "only Marine aircraft would attack targets in the vicinity of Marine ground forces."[9]

Offer to Assist in War on Terrorism

As the war on terrorism accelerated, Carey again offered his support and willingness to assist the commandant of the Marine Corps. In a May 19, 2003, letter to Carey, General M. W. "Mike" Hagee responded. General Hagee said, "Your personal pledge of support means a great deal to me, and I want you to know that I will not hesitate to call on you should the need arise."[10] General Carey said that he did not receive any requests from Hagee.

Active Lifestyle

Long after he retired, the General continued his lifelong dedication and commitment to physical fitness. At 85, 30 years after his retirement, General Carey rode in a 100-mile bicycle race in the West Texas heat on August 24, 2013. The General rode in annual cycling event called "Hotter 'N Hell Hundred" in Wichita Falls, Texas, with his youngest daughter Melody. Wichita Falls Bicycling Club Executive Director Ben "Chip" Filer said that only nine people between ages 80 and 85 participated that day. Mr. Filer added that 8,400 people pre-registered for the race.[11] The event's website bills the race, instituted in 1982, as one of the oldest and largest cycling events in the U.S.

Maintaining an active lifestyle, the retired General rode in the Hotter 'N Hell Hundred bike race in Wichita Falls, Texas, up to age 85. Carey rode in the 2009 race at age 81. (Courtesy Hotter N Hell Hundred, 2009)

One-Handed Pushups

The General was proud of his physical fitness. During his career and in retirement, General Carey often demonstrated his ability to do one-handed pushups. Colonel Pendergast recalled the General challenging his officers to beat him at one-handed pushups during the 1970s and '80s. According to Pendergast, he never saw anyone do more than the General's 20–25 pushups. Vietnam veteran and fellow Marine Frank Walker remembered the General's one-handed pushup challenge when Carey was well into his retirement years.

Honoring Those Who Served in Korea

The September 27, 2019 return of a Marine's remains again connected Carey to his service in Korea. That day, David Tarrant of *The Dallas Morning News* wrote about the returned remains of a Texas Marine killed following the Chosin Reservoir battle. Enemy fire took the life of Private First Class Grady J. Crawford, 21, of Dallas, Texas, on December 1, 1950, at the Chosin Reservoir. Private Crawford served with 4th Battalion, 11th Marines, 1st Marine Division (4/11) as an artilleryman at Yudam-ni. His responsibility on December 1, 1950, was to provide cover for evacuating Marines. No one saw Private Crawford after that day. His parents received a telegram telling them that their son was missing. In 1954, remains of American service members found on the western side of the Chosin Reservoir were part of an exchange of war dead between the United States and North Korea, known as Operation *Glory*. The military identified some of the remains. The unidentified service members ended up in unmarked graves at the National Memorial Cemetery of the Pacific (Punchbowl Crater) in Honolulu.

Technological advances led to the exhumation of many of the previously unidentified Korean War dead in 2012. The Defense POW/MIA Accounting Agency (DPAA) identified one set of remains as X-14896. That was Private Crawford. Fortunately, his remains were a nearly complete skeleton. Scientists used dental, anthropological, and skull analysis, as well as circumstantial and material evidence to make the identification. On July 15, 2019, Marine Corps officials contacted Private Crawford's sister-in-law, Nancy Crawford Dice, to tell her that the DPAA had identified her brother-in-law's remains. On September 27, Mrs. Dice and her four daughters, the private's nieces, met the flight on the tarmac at Dallas Fort Worth International Airport carrying Private Crawford's flag-draped casket. A seven-member Marine honor guard met the flight. Crawford's casket went to Restland Cemetery in Dallas for burial next to his brother Bill, a Korean War veteran who served in the Merchant Marine.[12] General Carey attended the burial wearing his dress blues uniform. He approached the casket, alone, rendered a solemn salute, and after the ceremony expressed his admiration and respect for Private Crawford privately to the attending family members.

General Carey took time and interest with a retired North Texas high school science teacher, Sherri Steward Ganz. She said, "There is something special about General Carey. He cares so deeply about veterans." Mrs. Ganz added, "We need heroes."

Her paternal uncle, David Steward, falsified his birth certificate, ran away from home, and joined the Army at the age of 16. The Army sent him to Korea. Although the family advised the Army of the youthful private's age, it was too late. David Steward lost his life to enemy fire on September 21, 1950—not quite eight months past his 16th birthday. Mrs. Ganz's father, William Steward, suffered wounds during World War II when he served in the European Theater of Operations with the U.S. Army. At that time, the Army said he had "combat fatigue." He rejoined the Army prior to the Korean War. He helped train soldiers and ultimately went to Korea where he was wounded again. Mrs. Ganz described her father as "tortured soul" who never fully overcame "his demons." In 1984, doctors finally diagnosed him with post-traumatic stress disorder, commonly referred to as PTSD. After nearly 40 years, he began receiving treatment.

When Mrs. Ganz's mother died in 2020, General Carey made the two-and-a-half-hour drive to Atlanta, Texas, to attend Mrs. Steward's funeral. Mrs. Ganz said the General, then 92, wore his dress blue uniform for the service.[13] In an email to the General Mrs. Ganz wrote:

> And finally, General Carey, you have shown me what a wonderful leader and magnificently compassionate human being looks like. I grew up in the shadow of the Korean War, the daughter of a combat veteran who was wounded in body, in mind, and in heart. The toll of war's savagery was palpable to me, even as a very young child. You took me "under your wing," General Carey. You made me feel that I was somehow special enough to garner the attention of a great hero, a great leader. You spent hours teaching me about the Korean War; the terrible mistakes made and the lessons learned there. As you have encouraged me to continue writing the story of two small-town Texas combat veterans, the resemblance of thousands of others who sacrificed all in the hallowed name of freedom. Your encouragement kept me from giving up. There is nothing I can do to adequately express my gratitude for you, General Carey. All I can say is that you have made me a better person. And I will never forget what you have done for Korean veterans … a little soldier's daughter from Atlanta, Texas. God Bless you, sir and thank you from the bottom of my heart for helping me.

In 2016, she accompanied the General to an event in Seoul, South Korea honoring American service members for their support during the Korean War. The Presbyterian Church in South Korea sponsored the program.

A fellow Marine three-star general and long-time friend, Charles H. "Chuck" Pitman, an Agent Orange victim, struggled with cancer. General Carey learned that Pitman had no primary care physician and introduced him to the North Texas VA Health Care system. General Carey visited him every month. Pitman, a Midwesterner, grew up as an orphan. Like General

Carey, Pitman was a mustang. Lieutenant General Pitman was a highly decorated helicopter pilot during the Vietnam War. He lived in Fort Worth, about 50 miles from Carey. On February 13, 2020, Carey learned that his old friend was near death. Carey went to the hospital and squeezed Pitman's hand. A few minutes later, Pitman died.[14]

At 3:30 in the morning of July 14, 2021, General Carey left his home to meet a flight to Dallas Fort Worth International Airport. An American Airlines airplane carried the remains of an Army major missing since the Chosin Reservoir fight on December 1, 1950. The General, dressed in a navy blue blazer, wore a tie with the Marine Corps logo, and placed his military ribbons on the left side of his coat. When interviewed about the Korean War by reporter Ben Russell of the Dallas NBC television affiliate, Carey spoke in a strong voice when he said, "We have to honor the warriors. It was a tough, tough fight." Joining the General that morning were Korean War veterans who formed an honor guard.

Major Harvey Storms, a Texas native and a Texas A&M University graduate, suffered multiple wounds at the east side of the Chosin Reservoir. Storms refused medical care, continued to fight, and led his troops. Eventually, fellow soldiers placed the injured major on a truck loaded with other wounded troops. That was the last time that anyone saw Major Storms alive. On that same day, Carey fought on East Hill, about 5 miles from Major Storms. In 2017, Kim Jong Un, Supreme Leader of North Korea, gave the United States containers holding the remains of 55 American service members during a meeting with President Donald J. Trump in Singapore. The remains went on to the DPAA at Joint Base Hickam, Honolulu, Hawaii. The painstaking process of identifying the remains took until 2019. Covid 19 further delayed the process. The DNA of one of the major's sons confirmed Storms' identity.

Following the airport ceremony in Texas, the major's remains went to Washington, D.C., for burial in Arlington National Cemetery in northern Virginia. All four of the major's sons, their wives, and his 38 grandchildren and great-grandchildren attended the service.

Mrs. Ganz coordinated the Dallas ceremony, arranged for General Carey to attend, and flew to Virginia to join the major's family for the Arlington National Cemetery ceremony.

On October 13, 2021, General Carey attended the 98th birthday celebration of fellow Marine Hershel "Woody" Williams, the last surviving World War II Medal of Honor recipient. Mr. Williams received the Medal of Honor for his heroic actions at Iwo Jima. It was the first time the General met Mr. Williams.

General Carey praised Mr. Williams for his heroism. He took the time to point out that Marines on Iwo Jima outnumbered the enemy by 3:1. At the Chosin Reservoir, however, communist forces outnumbered the Americans by 8:1.

In 2010, Mr. Williams established the Hershel "Woody" Williams Congressional Medal of Honor Education Foundation, Inc. The organization works with the public and community leaders to build permanent Gold Star Families Memorial monuments. Gold Star families are defined as families who lost a loved one in a combat death. In addition, the foundation provides scholarships to Gold Star surviving children. According to the foundation's website, there are 88 Gold Star monuments across the nation as of 2021.[15] One, dedicated on May 13, 2021, is located in Frisco, Texas, about 30 minutes from the General's home.[16] Williams died on June 29, 2022.

In addition, General Carey spent time with wounded Iraq and Afghanistan War veterans at Brooke Army Medical Center in San Antonio, Texas, about four hours south of Dallas. There, the hospital treats some of the most seriously wounded veterans including amputees.

While General Carey stood with world leaders, led Marines on the ground and in the air, received dozens of medals, and earned 11 promotions his impact on individuals tells a great deal about the character of Richard E. Carey.

Honors

During and after his career, General Carey received honors from the civilian community recognizing his accomplishments in the Marine Corps. Three came from his native state of Ohio. Franklin County (including the city of Columbus) issued a proclamation calling November 11, 1977 "Major General Richard E. Carey, USMC Day." In its proclamation, members of the Franklin County Board of Commissioners said that the General earned recognition "for giving unselfishly of his time and energies to make this a better community." Although the General did not always have complimentary things to say about the media, the Press Club of Ohio honored him on September 7, 1979. He was one of six Ohioans recognized at the dinner. Proceeds from the dinner, ironically, went to provide scholarships for Ohio State journalism students. Other honorees selected for the event included John Havlicek, an Ohio State graduate who starred for the National Basketball Association's Boston Celtics, and R. David Thomas, founder and chairman of Wendy's restaurants. Also honored were George M. Steinbrenner, owner of the New York Yankees baseball team; Ray Ross, director of the United Auto Workers Region 2 A; and Louis B. Seltzer, retired editor of *The Cleveland*

Press. In 2001, West High School in Columbus inducted General Carey into the school's Hall of Fame.

In 2011, General Carey won recognition for his leadership of the Marine Corps Marathon with his selection to the Marine Corps Marathon Hall of Fame.[17] His Marine Corps Marathon Hall of Fame award said:

> Lieutenant General Richard E. Carey was tremendously instrumental in solidifying "The People's Marathon" as one of the most recognized and largest marathons in the United States. Through his determination, the Marine Corps Marathon was reorganized from its origins at Marine Barracks 8th and I to Marine Corps Base Quantico where it has grown and developed into one of the most professionally organized marathons in the world. Carey participated in two MCMs, achieving his best finish time at 3:19 in the sixth MCM in 1982.

Congressman Sam Johnson, a Republican representing the third Congressional District in Texas, developed the Congressional Veteran Commendation award. The award recognized both wartime and peacetime service by residents of his North Texas district. The congressman established a group of eight community leaders who aided him in the selection process. Nominations came from district constituents of the congressman. In 2012, General Carey received the award.

A fellow Marine, also honored that day, praised General Carey. Retired Marine Gunnery Sergeant Timothy Dowd said:

> Sitting on the stage, though with the General, this was a man who he [*sic*] did some stuff brother that you and I can't even come close to. So as I was sitting next to him, I was just humbled. He is a man that personifies everything that you and I were taught about. He sat in a position that personified what it means to be a Marine.

General Carey said this about his career, "The Good Lord was looking out for me. I've had more than nine lives, I can tell you that." In addition to recognizing his military career, Congressman Johnson honored the General for his involvement with the Veterans Administration of North Texas System (health care).[18] The congressman and the General both served in Korea and Vietnam. Both flew fighter aircraft. Both were Silver Star, Distinguished Flying Cross, and Purple Heart recipients. Both lived in Plano. Congressman Johnson flew for the Air Force and retired as a full colonel after 29 years of service. A former POW, he spent nearly seven years in captivity.

General Carey received the Albert Nelson Marquis Lifetime Achievement Award in 2018. Achievements, leadership, and success in his field led to this honor. An October 19, 2018, Marquis Who's Who press release stated, "Factors such as position, noteworthy accomplishments, visibility, and prominence in a field are all taken into account during the selection process."[19] The organization previously honored the General with that award in their 1982/1983 edition.

General Carey received the Megellas Award from the America's Future Series in 2015. The award honors U.S. Army Lieutenant Colonel James "Maggie" Megellas. Megellas, who served in World War II, was the most decorated member of Army's 82nd Airborne Division. Past recipients include retired generals David Petraeus (Army) and Joseph Votel (Air Force), and retired Admiral Patrick Walsh (Navy). General Joseph F. Dunford, the 2022 recipient, a former Marine Corps commandant and retired JCS Chairman, said this about General Carey after receiving the award:

> I'd also like recognize Lieutenant General Richard Carey ... General Carey is a former Megellas Award recipient and he's well known in Dallas. My Dad and General Carey were at the Chosin Reservoir in 1950. General Carey is one of the icons of the Corps and I've always been proud to follow in his footsteps.

Lieutenant General Richard E. Carey USMC (Ret) has also been awarded the following medals and honors:

- Distinguished Service Medal
- Silver Star Medal
- Defense Superior Service Medal
- Distinguished Flying Cross
- Legion of Merit (2)
- Air Medal (16)
- Purple Heart
- Bronze Star "V" (2)
- Joint Service Commendation
- European Occupation
- Humanitarian Service (3)
- United Nations Medal
- Korean Service (4 Battle Stars)
- Vietnam Service (3 Battle Stars)
- Korean Presidential Unit Citation
- Vietnam Cross of Gallantry with Palm
- World War II Victory Medal
- Presidential Unit Citation (4)
- Navy Unit Commendation (2)
- Marine Meritorious Unit Commendation
- Combat Action Ribbon

November 10

For the men and women who served in the Marine Corps, each November 10 is a significant day. On November 10, 2021, Marines gathered to celebrate the 246th anniversary of the beginning of the Corps. General Carey attended a celebratory luncheon in Dallas that day. For the General, 2021 marked the 75th anniversary of the year that he first put on the uniform of a Marine at Parris Island. At the luncheon, an Irving High School (Texas) Marine Corps JROTC cadet shared the history of the Corps. In a special ceremony, the cadets presented the birthday cake. At these events, tradition calls for the oldest and the youngest Marine present to receive the first pieces of cake. One former Marine, born in 1926, had the first piece of cake. The second piece went to a former Marine born in 1994. General Carey, wearing his red Marine Corps blazer adorned with the ribbons he earned, led the attendees in singing the Marine Corps Hymn. Without notes and speaking from the heart, General Carey addressed his fellow (and future) Marines. He said that he "cherished every single moment in the Marine Corps." General Carey pointed out that we face "tough times in our country right now and we can always count on our Marines to step forward." The General proudly called the Marine Corps "the world's greatest military organization always ready to react and help." He added that, "I've had a wonderful life because of the Marine Corps." Citing his lifelong Christian faith, General Carey said, "Christianity carried me through many battles." The General added that Christianity helped build our nation. Finally, General Carey urged the Marines to "Always step forward, don't hold back, speak your piece and say what's right."

Following the ceremony, fellow Marines stopped by the General's seat to shake his hand. Some asked him to pose for a picture. He remained standing. Carey spoke with each person as if he or she was only one in the room.

CHAPTER 20

The Chosin Few Monument Project

Across the United States, Americans recognized and honored those who fought and died at the Chosin Reservoir. One of the first memorial honors for the Chosin Few happened when the United States Post Office issued a stamp recognizing Korean War service members on July 26, 1985. The stamp showed troops moving from the Chosin Reservoir to Hungnam.

The Marine Military Academy in Harlingen, Texas, named the south entrance to the campus as the Chosin Few Memorial Gate on May 8, 1999. The plaque reads:

> During the winter of 1950–51, a determined force made up primarily of U.S. Marines along with soldiers, sailors, airmen, and our allies fought their way from the area of the Chosin Reservoir to the Sea of Japan
>
> This Memorial Gate is dedicated to the gallant men who fought, suffered and died in the freezing hell. It is dedicated to the memory of all who perished in it by those who survived that terrible ordeal
>
> May we never forget the sacrifice which those men made, nor take for granted the freedom for which they fought
>
> Live on in our memory forever, you who are members of this eternal band of brothers and walk the "Chosin Way"

The Marine Military Academy is a private boarding school for boys that also has an Iwo Jima monument on its campus.[1]

Other communities around the country honored those who served at the Chosin Reservoir. On May 31, 2001, members of the Chosin Few Chapter of New York and Long Island dedicated a memorial at Rockville Centre, New York.[2] The Southwest Florida Chapter of the Chosin Few in Cape Coral dedicated a monument honoring each branch of service that served at the Reservoir. That monument lists the names of all Chosin Reservoir Medal of Honor recipients. On the monument is this inscription:

> Whatever we were in that frozen long-ago and whatever we are now, we are forever a fraternity of honor, a band of brothers. We are the few—the Chosin Few.[3]

The first monument honoring the Chosin Few at a Marine Corps base went up at Camp Pendleton on September 15, 2010, on the 60th anniversary of the Inchon landing. Attending the dedication of the 3,000-pound granite monument was Marine Corps Commandant General James T. Conway. General Conway, who retired shortly after the event, said:

> Korea is often a forgotten war that many consider a police action. We in the Marine Corps do not see it that way. We see it as a tremendous bright spot in our legacy.

A story about the dedication, written for the Camp Pendleton newspaper, covered a brief history of the Chosin Reservoir.[4] There was an omission. Nothing in the story mentioned that thousands of Marines who went on to fight at the Chosin Reservoir battle briefly trained at Camp Pendleton during the summer of 1950. Members of George 3/1—including a second lieutenant named Richard E. Carey—trained there.

In the Midwest, Indianapolis, Indiana, and Springfield, Illinois, honored the Chosin Few. In Indianapolis, the Chosin Reservoir Memorial Statue is located on Chosin Reservoir Memorial Parkway. In Springfield, a Korean War Memorial also commemorates the Chosin Reservoir. That monument stands near the tomb of President Abraham Lincoln.

A portion of Route 35 running through Monmouth County, New Jersey, honors those who served at the Chosin Reservoir. A sign placed along the highway reads,

> Chosin Few Memorial Highway
> Dedicated to our fallen brothers
> Battle of the Chosin Reservoir
> Korean War

A former Marine who served at the Chosin Reservoir, Michael Sheehan, led the effort to get the highway named and the sign placed. First, the New Jersey legislature authorized the naming of the highway. In 2011, Governor Chris Christie signed the legislation. The project could not use state funds. In 2017, local officials placed the sign. Sadly, Mr. Sheehan died before seeing the official naming of the highway completed. His widow, Lynnore Sheehan, attended the ceremony.[5]

Although those who served at the Chosin Reservoir received recognition in local areas across the United States, no national monument existed. Lieutenant General Richard E. Carey, the one-time second lieutenant who served at East Hill, decided that the "Chosin Few" needed more recognition on a national scale. Carey took charge, as he did many times in his career. His drive, skills, leadership, and faith helped him see the project through to completion. Carey's leadership resulted in Chosin Few Monuments at the National Museum of the Marine Corps in Quantico, Virginia, and one at the Dallas Fort Worth National Cemetery in Dallas, Texas. The Quantico monument went from an idea that initially generated push back within the Marine Corps veteran community to an architect's rendering. Then came funding drives and publicity from 2012 to 2017. Initial discussions about the proposed national monument took place at the Chosin Few Reunion Convention during the summer of 2012 in San Antonio, Texas. Mark Austin Byrd, a Marine Cobra helicopter pilot in Vietnam and a sculptor, attended that convention with General Carey. Mr. Byrd designed materials for the General's presentation. The General pitched the monument concept to the Chosin Few's Board of Directors. The group voted no. Then, General Carey made a similar presentation to all of the members attending the convention. Again, he received a negative response, according to Mr. Byrd. Finally, the North Texas Chapter of the Chosin Few agreed to take on the project alone, Mr. Byrd said.[6]

In addition to opposition from the national Chosin Few organization, this project faced two major two roadblocks. First, two previous attempts to build a national monument honoring the heroics of the Chosin Reservoir failed. Sculptor Felix DeWeldon, creator of the Marine Corps War Memorial (Iwo Jima Monument) dedicated in Arlington, Virginia, in 1954, also developed a rendering for a proposed Chosin Few Memorial in the late 1980s. The group leading the project estimated the cost to be $5 million.[7] That project failed. Second, Carey faced two personal challenges. His wife's health rapidly declined during that time period and his youngest daughter suddenly and unexpectedly died in 2013. Despite his personal situation, the General pressed forward. Carey said, "God wanted this story told." So did General Carey. A negative response to General Carey was simply an opinion waiting to be changed.

As Carey began organizing a team in North Texas, he quickly found he needed to convince people that "We would succeed and get it done." Carey added, "We had people in Dallas who made it happen." Even fellow Marines doubted the idea. People at Quantico where the monument stands initially raised objections.[8]

The Monument Team in Dallas

When the North Texas Chapter of the Chosin Few (NTCF) began the Chosin Few Monument project, the group only contemplated a national monument. The late Bruce Woodward, a former Marine Corps corporal and veteran of the Chosin Reservoir, served as chairman of the North Texas Chapter of the Chosin Few in 2012. He was one of many Marines called to serve in Korea who did not go through boot camp. His widow, Fran Woodward Kreekon, said that her husband learned to fire his weapon while on the ship to Inchon. Woodward organized the North Texas Chapter, aided in the fundraising, and contributed money to the project. Woodward sent out an initial fund-raising letter in 2013.

Watson Crumbie, a member of the Marines 1st Division at Yudam-ni, joined the effort to build the national monument. He served as co-chairman of the group driving the project. Acknowledging that their efforts received pushback from other Marines, Crumbie said, "I didn't understand that. I believed in General Carey." Crumbie said Carey served as the group's senior advisor, worked closely with the sculptor, Mr. Byrd, and led fund-raising efforts. During meetings, Crumbie said, Carey's leadership style was, "like a general."

Helping to publicize the Chosin Few Monument, the General appeared on a Dallas television station newscast on May 23, 2014. Speaking about the Chosin Reservoir fight, Carey said:

> As a result of that battle, South Korea survived. Today of course, that's [South Korea] the balance between the United States and China. That provided our balance to China to hold them down. Otherwise, they'd be controlling Asia now.[9]

Monument Fundraising

To Mrs. Woodward Kreekon, the monument project was personal. First, she wanted to finish the work that her late husband Bruce started in 2012. Second, veterans were an important part of her life. Three of her uncles served in World War II. One lost a limb. As a child, her parents brought her to visit one of her uncles at McCloskey Army Hospital in Temple, Texas.[10]

While acknowledging that she never did anything like major fundraising before, Mrs. Woodward Kreekon sought out an expert: her cousin, Texas A&M University Chancellor John Sharp. Not only did Chancellor Sharp understand fundraising for a major university, but he also personally raised money for his own political campaigns. He served two terms as the Comptroller of Public Accounts for the state of Texas. Chancellor Sharp shared ideas with Mrs. Woodward Kreekon.[11]

Initially, Mrs. Woodward Kreekon wrote monument fund-raising letters to an estimated 2,000 Chosin Few veterans. She received contributions from 15 percent of those who received the letter. Each contributor received a hand-written thank-you note from Mrs. Woodward Kreekon.[12] The response to the mail-appeal was significant and larger than expected. "The average direct mail response for prospect list was 4.9% last year [2019]," according to Maddie Shepherd. Ms. Shepherd wrote "12 Direct Mail Statistics You Should Know in 2021."[13] Working with General Carey and Korean Marine Peter Oh, Mrs. Woodward Kreekon also contacted foundations and the Korean-American community. In addition, the group reached out to the Republic of Korea. General Carey said, "It wouldn't have happened without her [Mrs. Woodward Kreekon]."[14]

The Republic of Korea never forgot the Americans who fought and died on their behalf during the Korean War. In honor of the Chosin Few, the citizens of the Republic of Korea along with the Korean Patriots Association contributed more than $400,000 to help build the national monument. In addition, the following business leaders contributed more than $200,000 to the effort:

- Timothy T. Day (a Marine veteran), founder of Bar-S Food Company and chairman of Timothy T. Day Foundation, Inc. through his foundation.
- Ellen Gordon, president of Tootsie Roll Industries
- The late T. Boone Pickens, founder of Mesa Petroleum.

Some individual contributions honored Carey's late daughter Melody and Mr. Woodward.

In addition, the following were major contributors to the Dallas-area monument:

- The Honorable Craig Penfold, Texas State District Judge (Retired)
- Ellen Gordon, president of Tootsie Roll Industries
- FedEx Chief Executive Officer Fred Smith (a Marine veteran)
- Major Richard "Dick" Agnew (U.S. Army (Ret)
- Roy Upshaw, owner of Taco Casa Restaurants.

The Monument

Both monuments have eight panels honoring the entire operation at the Reservoir with seven containing separate battle scenes. The Quantico monument is an octagon with eight panels. Eight panels make up the rectangular monument in Dallas. The panels in both monuments include a description of those battles. Brief panel descriptions are:

Jangjin (Chosin Reservoir) Panel

Honoring the entire operation is the Jangjin (Chosin Reservoir) panel. The Korean name for the area is Jangjin, but U.N. forces used Japanese maps. The Japanese called the area Chosin while occupying Korea during World War II. American service members referred to the reservoir as Chosin and called themselves the "Chosin Few."

The Chinese believed that by annihilating the 1stMarDiv, 7th U.S. Army Division, and 41 Independent Commando, British Royal Marines, they would force the withdrawal of UN forces. Then, the Chinese would take the entire Korean Peninsula. The Chinese ultimately failed.

East of Jangjin (Chosin) Panel

The panel honors the U.S. Army's 31st Regimental Combat Team (RCT) that included the 31st and 32nd Regiments of the 7th Infantry Division. Under attack by an estimated 20,000 Chinese troops on December 1, 1950, Lieutenant Colonel Don Faith organized a convoy of trucks headed to Hagaru-ri. Enemy forces destroyed the convoy, known as Task Force Faith, and killed Faith. An estimated 900 soldiers escaped across the frozen reservoir to Hagaru-ri.

Yudam-ni Panel

The Yudam-ni panel recognizes the five-day battle fought by 5th and 7th Marines of the 1stMarDiv as the Chinese surrounded the Marines. The Marines broke out by attacking 14 miles southeast to Hagaru-ri. Those able to walk marched into Hagaru-ri singing the Marine Corps Hymn.

Toktong Pass Panel

The Toktong Pass panel honored Fox Company of 2nd Battalion, 7th Marines (2/7). Surrounded by the Chinese, Fox Company suffered 30 percent casualties. Two members of Fox Company, Captain William E. Barber, the CO, and Private Hector Cafferata, received Medals of Honor for their actions. Fox Company held the hill overlooking the pass until rescued by the 1st Battalion 7th Marines (1/7) led by Lieutenant Colonel Ray Davis who also earned the Medal of Honor.

Hell Fire Valley Panel

Task Force Drysdale, led by Lieutenant Colonel Douglas B. Drysdale, commanding officer of 41 Commando British Royal Marines, attacked through what survivors called Hell Fire Valley to provide reinforcements at Hagaru-ri.

The Chinese inflicted heavy losses on the task force, capturing groups of Marines and soldiers from the U.S. Army. George Company, 3rd Battalion, 1st Marines (3/1) and 41 Commando British Royal Marines and 16 tanks made it to Hagaru-ri.

Hagaru-ri Panel

This panel honors the battle at East Hill and the engineers who built the airstrip at Hagaru-ri enabling the Marines to evacuate more than 4,000 casualties and bring in replacement forces and nearly a million pounds of supplies and ammunition.

Koto-ri Panel

U.N. units fought from Hagaru-ri to Koto-ri. The Chinese surrounded units that included members of 1stMarDiv and remnants of the U.S. Army's 7th Infantry Division. A darkened sky and heavy snow kept fighter aircraft support from aiding the ground forces. A single star appeared. The sky cleared.

Carey at the Chosin Few Monument dedication on May 4, 2017, in Virginia with Joint Chiefs of Staff Chairman General Joseph F. Dunford (right), the second Marine to ever hold that post. Korean Marine, and long-time friend of Carey's, Peter Oh is in the background. Mr. Oh died on November 21, 2022. (Carey family collection, 2017)

Fighter planes flew in the morning and the forces moved to Funchilin Pass (Hwangch'o-Ryong).

Topping both monuments is the Star of Koto-Ri. The star on the National Monument is larger with a slightly different design than the star on the monument in Dallas. On that panel are these words, "We few, we Chosin few, we eternal band of brothers." That star became the logo of the "Chosin Few." Survivors wear lapel pins called the Star of Koto-Ri.

Funchilin Pass Panel

At the Funchilin Pass, the Chinese destroyed the bridge that would take the U.N. forces to the sea. The U.S. Air Force airdropped Treadway bridge sections. Engineers replaced the bridge and the drive to the sea continued. This panel also lists the names of the 17 Medal of Honor recipients from the Chosin Reservoir battles including 14 Marines. The list can be seen in the table below.

Table 1: Chosin Few Medal of Honor Recipients

Name	*Rank*	*Unit and Branch*	*Home State*
William E. Barber	Captain CO	F Company 2/7 Marine	Kentucky
William E. Baugh	Private First Class	G Company G 3/1 Marine	Kentucky
Hector A. Cafferata	Private	F Company 2/7 Marine	New York
Raymond G. Davis	Lieutenant Colonel CO	1/7 Marine	Georgia
Don C. Faith	Lieutenant Colonel CO	32nd Regiment Army	Indiana
Thomas J. Hudner	Lieutenant (J.G.)	Fighter Squadron 32 Navy	Massachusetts
James E. Johnson	Sergeant	J Company 3/7 Marine	Idaho
Robert S. Kennemore	Staff Sergeant	E Company 2/7 Marine	South Carolina
Frank N. Mitchell	First Lieutenant	A Company 1/7 Marine	Texas
Reginald D. Myers	Major XO	3/1 Marine	Idaho
John U. D. Page	Lieutenant Colonel	X Corps Artillery Army	Minnesota
Lee H. Phillips	Corporal	E Company 2/7 Marine	Georgia
James I. Poynter	Sergeant	A Company 1/7 Marine	Illinois
Phillip D. Reem	Second Lieutenant	H Company 3/7 Marine	Pennsylvania
Carl L. Sitter	Captain CO	G Company 3/1 Marine	Missouri
Archie Van Winkle	Staff Sergeant	B Company 1/7 Marine	Alaska
William G. Windrich	Staff Sergeant	I Company 3/5 Marine	Illinois

Reaction to the Dedication at Quantico

When General Carey saw the monument at the dedication Quantico on May 4, 2017, he first offered a prayer of thanks, "with God's guidance for what I helped do. Despite two prior failures, by prayer and effort, we got this done. God wanted this story told." He added, "I was absolutely overwhelmed with the monument and was totally gratified that it was done." As he stood at the dedication ceremony as one of the day's speakers, General Carey said:

> I thought about the individual heroics of the Marines. I saw examples of it myself. Many did not recognize the importance of that battle [Chosin]. Had we pulled out of Korea as a result of that battle, South Korea would not exist today.[15]

Former Marine Corps Commandant General Joseph F. Dunford, Jr., chairman of the Joint Chiefs of Staff, spoke at the Quantico dedication. General Dunford's father, Joseph F. Dunford, Sr. served at the Chosin Reservoir with Baker Company 1/5. Mr. Dunford also attended the dedication.

Mrs. Ganz boarded the Southwest Airlines flight to the ceremony with the General and others from North Texas. Mrs. Ganz made sure the flight crew knew that General Carey was on the flight. As a result, the flight's captain asked passengers to let the General and his group be the first people off the flight. Mrs. Ganz attended the Quantico ceremony with General Carey.

South Korea's President Visits Chosin Few Monument

On June 28, 2017, South Korean President Moon Jae-in, in his initial visit to the United States, made Quantico his first stop in order to see the monument. Marine Corps Commandant General Robert B. Neller met the South Korean president and offered a brief comment when he said, "That the [Chosin Reservoir] legacy lives on today as we affirm the bonds our two nations share."

For President Jae-in, the visit was both part of his role as South Korea's leader and very personal. His mother and father were among the thousands of North Korean refugees rescued by Americans like General Carey. His parents were two of the 14,000 refugees placed on the United States Merchant Marine Victory ship call SS *Meredith Victory*.[16] The ship was designed to hold a crew of 60, but Captain Leonard LaRue ordered the offloading of the ship's cargo. Refugees filled the cargo holds and deck. The ship, later referred to as the "ship of miracles," took the refugees from Hungnam to Pusan. Of the 193 ships that carried refugees, the *Meredith Victory* took more people than any other ship. An estimated 100,000 people fled North Korea on the ships.[17]

Most of the refugees stood during the three-day trip. Five babies were born during the voyage. The ship's crew received recognition: South Korea awarded the crew the Korean Presidential Unit Citation. In addition, the United States Merchant Marine awarded the SS *Meredith Victory* crew with its highest honor—the Meritorious Service Medal.

Honors for the ship continued over the years. President Eisenhower signed an Act of Congress designating the *SS Meredith Victory* a "Gallant Ship," in 1960. The Department of Transportation called the voyage "The greatest rescue in the history of mankind." Perhaps the ship's crew most impactful recognition came in a hand-written note from one of the refugees on the ship. Translated into English the note said, "We ever thanks American assistance. Thanks U.S. Forces fighting in Korea."[18]

Chosin Few Monument in Dallas

The idea of a second monument occurred right after the dedication ceremony at Quantico. Taking the long-term view, General Carey envisioned additional placements of Chosin Few monuments in other locations besides Quantico. He pushed hard to put a replica of the monument at the Dallas Fort Worth National Cemetery. The Metroplex Military Charitable Trust (MMCT) sponsored the drive for the Dallas Chosin Few Memorial project. General Carey still serves the MMCT as the presiding trustee.

Getting there was a "monumental process," General Carey said. The General and his team raised funds and Mark Byrd's sculpture was completed. Over a four-year period, General Carey's team navigated a number of bureaucratic hurdles with the federal government.

With an objective to aid fundraising for placement of the Chosin Few Monument in Dallas, General Carey narrated a 10-minute presentation videoed after the dedication ceremony ended in Virginia. During General Carey's narration in the video, he briefly summarized the actions depicted on the monument. Then 89, the General spoke without using notes.

The video also showed General Carey meeting with a delegation of South Korean leaders who attended the dedication ceremony. Carey mentioned the possibility of adding monuments in other parts of the United States.[19]

The Dallas Monument Design

Above the panels on the Dallas monument are scenes representing the weather, terrain, and equipment at the Chosin Reservoir. Those scenes replaced the original bas-reliefs used on the monument at Quantico. (Artists create a bas-relief by sculpting onto a 2D plane to create and accentuate figures and objects, producing a 3D appearance, which shows all angles with little distortion). In addition, there are bas-reliefs of distinguished men who served at the reservoir including the 17 Medal of Honor recipients.

Chosin Reservoir Monument as an Educational Tool

From General Carey's perspective, he sees placement of the monument at the cemetery as a means to help teachers to provide an opportunity to educate schoolchildren about the Korean War. Larry Williams, Director of the Dallas Fort Worth National Cemetery, added:

> The monument will be a great tool to help educate not only schoolchildren, but also many adults. You've got to remember, the Korean War is the forgotten war. Many adults don't know anything about it. I'm excited to get it done. With our Korean War veterans passing, history is being lost and forgotten.[20]

Even in Texas, with an estimated 1.4 million veterans (second only to California with an estimated 1.5 million veterans) public schools offer limited coverage of the Korean War.[21] The Texas Education Agency (TEA) provides direction for the state's coverage of the Korean War for high schools. The Korean War is part of a yearlong study for high school juniors (third year). Here is the TEA curriculum covering the Korean War. The Korean War is covered under U.S. history since 1877. Texas schools are required to cover the following essential knowledge and for social studies as it relates to the Korean War:

> Explain reasons and outcomes for U.S. involvement in the Korean War and its relationship to the containment policy.[22]

Jenny Gaona, TEA's social studies content specialist, said that Korean War battles are not included in the requirements. By comparison, coverage of the American Revolutionary War and the Civil War includes four battles for each of those conflicts, Ms. Gaona said. However, she explained, each local independent school district (ISD) then develops a local curriculum to cover that material. In addition, Ms. Gaona said local districts might, as an example, discuss battles or bring in knowledgeable speakers on the Korean War to speak to their classes.[23]

Jeremiah Rush, Frisco Independent School District (ISD) Social Studies Coordinator for grades 6–12 said approximately two hours of classroom time is dedicated to the Korean War during the academic year. Mr. Rush said the district uses information from the Korean War Legacy project that includes an oral history interview with General Carey.[24]

Texas Tech University's Dr. Kelly Crager, who heads the Oral History Project for the Vietnam Center and Archive, said this about the lack of classes on the Korean War:

> Unfortunately, the "Forgotten War" is still largely forgotten in lesson plans around the country. I'm certainly no expert in this area, but I saw it when I was in grad school and when I was teaching. The survey courses have so much to teach (and more to teach each semester) that so many important topics get short shrift. Seems to me that a one or maybe two-hour lecture on Korea would be all instructors have time for in a basic history class.[25]

Dr. Andrew Mitchell, a history professor at Grove City College, a private school in Western Pennsylvania, offered his thoughts on the Korean War from an academic perspective when he said:

> As someone who regularly glosses over the Korean conflict in my US Military History class, I am, nevertheless struck by the aura of pathos that surrounds our "forgotten war." Involving momentous amphibious operations in a distant, East Asian theater, it nevertheless lacked the initial tragedy of a Pearl Harbor or a Gulf of Tonkin to seize the American imagination. While Truman and Eisenhower provided honest and articulate leadership, most American military commanders in Korea were considerably more modest than the titanic figures—and egos—of the brass who commanded "the greatest generation" from 1941–45. Too close to World War II, and too far away from the tensions surrounding Vietnam, the Korean War comes off a little shabby, seemingly not significant enough either to boast about or to protest.[26]

Stephen R. Taafe, author of *MacArthur's Korean War Generals*, said this about teaching about the Korean War: "As for Texas public schools, I would also be amazed if the teachers know much about the Korean War, let alone the students." He is also a professor of history at Stephen F. Austin University in Nacogdoches, Texas. Dr. Taafe presents a lecture on the Korean War in his survey classes.[27]

In General Carey's view, if future teachers do not study about the Korean War, it would be difficult for them to teach students about that war.[28]

The Sculptor—Mark Austin Byrd

Beginning in 2012, Mr. Byrd worked closely with General Carey on both Chosin Reservoir Monuments. They shared several things. Both served as Marine officers in Vietnam. Both were aviators. Both faced enemy fire.

Both earned the Distinguished Flying Cross. Both are detail oriented. Both considered careers in medicine. Both are passionate about honoring those who served in the military. They first met while attending the funeral of a Vietnam veteran they both knew.

Mr. Byrd served in the Marine Corps for five years. While in Vietnam between 1969 and 1970 as a first lieutenant, Mr. Byrd flew UH-1E gunship helicopters and AH-1G Cobras as a member of Light Helicopter Squadron Attack (HMLA-367). On December 2, 1969, Lieutenant Byrd, serving as a Cobra co-pilot, provided machine gun fire to enable rescue helicopters to extract four fellow Marines from a mountainous jungle area near the Ho Chi Minh Trail. For his efforts, Lieutenant Byrd received the DFC. His citation reads in part:

> … he provided a continuous flow of vital information, coordinated his fire with that of supporting Cobra gunships, and delivered accurate machine gun fire that the North Vietnamese fire was suppressed sufficiently to permit transport helicopters to enter the precarious area on two separate occasions and extract the downed crew.

While serving in Vietnam between 1969 and 1970 Lieutenant Byrd flew 642 combat missions and in addition to his DFC earned 32 Air Medals.[29]

Following his tour in the Marines, Mr. Byrd pursued a master's degree in architecture. Although he did not complete the degree, he worked with architectural firms as a lead designer and construction manager for 25 years before finding his true passion as a sculptor.[30]

He came to sculpture later in life, although as a small child he often built clay models. Mr. Byrd met Lena Beth Frazer, a sculptor who taught him not only how to make bronze art, but how to prepare his work for sale. Initially, he sculpted wildlife and then his work evolved. His first military-related project was a bust of Army Master Sergeant Roy Benavidez, a Texas Medal of Honor recipient from the Vietnam War.[31] The United States Military Academy at West Point displays that bust—the first enlisted man so honored there, Mr. Byrd said. His wife Jenelle Armstrong Byrd, a portrait artist, collaborates with her husband on all of their projects. Mr. Byrd's chance meeting with General Carey led to an opportunity. The General recommended Mr. Byrd to work on a Vietnam Memorial in Arlington, Texas. Other military sculpture commissions followed including annual bronze awards for Marines.[32]

Among military memorials designed by the Byrds are the Medal of Honor Memorial in Gainesville, Texas, and a statue of Captain Lance Sijan, Medal of Honor recipient at the Hall of Heroes at the United States Air Force Academy in Colorado Springs, Colorado. Other monuments include World War II hero Audie Murphy (World War II's most decorated soldier) and the Marine Corps Engineers Memorial at the National Museum of the Marine Corps.

With the General's eye for talent in just about any area, the Carey-Byrd team led the Chosin Reservoir Monument project in Dallas. As project meetings began, Mr. Byrd learned several things about General Carey. First, the General did not understand, nor did he accept no for an answer. The General took a "no-nonsense" approach to the project and was "The rock who kept it going," Mr. Byrd said. He described the General as "a great delegator." While Mr. Byrd developed the design and built the project from a clay model, General Carey provided the ideas and wording for the eight panels. The General inspired the scenes at the top of the panels.

While concept and design were important to the development of the monument, funding the project was another challenge. To support the fundraising, Mr. Byrd developed hard-hitting professional marketing materials. When Korean government officials showed interest in the project, they requested a budget. Working with the committee, Mr. Byrd incorporated the budget in a brochure.[33]

As the group met the funding goals, Mr. Byrd's clay models went to a foundry. The foundry workers cast the models into bronze. Eventually, the wording on each scene had to be proofread. Then each scene needed packing in separate crates for shipment. Throughout the project, Mr. Byrd worked closely with the architects, engineers, and the National Museum of the Marine Corps in Triangle, Virginia. To obtain the site for the monument, the committee needed to raise $250,000. After reaching that goal, the Dallas group held discussions with Museum leaders. There was disagreement over the wording. Folks from the Museum wanted to use fewer words. The rationale—visitors would not read lengthy copy. That response did not go over well with General Carey, Mr. Byrd said.[34] Apparently, Museum leaders did not know they were dealing with a man who grew up in the Depression, ran track after rupturing a kidney, faced near-death experiences seven times in Korea, had no college degree until he was 43, helped raise seven children, and faced personal tragedies in his own family. General Carey's wording is on the monument with no changes from the Museum.

One more challenge came close to stalling the project—the name. The word Chosin appeared on maps drawn by the Japanese during their occupation of Korea during World War II. Veterans of the battle at the Reservoir call themselves the "Chosin Few." The Korean name for the area is Jangjin. To satisfy both the Korean government and American Korean war veterans a compromise produced this wording on the monument—Jangjin (Chosin) Reservoir Battle.

The team of Mark Austin Byrd and his wife Jenelle Armstrong Byrd attended the dedication of the Chosin Few Memorial in Dallas. Mark designed the sculpture and Jenelle designed the portraits of the Chosin Few veterans displayed on the monument. (David Alvey, July 9, 2022)

Chosin Monument Ground Breaking Ceremony in Dallas

In addition to the monument in Virginia, Mr. Byrd worked with General Carey on a second monument. A ground breaking ceremony for the placement of the monument at the Dallas Fort Worth National Cemetery (another project that also resulted from the General's leadership) took place on General Carey's 94th birthday—January 10, 2022. Sun Lae Hung, head of the mission for Korean Consular Office in Dallas and Sung-Joo-Yoo, president of the Korean Society of Dallas, attended the event.

General Carey addressed the estimated 50 attendees. He pointed out the success in Korea resulted in a continuing free South Korea. South Korea has the fourth largest economy in Asia. Only the economies of China, India, and Japan are larger than South Korea's, the General said.

Regarding the Chosin Reservoir, General Carey said that in his view, "China was glad to see us go." He praised the bravery and courage of those he fought with in Korea. The General added, "We had a will to win. Thank God, He was on our side."

During the ground breaking ceremony for the Dallas Chosin Few Monument, Mr. Byrd announced that U.S. Army Major Harvey Storms' picture would be on the monument. His remains came through Dallas on the way to Arlington National Cemetery in 2021.

In addition to the ground breaking ceremony, attendees surprised General Carey with a birthday cake that he cut with a K-Bar combat knife provided by Vietnam veteran Gene Pugh, who served with the U.S. Army Special Forces. Mr. Byrd presented the General with a sculpture of his friend, the late Marine Corps Commandant General Barrow.

The Dallas monument has four panels on each of its two sides with the same descriptions as the national monument. The Dallas monument includes sculptured portraits of those who performed heroic acts at the Chosin Reservoir. One of those sculptures is titled "Every Marine a Rifleman."

As with the national monument, the Dallas effort was a lengthy process involving the Dallas Fort Worth National Cemetery, the Veterans Administration, General Carey's group, the Metroplex Military Charitable Trust, and the Byrds. During the building of the Dallas monument, Mr. Byrd provided the preliminary design, produced the sculpture, and managed the design process. Again, he worked closely with General Carey. The General and his team also coordinated the placement of the monument with the Veterans Administration during a five-year period. The VA has responsibility for the Dallas Fort Worth National Cemetery. A portion of the money raised for the Dallas project will support maintenance of the monument.

Dedication of the Monument in Dallas

On July 9, 2022, more than 200 people joined General Carey and 10 other Chosin Reservoir veterans for the Chosin Few Memorial dedication in Dallas. Members of the General's family including children, grandchildren, and great-grandchildren attended the ceremony. Descendants of the Chosin Few veterans also attended. The temperature that morning was more than 150 degrees warmer than the freezing temperatures those eight Marines faced at the reservoir between November and December 1950.

In addition to General Carey, two Chosin Few veterans spoke. World War II and Chosin Reservoir Marine veteran Watson Crumbie introduced fellow Chosin Few members. The Chosin Few veterans in attendance included: Rayburn Blair, Felix Byrd, Thomas Beard, Orace Edwards, Charles Floyd, James Haun, John Y. Lee (a Korean who served as a translator), Larry Lucido, Herbert Odell, and Lieutenant General Philip Shutler, USMC (Ret). Shutler, a 1948 U.S. Naval Academy graduate, was one of four Chosin Reservoir veterans who rose to three-star general. The other Chosin Reservoir veterans who became lieutenant generals were Stephen Olmstead and the late John "Jack" N. McLaughlin. Both Carey and Olmstead were members of George 3/1 while serving in Korea. General Olmstead was the last surviving Marine officer from the Chosin Reservoir Battle on active duty when he retired in 1989. Olmstead died on July 20, 2022, at age 92.[35]

Descendants of Chosin Reservoir veterans at the ceremony included Bobbie Broyles (and her husband Stephen). She is the daughter of U.S. Army Lieutenant Colonel Don Faith. Faith commanded the 31st RCT (reconstituted as Task Force Faith). Mrs. Broyles' father lost his life while leading the task force south for Hagaru-ri. Also attending was Sandy Thompson Carroll (and her husband Dave). Her father, Air Force Lieutenant Royal S. Thompson, led the C-119 drop of Treadway Bridges.

Anne Swenson represented the Chosin Few. Her father, Colonel Warren Wiedhahn, USMC (Ret) in 2022 served as the president of the Chosin Few, the organization of Chosin Reservoir veterans. The group's purpose is "to reunite the survivors of that epic campaign for life."[36] Colonel Wiedhahn was unable to travel to the dedication.

Mark Austin Byrd, the sculptor of the memorial, told the audience that the battle of the Chosin Reservoir was one of the three most important battles in Marine Corps history including Belleau Wood in World War I and Iwo Jima in World War II.

For General Carey, the dedication was the culmination of nearly a decade's efforts. The General's resolve overcame naysayers. He built a team to get the monument built and helped raise funds. Carey's appearance at the ceremony was in doubt after he fell five weeks earlier. Taken to the hospital by ambulance, doctors discovered that the General suffered from a blood infection. Treatment quickly began. After a few days, General Carey went to a rehabilitation center. Patients at the center listed a goal for their stay on a wallboard in their rooms. In typical General Carey fashion, his goal—"get out of here." After five days, the General returned home and prepared for the dedication.

Despite a heat advisory and the temperature topping 100 degrees, General Carey never removed his navy blazer. In his remarks, lasting approximately seven minutes, the 94-and-a-half-year-old Chosin Reservoir veteran spoke without notes. He said,

> The battle of Chosin was equal to Iwo Jima. Our one division fought eight Chinese Communist divisions. It wasn't an easy task to fight our way out. We had the guts to do it. It was a tough battle. Many, many brave Marines never made it back [home]. I feel like crying for all those guys. Our troops who were there will never be forgotten.

A flyover by Marine aviators in two F-18s capped the ceremony. Flight lead Major Jesse McGough and Captain Michael Fineis, members of VMFA-112, flew the fighter jets. The pilots serve in Marine Air Group 41 (MAG-41), 4th Marine Air Wing (MAW) at Naval Air Station, Joint Reserve Base in Fort Worth, Texas. When General Carey served at HQMC in the 1970s, he worked on the development of the F-18.

At a post-ceremony reception at Dallas Baptist University, Myoung-Joon Kim, Head of the Mission of the Consulate of the Republic of Korea in Dallas, spoke. Kim summed up the results of the Chosin Reservoir Battle with these four words, "That saved our country."

Also at the dedication was John Y. Lee, a Korean who served as a translator at Hagaru-ri. In 1950, Lee, 21, attended Korea University in Seoul. He grew up in Panmunjom, North Korea. Speaking at the reception with a great deal of emotion, Lee praised General Smith and General Carey. Smith continually defied orders from Army X Corps commander, Major General Edward "Ned" Almond to swiftly attack to the Yalu River. Smith instead reinforced Koto-ri. In addition, Lee praised Carey's use of the intelligence information provided by the line crossers. He said that Carey's recommendation

Through General Carey's efforts, the Chosin Few Memorial that includes the Star of Koto-Ri was dedicated at the Dallas-Fort Worth National Cemetery on July 9, 2022. (Jane L. Mesches, November 17, 2022)

saved 1st Division's headquarters (including Hagaru-ri). In a July 14, 2022, email Lee added this comment, "The successful defense of Hagaru-ri was a miracle."[37]

According to Lee, appreciative Marines aided his efforts to enter Yale University in 1954. Lee earned both a Bachelor of Arts and Juris Doctorate from Yale. Over the years, Lee said that he practiced law in New York, Washington, D.C., and Seoul. For 20 years, Lee served as an attorney for the U.S. Forces Command in Korea and spent two years with the Justice Department. Lee came to the dedication from Florida.[38]

General Carey spoke at the dedication of the Chosin Few Memorial. He told the audience, "Our troops there will never be forgotten." (Jim Nelson Black, July 9, 2022)

Four generations of the Carey family attended the Chosin Few Monument dedication in Dallas. (Jim Nelson Black, July 9, 2022)

CHAPTER 21

Family

While General Carey's career put him in dangerous and challenging situations, nothing could prepare him for the difficult family situations that he faced. Between 2005 and 2020, he dealt with his wife's nearly 15-year battle with Alzheimer's, the deaths of one daughter and one son, and a missing son.

Dena's Fight with Alzheimer's Disease

From a two-page hand-written note from former President Reagan, the world learned that the nation's 40th president faced the earlier stages of Alzheimer's Disease. In his own words, on November 5, 1994, the former president said:

> My fellow Americans, I have been told that I am one of the millions of Americans who will be afflicted with Alzheimer's Disease. In opening our hearts [Nancy and I], we hope that this might promote greater awareness of this condition. Unfortunately, as Alzheimer's Disease progress, the family bears a heavy burden.[1]

The New York Times, as an example, reprinted the entire Reagan letter on November 6, 1994.

When Reagan's announcement came out, President Bill Clinton was addressing a Democratic Party event in Oakland, California. The 42nd president shared the news with the audience. Clinton said, "It touched my heart." President Reagan's doctors also issued a statement about his condition that said, "Additional testing and extensive observation over the past few weeks leads us to conclude that President Reagan is entering the early stages of this disease."[2]

That Saturday afternoon, General Carey, along with the rest of the nation, learned about the former president's situation. For the General, it was a bit more personal. General Carey and President Reagan met several times when the president came to Quantico for horseback riding. The General's home had an

Dena Carey, the General's wife of 58 years, spent the last 14 years of her life battling Alzheimer's disease. (Carey family collection, 1982)

autographed photo of the president with General Carey. The picture showed General Carey greeting the president arriving at Quantico in the early 1980s. General Carey admired the 40th president. For him, the news about President Reagan was more personal than it was for most people.

About a year after President Reagan died in 2004 at 93, Alzheimer's struck the Carey family, when the General's beloved wife Dena learned that she faced early stages of the disease. At that time, Dena Carey found out that she was one of four million Americans facing an incurable disease. Unfortunately, family members of Dena's had suffered from Alzheimer's disease. By 2004, in the 40 counties making up the North Texas area, 40,000 people suffered from the affliction, according to the North Central Texas Chapter of the Alzheimer's Association.[3] Dena Carey, 69 when doctors diagnosed her with early-stage Alzheimer's Disease, faced a difficult time. For the Carey family, that news began the start of a long and sad journey. The Alzheimer's Association said, "People living with Alzheimer's die an average of eight years after first experiencing symptoms, but the duration of the disease can vary from three to 20 years."[4]

Alzheimer's Research

Alzheimer's Disease, first identified in the early years of the twentieth century, is the sixth highest cause of death in the United Sates. Research indicates that the disease begins in the part of the brain that regulates thinking and memory skills. As the disease spreads, the loss of brain cells results in the failure of other body systems.[5] Over time, cognitive abilities decline. Alzheimer's sufferers become dependent on others for their care as body functions shut down.[6] Scientists continue the search for a cause and cure for the disease.[7]

During his career in the Marine Corps, General Carey faced enemy ground fire in Korea and suffered a wound and frostbite. He saw fellow Marines die. As a young officer, he dodged death at least seven times. In Vietnam, Carey flew close-air-support sorties less than 100 feet from communist ground troops. In retirement, political battles tested his mental and moral fiber. Nothing in combat or politics prepared General Carey for the next 14 years as Dena battled a disease with no cure.

The General described the situation as "a very difficult thing … so frustrating." He called on his Christian faith to guide him through this challenge. First, he came to understand that this was "God's way." While Dena's disease would be hard to take over the next 14 years, the General said, "Christianity taught me that [Alzheimer's] was God's way and I was more able to accept it." Over time, General Carey watched Dena's decline. "It wasn't easy, but I could accept it with God's help."

A red flag for Dena came when she began making mistakes while she prepared dinner. She realized the problem and did not know why. As the General explained, "She was a great cook." They both knew that something was wrong. They scheduled an appointment with their doctor. Dena had a complete physical. Following that appointment, Dena took an extensive series of tests. The diagnosis—early stages of Alzheimer's. Dena, who over the years planned parties, graced social events, and served as the ultimate grandmother, would never get better. General Carey said that he did not take that news "very well." He said that learning the diagnosis was "hard to believe and very sad."[8]

The Carey Family Faces Dena's Struggle

General Carey learned about the three stages of the disease that slowly took Dena away from him and their family.[9] First came the mild stage. Dena faced the challenge of coming up with the right word. At times, she forgot the names of people she just met. Other times, she forgot material that she just read. Social situations became difficult. Dena had trouble planning and organizing things. Occasionally, she misplaced things.

As the disease progressed, Dena became more forgetful. She had difficulty recalling personal events. At times, Dena became moody and withdrawn. Occasionally, she was confused about her location or the day. Dena needed help when selecting clothes. She had trouble sleeping. Her behavior changed.

General Carey said prior to the diagnosis, he and Dena bought a recreational vehicle (RV). Dena and the General planned to tour the country visiting special places, family, and friends from 38 years in the military. When the Careys learned Dena was in the early stages of Alzheimer's, they sold the RV.

During the first five years following the initial diagnosis, Dena's health gradually declined. By 2010, Melody, the youngest of the Careys' seven children, knew that her mother's health was in decline and came home to help. The General described Melody as "very dedicated to her mother." Even her grandchildren noticed a difference in their grandmother. Early on, Dena would greet family friends as if she recognized them. Eventually, she lost the ability to recognize people.

If dealing with Dena's condition was not enough, another tragedy hit the Carey family. On October 21, 2013, 48-year-old Melody died. An athlete, her death was completely unexpected. Melody died less than two months after she and her father rode together in the "Hotter 'N Hell Hundred" bike race. The General now not only dealt with his wife's declining health but also had to arrange the funeral for his youngest child. In addition to losing a child, General Carey lost Melody's assistance with her mother. Dena attended Melody's funeral. It would be one of her last public outings. Following Melody's death, Dena's health rapidly declined. Over the next year, Dena lost her ability to speak. Despite all of her health problems, the General said that Dena always recognized him. Eventually, her husband was only person that Dena recognized.[10]

During Dena's struggle, Tamara, his older daughter, traveled to Plano from her South Florida home. The Careys' son Bill and his wife Julie, a nurse, lived about 7 miles from the General in nearby Parker, Texas. They aided with visits and helped with grocery shopping.

As Dena's condition worsened, she entered the severe stage of Alzheimer's. By that time, she needed round-the-clock care. Along with not being able to speak, Dena struggled with the ability to walk, sit, and swallow. In 2014, the General finally placed Dena in an assisted living facility located a few minutes from the Carey home. Over the next 1,500 plus days, General Carey visited Dena every single day. They shared dinner together every evening. In Dena's final weeks, General Carey fed the woman he loved. Every time that the General visited Dena, he said that she greeted him with the loving smile that he had known for nearly 60 years. General Carey said that the couple communicated with their hands. Dena answered yes by squeezing her husband's hand, the General said. Throughout Dena's time at the assisted living facility, General Carey described her four attendants as "very caring." He added, "They were spectacular. They spent all their time and effort helping patients."

Throughout Dena's declining health, General Carey's friends from the Metroplex Marines rallied around the senior Marine officer in the Dallas area. The Metroplex Marines, particularly Frank Walker, made sure that the General attended their luncheons held the first Thursday of each month. General Carey said of his fellow Marines, "They are a great group."

Maudine "Dena" Adcock Carey died on June 12, 2019. The proud native Texan died in her home state.

General Carey shared this very personal and emotional part of his life in hopes that it would assist others dealing with the disease in their family. "I want to help people," he said.

Dena's burial took place at the Dallas Fort Worth National Cemetery on June 19, 2019. The General was part of the community leadership group that helped get that cemetery built. One day, General Carey will join Dena in the same burial plot. His remains will go above Dena's remains. The General regularly places flowers at her grave. Dena's family described her this way in her obituary written prior to her funeral:

> … a pure stature of a woman; had the smile of a Princess, the grace of a Queen, and a laugh that could melt a King. Dena was a perfect wife with style and finesse, not only in her flawless wardrobes but also in her home. As a military wife, she could throw the parties of all parties and be the belle of the ball at the same time. She stood fierce and strong behind her husband and supported his (nearly) 38 years in the Marine Corps. She raised and nurtured seven successful children; all could not have asked for a better mother and best friend. Her love of dancing, golf, homemaking, travel, and storytelling left you eager to be around her.[11]

For the General, Dena was not the first member of his family to face Alzheimer's Disease. In the late 1940s, his father, Timothy Carey, suffered from the disease while in his early 50s.

Hoping that Dena's struggles with Alzheimer's would help others the Carey family asked that instead of flowers memorial contributions go to the Alzheimer's Research and Prevention Foundation (ARPF). ARPF, founded in 2003, funds Alzheimer's prevention integrative medicine research and provides educational support on Alzheimer's prevention.[12]

Death of a Son

Just over 15 months after Dena's death, the General's third oldest son, Michael Ramsey Carey, died on August 29, 2020. He was five weeks away from his 67th birthday. Michael Ramsey was a long-time resident of Asheville, North Carolina. For many years, he lived near his birth mother. Michael served in the United States Navy as seaman on the USS *Niagara Falls*. The ship carried supplies in the Pacific and spent time between North and South America. Following his service in the Navy, Michael worked in the home construction and hospitality industries. Growing up, he shared his father's love of running. Michael ran cross-country in high school and as a high-school freshman earned ranking as number four in the state of Virginia. Disabled in later life with heart trouble, he died in the Hospice Unit of the Charles George Veterans Administration Medical Center in Asheville. Michael loved the Blue Ridge Mountains of Western North Carolina and asked that his survivors spread his ashes in the mountains.[13] Between 2013 and 2020, General Carey lost his wife and two of his seven children.

The General described Michael as a loner. Until entering high school, Michael lived with his mother. Carey reached out to his ex-wife and arranged for Michael to join his brothers and sisters when he was in high school. Michael never married, although he had a long-term relationship with a woman. Carey said he believed at the end of his life Michael "lost his will to live." He described his son as "self-sufficient" and said he "did not want any help."[14]

Surviving Children

Within the blended family, General Carey adopted Dena's sons, Bill, Robert, and Michael Scott. The three boys joined Paul and Michael Ramsey. Dena and the General had two daughters named Tamara and Melody. Carey is proud of the fact that all five of his sons served in the armed forces—one in the Marine Corps, three in the Navy, and one in the Army. The General's oldest son, Bill, served as an officer in the Marine Corps. Dena and the General

General Carey commissions his grandson Cole (Bill's son) as an ensign in the United States Navy in 2020. (Frank Walker, 2020)

Tamara Carey joins her four brothers and parents for a family photo in Texas in 1962. (Carey family collection)

pinned on his gold bars after he earned his commission as a second lieutenant. After his time in the Marine Corps, Bill had a career in hospital equipment sales. He continues to serve in retirement working as a school bus driver. Bill's son, Cole, enlisted in the Marine Corps, served for four years, went to Texas Tech University, and graduated with an engineering degree. Cole then earned a commission in the Navy. In 2022, he is in Navy fighter pilot training in Corpus Christi. General Carey's son Paul is a retired Defense Intelligence Agency analyst, after serving in the Navy. Paul enlisted in the Navy, earned a commission, and retired as a lieutenant commander. He lives in Virginia. Bob also served in the Navy in the nuclear submarine program. After Bob finished his tour of duty in the Navy, he worked for power companies. He lives in Arkansas. In retirement, he consults on nuclear power company projects. The General's older daughter, Tamara (Tammie), works in the travel industry in Florida. She regularly returns to Texas to see her father. Tamara takes charge of the General in arranging both medical appointments and housekeeping for her father. Bill, Bob, and Paul defer to Tamara regarding their father. General

The Careys pinned on son Bill's 2nd Lieutenant's bars when Bill earned his commission in the United States Marine Corps in 1976. (Carey family collection, 1976)

Carey often mentions that his children "watch out for me." The General has not seen Michael Scott in nearly 15 years.

Tamara shared one story about a teenage dating experience as a general's daughter with five older brothers. She said when she was in middle school a boy came to take Tamara to her first dance. The General and her brothers quizzed the young about his life's plans. The young man did not have another date with Tamara.

Epilogue

General Carey combined drive, resilience, commitment, Christian faith, and strong convictions in building a life of achievement in the Marine Corps and beyond.

General Carey's Marine Corps experience, with the benefit of hindsight, offered his assessment about the nation's military involvement between 1950 and 1975. The General spoke about Korea, Vietnam, and the *Mayaguez*. He said that "Too often politics drove decisions for the warriors. Many times, the military is not the answer. We go too quickly." Carey the warrior understood the importance of not just jumping into battle.

When asked what advice he would offer his 22-year-old self following his military and retirement years, General Carey replied, "Whatever you are tasked to do, put in every ounce of your capability to get the job done." He also pointed out the need to help other people.[1] The General lived those ideals.

While he would go on to significant achievements in aviation and senior leadership roles, General Carey always came back to his time in the Korean War. Carey learned from Marine Corps leaders such as O. P. Smith and Chesty Puller. The skill and professionalism of World War II officers and NCOs stayed with him. Carey's Korean battlefield experiences influenced his decisions and command philosophy throughout his career. When Carey retired, his Korean War service received recognition from General Barrow, then the commandant of the Marine Corps.

In Korea, 2nd Lieutenant Carey and his fellow Marines faced brutally cold temperatures, snow, and treacherous roads. Casualties on both sides would be high. From November 27 to December 15, 1950, Americans, along with United Nations' (UN) allies at the Chosin Reservoir, endured wind chill factors that dropped to an estimated 65 degrees below zero, heavy enemy fire, significant casualties, and thousands of advancing Chinese soldiers. The ground froze 19 inches deep making entrenchments of fighting holes (fox holes) almost impossible.

At times, Marines stacked dead Chinese soldiers around their fox holes as protection from both the enemy and the elements. Along with the harsh weather, troops of the UN faced another challenge. Chinese Communist Forces badly outnumbered them by eight-to-one. The Chinese encircled the UN forces. Despite those odds, with the Marines taking the lead, the western troops fought their way out of the trap and back to the coast.

In retirement, the General spoke often about Korea. He never wanted anyone to forget about Korea and that war's significance in American history. In oral history interviews, General Carey devoted hours of time in discussing it. When invited to speak, the General many times shared his Korean War experiences—especially the days that included the Chosin Reservoir campaign.

From high school to the Marine Corps and into his tenth decade of life, Carey focused on helping people. Growing up in a single-parent home during the Depression with strong Christian faith was Carey's boot camp for life. Helping others was no empty platitude. From moving up a weight class during a high school wrestling match to building monuments to honor the Chosin Few, Carey spent a lifetime helping other people.

To combat drug trafficking and abuse in the Marine Corps, Carey introduced detection and prevention programs while serving as Commanding General at Quantico. To help achieve those objectives, Carey utilized internal media and increased efforts toward morale and recreational activities. Part of that effort involved heightened security procedures at the entry points of the base to prevent drugs from coming into Quantico. In addition, a stepped-up urinalysis program identified drug users on base.

General Carey emphasized professional education at Quantico. He said, "We've turned our whole education system around to direct our efforts toward this goal, to teach Marines to fight and to win, and to win at the level where they'll be involved." Those who led the Marine Corps into the 21st century benefitted from Carey's vision of training and development.

As a lifelong advocate of physical fitness, the General introduced the "Survival of the Fittest" competition. Quantico units competed in boat races, orienteering, cycling, and swimming. In addition, Carey brought the responsibility for the Marine Corps Marathon to Quantico.

Helping others came in large and small segments. In Korea, he arranged to get better food for his troops. In Vietnam, he applied battle-tested tactics to get ice cream to ground Marines as they faced enemy fire. Carey's bike riding raised funds for an Ohio charity. The General pushed for more funds to combat alcoholism in his native sate. He visited a hospitalized Marine Medal of Honor recipient who suffered from alcoholism, wrote a personalized letter to a forward-based young Marine, met a flight bringing home the remains of a Chosin Reservoir veteran, helped a fellow General obtain medical care, and attended the funeral of the widow of a war-time PTSD victim.

Carey also understood that small gestures made a difference. He took in two small dogs needing a home. Visitors leaving Carey's home are always walked to their cars regardless of the time of day or the weather.

While Carey knew the needs of wounded veterans, he also showed compassion for their family members who often served as caregivers, understanding that they also needed time for themselves. As a result, he led an effort to get vans and volunteer drivers to take wounded veterans to the VA hospital. Carey knew the importance of family members being close to a hospitalized veteran. To achieve that, Carey raised funds for Fisher House so families would have no-cost lodging while their loved ones were hospitalized. After learning families had to drive hundreds of miles to get to a veterans' cemetery, Carey actively became involved in bringing a veterans' cemetery to North Texas.

When his military career ended, Carey never sought high paying corporate jobs. His post-Marine Corps roles reflected on his desired to help other people with "every ounce" of his capability. Carey's experience and commitment took the General to his latest challenge—honoring those who served at the Chosin Reservoir with a monument. Despite the fact that others failed to do that and opposition from some in the Marine Corps community, Carey remained undeterred. The General built a team who shared his passion and commitment. No figurehead, Carey battled bureaucrats, raised funds, and personally reviewed every word on the monument plaques. Following the dedication of the national monument honoring the Chosin Few, Carey immediately set his sights on placing monuments across the country. The first one was dedicated in the General's adopted home of Texas.

Glossary

Ace—designation of a pilot who downed five or more enemy aircraft.

Aid Station—area set up near combat units to provide initial medical care.

Amphibious—a unit deployed to land from the war (usually an ocean) and occupy an area.

Battalion—three or more companies or batteries.

Billet—assigned position or job in the Marine Corps.

Boot Camp—place where new recruits receive their initial Marine Corps training.

Brigade—in the Marine Corps, a task-organized formation consisting of a regiment (three battalions) of infantry, at least a battery of artillery, a composite group or squadron of aircraft, and a logistical unit.

CAS (Close Air Support)—air action, including air strikes by fixed or rotary-winged aircraft against hostile targets, in direct support of and near friendly ground forces.

CINCLANT—Commander in Chief of Atlantic Forces.

CINCPAC—Commander in Chief of Pacific Forces.

Company—three to four platoons that serve under a battalion. Usually commanded by a captain.

Congressional Medal of Honor (also known as Medal of Honor or MOH)—highest military award for valor, usually presented by the president of the United States.

CP (Command Post)—in combat, a unit's headquarters in which the unit commander is located or from which such commander operates.

C-rations—Marine-carried individual meals carried in areas without kitchen facilities that include pre-cooked food in cans.

DCSA (deputy chief of staff for aviation)—a lieutenant general based at Headquarters Marine Corps in charge of all Marine Corps Aviation units.

Debarkation—orderly process of Marines leaving a ship with their equipment to enter combat.

DI (Drill Instructor)—a sergeant responsible for training enlisted recruits at boot camp. At Officer Candidate School, this position is known as "Sergeant Instructor."

Division— in the Marine Corps, a division usually consists of three infantry regiments, one artillery regiment, and task-organized additional attached specialty units.

DPPA (Defense POW Accounting Agency)—located in Hawaii, this organization tracks missing military members and identifies their remains once found.

FAC (Forward Air Controller)—ground controller of close air support.

FAC(A)—airborne controller of close air support.

FASTFAC—airborne controller of close air support in the backseat of a fast attack or fighter jet aircraft.

Fighter Squadron—unit of fighters, intercept operators, maintenance, and support personnel.

Foxhole—dirt hole dug for a Marine to take cover during combat—also known as a "fighting hole."

Frequent Wind—name of the operation for the evacuation of Saigon, April 1975.

G-1—at the division level or above, the G-1 is responsible for administration. The designation applies to both the unit and commanding officer of the G-1 unit.

G-2—at the division level or above, the G-2 is responsible for intelligence. The designation applies to both the unit and commanding officer of the G-2 unit.

G-3—at the division level or above, the G-3 is responsible for operations. The designation applies to both the unit and commanding officer of the G-3 unit.

G-4—at the division level or above, the G-4 is responsible for logistics. The designation applies to both the unit and commanding officer of the G-4 unit.

Grunt—nickname for Marine rifleman.

Gunny—a shortened version of the gunnery sergeant rank.

H—first letter in a helicopter squadron or the first letter in the division rifle company, e.g. How Company.

Hill [number] e.g., Hill 1081—method of naming local hills by the height of the hill above sea level. Hill 1081 in Korea was 1,081 meters above sea level.

HMH—Heavy Marine Helicopter squadron containing CH-53s.

HML—Light Marine Helicopter squadron containing Hueys.

HMLA—Light Marine Attack Helicopter squadron initially containing Huey gunships and Cobras in Vietnam; it now contains AH-1Z Vipers.

HMM—Medium Marine Helicopter squadron, containing CH-46s in Vietnam and Ospreys today.

HQMC (also known as HMC)—Headquarters Marine Corps, located at the Pentagon.

I&I (Inspector-Instructor)—active-duty Marine used to support Reserve training and keep unit moving between the drill periods.

JCS (Joint Chiefs of Staff)—leaders of Army, Navy, Marine Corps, and Marine Corps reporting to the chairman JCS. The chairman reports to the president of the United States as the senior military advisor.

Log Book—a pilot's personal flying record containing the following information: type of aircraft flown, date, time, length of flight, and flight purpose. Log books remain with pilots throughout their careers.

LZ (Landing zone)—area for an aircraft to land.

MAB—Marine Amphibious Brigade.

MAG (Marine Aircraft Group)—multiple squadrons of fixed-wing and/or rotary wing aircraft.

MAW (Marine Aviation Wing)—multiple Marine Aircraft Groups report to the Wing.

MCAS (Marine Corps Air Station)—base for Marine aviators, airstrip, maintenance, support, and staff.

MCB (Marine Corps Base)—large base for Marine Corps ground units.

MEB—Marine Expeditionary Brigade.

MSR (Main Supply Route)—road used to move combatants and their equipment, in a combat area. In Korea the routes were often single-lane dirt roads.

NATO (North American Treaty Organization)—a mutual defense pact among the United States and European allies. Established following World War II, it originally had 15 member countries.

OCS (Officer Candidate School)—in the Marine Corps, where future officers received their initial training prior to earning their commission as second lieutenants.

Ordnance—military weapons and ammunition.

Platoon—a unit made up of squads reporting to a platoon commander, who is often a second lieutenant.

PT Boat (Patrol Torpedo Boat)—this small-engine boat was used by the U.S. Navy during World War II.

Quantico—shortened name for Marine Corps Base Quantico, Virginia, where all Marine officers receive their initial training before and after being commissioned and where training and education programs are both developed and implemented.

RIO (Radar Intercept Operator)—flies with a fighter pilot handling navigation. Also called "guy in the back" (GIB) or "back seater."

SEATO (Southeast Asia Treaty Organization)—countries including the United States organized for the mutual protection of Southeast Asia.

SITREP (Situation Report)—summary of activities provided to commanders.

S-1—below the division level, the S-1 is responsible for administration. The designation applies to both the unit and commanding officer of the S-1 unit.

S-2—below the division level, the S-2 is responsible for intelligence. The designation applies to both the unit and commanding officer of the S-2 unit.

S-3—below the division level, the S-3 is responsible for operations. The designation applies to both the unit and commanding officer of the S-3 unit.

S-4—below the division level, the S-4 is responsible for logistics. The designation applies to both the unit and commanding officer of the S-4 unit.

Task Force—a military organization designed to accomplish a specific mission.

TBS (The Basic School)—training program for newly commissioned second lieutenants. Training covers all facets of the Marine Corps. When General Carey completed the program, it was 36 weeks long. In 2022, it is 28 weeks long.

USMC—United States Marine Corps.

USS—United States Ship.

USNS—United States Naval Ship.

V—the first letter in the name of a squadron flying fixed-wing aircraft (V is taken from the first letter of the French verb *voler*—to fly).

V-5—U.S. Navy World War II flight training program.

Viet Cong—communist forces in South Vietnam, also known as VC or National Liberation Front (NLF) of South Vietnam.

Wing Commander—commander of an aviation wing. The USMC equivalent of a division commander.

XO (Executive Officer)—second-in-command in a unit with responsibility for directing administration, logistics, intelligence, and operations.

Yank—nickname for an American service member.

Yankee imperialism—charge of takeover of a country by the United States.

Bibliography

Baker, Hal (ed.), *Transcripts—Robert B. Gault—Inchon—Chosin—10 July 1951 Korean War Project Record USMC 1025*. Maryland: United States Marine Corps History Division.

Carey, Richard E. (Lieutenant General USMC, Ret), written for *Battle Stories of the Korean War Heroes, My Last Mission*. The Sae Eden Presbyterian Church, 2011.

Dunham, Major George R. and Colonel David A. Quinlan, *U.S. Marines in Vietnam, The Bitter End 1973*–1975. Washington, D.C.: History and Museums Division, Headquarters U.S. Marine Corps, 1997.

George Company 3/1, *Volume II Majoni-Hagaru-Ri, 1950*, August 6, 1989, 17.

Holk, Major Richard P., U.S. Army, "Print Coverage of Military Conflict: the *Los Angeles Times* and the Vietnam War (A content analysis, 1964–1972)" written as a thesis for his Master of Arts degree in communication at California State University, Fullerton, in 1979.

Members of George Company, 3rd Battalion, 1st Marines (3/1), *Volume I Inchon Seoul.*

Minor, Augusta Denita, "A content analysis: attitudes of the *New York Times and the Washington Post* toward the Vietnam War as expressed in editorials (1968) (1981). Retrospective theses and dissertations. 18583. https:lib.dr.iastate.edu//dissertations. rrd/18583.

Mossman, Billy C., *United States Army in the Korean War Ebb and Flow November 1950–July* 1951. Washington, D.C.: Center of Military History United States Army, 1990.

Nelson, Christopher, Major, U.S. Marine Corps, "The Tet Offensive 1968: A 50-Year Reflection on the Impact of Information, Influence, and Culture," accessed August 21, 2021, https://www.usmcu.edu/Portals/218/LLI/MLD/Tet%20OffensiveCase_FINAL.pdf?ver=2019-02-26-152753-987

Parker, Lieutenant Colonel Gary W. and Major Frank M. Batha, *A History of Marine Observation Squadron* Six. Washington, D.C.: History and Museums Division, Headquarters, U.S. Marine Corps, 1982.

Quilter II, Colonel Charles J., U.S. Marine Corps Reserve, *U.S. Marines in the Persian Gulf, 1990–1991: With the I Marine Expeditionary Force in Desert Shield and Desert Storm*. Washington, D.C.: History and Museums Division, Headquarters United States Marine Corps, 1993.

Shulismson, Jack, Lieutenant Colonel Leonard A. Blasiol, U.S. Marine Corps, Charles R. Smith, and Captain David A. Dawson, *U.S. Marines in Vietnam: The Defining Year 1968*. Washington, D.C.: History and Museums Division, Headquarters U.S. Marine Corps, 1997.

Smith, Charles R. (editor), *U.S. Marines in the Korean War*. History Division, United States Marine Corps, Washington, D.C., 2007.

Endnotes

Chapter 1: The Early Years

1 *Occident*, yearbook of West High School, Columbus, OH, 1945.
2 Lieutenant General Richard E. Carey, USMC (Ret) interview with the author, June 8, 2021.
3 Lieutenant General Richard E. Carey, interview with the author, September 8, 2021.
4 Lieutenant General Richard E. Carey, interview with the author, May 28, 2021.
5 "Aviation Cadet Training Program (USN)," Military Wiki, accessed June 2, 2021, https://military.wikia.org/wiki/Aviation_Cadet_Training_Program_(USN)#1942-1945.
6 Interview with Lieutenant General Richard E. Carey, USMC (Ret) United States Marine Corps History Division GRC Archives, by Dr. Fred Allison, November 1, 2012. Accessed September 27, 2021.
7 Lieutenant General Richard E. Carey, interview with the author, May 28, 2021.
8 "A Brief History of the United States Marine Corps," accessed October 10, 2022, https://www.mclwestchester.org/knowledge-base/marine-corps-hymn-history/a-brief-history-of-the-united-states-marine-corps/.
9 Ibid.
10 Ibid.
11 Ibid.
12 "Marine Corps Values," Marines, accessed September 19, 2021, https://www.marines.com/life-as-a-marine/standards/values.html.
13 During World War I, 3.6 percent of total Marines died versus 2.6 percent for the Army and 1.4 percent for the Navy. In World War II, Marine deaths equaled 3.6 percent of total members of the Marine Corps in service. Army deaths hit 3.3 percent of those who served, and the Navy lost 1.4 percent of their members. In Korea, the Marine deaths were 1.06 percent. Army deaths were 1.04 percent of their soldiers. The Navy's deaths totaled 0.5 percent of their sailors. The Air Force lost 0.1 percent. Korea marked the first time Air Force casualty figures were separate from the Army. In Vietnam, the percentage of Marine Corps deaths topped the combined percentages of the Army, Navy, and Air Force. The Marines lost 1.8 percent while the three other branches combined losses totaled 1.1 percent of their total force. During Korea, the Marines had 12.4 percent of the total deaths in that war despite having only 7.4 percent of the total service members. Nese F. DeBruyne, "American War and Military Operations Casualties: Lists and Statistics," accessed September 19, 2021, https://www.census.gov/history/pdf/wwi-casualties112018.pdf.
14 "The Commandant of the Marine Corps and the JCS," accessed January 11, 2022, https://www.hqmc.marines.mil/Portals/61/Docs/OLA/The%20Commandant%20of%20the%20Marine%20Corps%20and%20the%20JCS.pdf.

15 "Boxer V (CV-21)," Naval History and Heritage Command, accessed May 29, 2021, https://www.history.navy.mil/research/histories/ship-histories/danfs/b/boxer-v.html.
16 "Captain's gig," Military Wiki, accessed June 18, 2021, https://military-history.fandom.com/wiki/Captain%27s_gig.
17 Lieutenant General Richard E. Carey, interview with the author, June 17, 2021.
18 Lieutenant General Richard E. Carey, interview with the author, June 15, 2021.
19 Lieutenant General Richard E. Carey, interview with the author, June 15, 2021.

Chapter 2: On to Korea

1 "U.S. Military Manpower—1789 to 1997," Alternate Wars, accessed October 16, 2021, http://alternatewars.com/BBOW/Stats/US_Mil_Manpower_1789-1997.htm.
2 Ibid.
3 Lieutenant General Richard E. Carey, interview with the author, June 17, 2021.
4 Lieutenant General Richard E. Carey, interviews with the author, May 28 and June 17, 2021.
5 Members of George Company, 3rd Battalion, 1st Marines (3/1), *Volume I Inchon Seoul*, 7.
6 Lieutenant General Richard E. Carey, interview with the author, June 17, 2021.
7 Interview with Richard E. Carey, OH0443. Vietnam Center and Sam Johnson Vietnam Archive, September 19, 2005, Lieutenant General Richard E. Carey Collection, Vietnam Center and Sam Johnson Vietnam Archive, Texas Tech University, accessed June 13, 2021, https://www.vietnam.ttu.edu/virtualarchive/items.php?item=OH0443.
8 Lieutenant General Richard E. Carey, interview with the author, June 15, 2021.
9 Interview with Richard E. Carey, OH0443. Vietnam Center and Sam Johnson Vietnam Archive, September 19, 2005, Lieutenant General Richard E. Carey Collection, Vietnam Center and Sam Johnson Vietnam Archive, Texas Tech University, accessed June 13, 2021, https://www.vietnam.ttu.edu/virtualarchive/items.php?item=OH0443.
10 The USNS *Simon B. Buckner* honored Army Lieutenant General Simon B. Buckner. General Buckner lost his life to enemy fire in Okinawa on June 18, 1945. He was one of three U.S. Army lieutenant generals killed in World War II.
11 "What is the Importance of the Inchon Landing During the Korean War?" accessed October 9, 2022, https://classroom.synonym.com/importance-inchon-landing-during-korean-war-8832.html.
12 Lieutenant General Richard E. Carey, interviews with the author, June 15 and June 17, 2021.
13 1st Marine Regiment 3rd Battalion—Special Action Report—August 28, 1950–December 15, 1950, Korean War Project-USMC-1357.
14 Ibid.
15 Andrew H. Hershey, "Marines at Pusan Perimeter Korea, 1950: You Take Command," Historynet, accessed March 27, 2022, https://www.historynet.com/marines-pusan-perimeter-korea-1950-take-command/.
16 1st Marine Regiment 3rd Battalion—Special Action Report—August 28, 1950–December 15, 1950, Korean War Project-USMC-1357.
17 Bob Harbula, interview with the author, June 22, 2021. Mr. Harbula served as a machine gunner with Lieutenant Carey as a member of George Company, 3rd Battalion, 1st Marines (G/3/1). He said that he fired his machine gun for the first time after arriving at Inchon on the way to Seoul. Before arriving at Camp Pendleton, Private Harbula had a ceremonial assignment at 8th & I Streets barracks in Washington, D.C. There he participated in parades, burial ceremonies, and guarded President Truman when he went to Shang Ra La, a presidential retreat

in the mountains of Maryland renamed Camp David by President Dwight D. Eisenhower. Mr. Harbula said that he volunteered for duty in Korea and received machine gun training while on the *Buckner*.

18 Bob Harbula, telephone interview with the author, June 22, 2021.

19 Lieutenant General Richard E. Carey, interview with the author, June 15, 2021.

20 1st Marine Regiment 3rd Battalion—Special Action Report—August 28, 1950–December 15, 1950, Korean War Project-USMC-1357.

21 Bob Harbula, telephone interview with the author, June 22, 2021.

22 "Navy Officer Praises Marine Courage at Inchon Landing," *Napa Journal*, October 15, 1950.

23 Hanson Baldwin, "MacArthur Inchon Plan Saved Korea," *Los Angeles Times*, November 13, 1950. Baldwin, a U.S. Naval Academy graduate, served on active duty in the Navy during the 1920s. He won a Pulitzer Prize for his reporting on the war in the South Pacific during World War II.

24 Associated Press, "Opposition at Inchon is mopped up," *Des Moines Register*, September 16, 1950.

25 "Wizardry … or luck," *Charlotte News*, October 12, 1950.

26 "4 ½ miles gained in southern offensive," *Indianapolis News*, September 16, 1950.

27 Lieutenant General Richard E. Carey, interview with the author, May 28, 2021.

28 Lieutenant General Richard E. Carey, interview with the author, June 15, 2021.

29 Interview with Richard E. Carey, OH0443. Vietnam Center and Sam Johnson Vietnam Archive, September 19, 2005, Lieutenant General Richard E. Carey Collection, Vietnam Center and Sam Johnson Vietnam Archive, Texas Tech University, accessed June 10, 2021, https://www.vietnam.ttu.edu/virtualarchive/items.php?item=OH0443.

30 Lieutenant General Richard E. Carey, interview with the author, March 23, 2022.

31 1st Marine Regiment 3rd Battalion—Special Action Report—August 28, 1950–December 15, 1950, Korean War Project-USMC-1357.

32 Lieutenant General Richard E. Carey, interview with the author, June 15, 2021.

33 Lieutenant General Richard E. Carey, interview with the author, June 15, 2021.

34 Interview with Richard E. Carey, OH0443. Vietnam Center and Sam Johnson Vietnam Archive, September 19, 2005, Lieutenant General Richard E. Carey Collection, Vietnam Center and Sam Johnson Vietnam Archive, Texas Tech University, accessed June 10, 2021, https://www.vietnam.ttu.edu/virtualarchive/items.php?item=OH0443.

35 Interview with Lieutenant General Richard E. Carey, United States Marine Corps History Division GRC Archives, by Dr. Fred Allison, November 1, 2012, accessed September 27, 2021.

36 In 1964, Ridge retired from the Marine Corps as a full colonel and went to work as a Department of Defense civilian employee. He held the post of assistant director in the office of the assistant secretary of defense for International Security Affairs. "Thomas L. Ridge," Wikipedia, accessed July 6, 2021, https://en.wikipedia.org/wiki/Thomas_L._Ridge.

37 1st Marine Regiment 3rd Battalion—Special Action Report—August 28, 1950–December 15, 1950, Korean War Project-USMC-1357.

38 "Veterans' Memoirs—Orace Leon Edwards," Korean War Educator, accessed September 27, 2021, http://www.koreanwar-educator.org/memoirs/edwards_orace/index.htm.

39 Ibid.

40 Third Battalion received information on movement to Majon-ni only one day in advance. In addition, the battalion had no rehearsal for the landing at Wonsan.

Chapter 3: A New Role—Chosin Reservoir Campaign

1 Interview with Richard E. Carey, OH0443. Vietnam Center and Sam Johnson Vietnam Archive, September 19, 2005, Lieutenant General Richard E. Carey Collection, Vietnam Center and Sam Johnson Vietnam Archive, Texas Tech University, accessed June 10, 2021, https://www.vietnam.ttu.edu/virtualarchive/items.php?item=OH0443.

2 Interview with Richard E. Carey, OH0443. Vietnam Center and Sam Johnson Vietnam Archive, September 19, 2005, Lieutenant General Richard E. Carey Collection, Vietnam Center and Sam Johnson Vietnam Archive, Texas Tech University, accessed June 10, 2021, https://www.vietnam.ttu.edu/virtualarchive/items.php?item=OH0443.

3 Ibid.

4 Charles R. Smith (editor), *U.S. Marines in the Korean War*, (History Division, United States Marine Corps, Washington, D.C., 2007), 255.

5 George Company 3/1, *Volume II Majoni-Hagaru-Ri, 1950*, August 6, 1989, 17.

6 Harris, an 11-year veteran of the Marine Corps, had just received command of 3/7. During World War II, he served on Corregidor in the Pacific. The Japanese took him as a prisoner of war. While fighting at the Chosin Reservoir, Harris went missing on December 7, 1950. Later, the Marines listed him as presumed dead. His father, Lieutenant General Field Harris, commanded the 1st Marine Air Wing (MAW) during the Korean War.

7 Smith, *U.S. Marines in the Korean War*, 221.

8 Ibid., 225.

9 Lieutenant General Richard E. Carey, interview with the author, July 8, 2021.

10 Second Lieutenant Richard E. Carey, "Post November 23 – December 6, 1950," undated report covering Hagaru-ri.

11 Ibid.

12 Ibid.

13 Smith, *U.S. Marines in the Korean War*, 255.

14 Ibid.

15 Interview with Richard E. Carey, OH0443. Vietnam Center and Sam Johnson Vietnam Archive, September 19, 2005, Lieutenant General Richard E. Carey Collection, Vietnam Center and Sam Johnson Vietnam Archive, Texas Tech University, accessed June 10, 2021, https://www.vietnam.ttu.edu/virtualarchive/items.php?item=OH0443.

16 Carey, "Post November 23 – December 6, 1950."

17 Lieutenant Richard E. Carey, interview with the author, January 12, 2022.

18 Interview with Richard E. Carey, OH0443. Vietnam Center and Sam Johnson Vietnam Archive, September 19, 2005, Lieutenant General Richard E. Carey Collection, Vietnam Center and Sam Johnson Vietnam Archive, Texas Tech University, accessed June 10, 2021, https://www.vietnam.ttu.edu/virtualarchive/items.php?item=OH0443.

19 Carey, "Post November 23 – December 6, 1950."

20 William Chapman, "Battalion loses 60 pct. of men, equipment," *The Albany (OR) Democrat-Herald*, December 11, 1950.

21 Interview with Richard E. Carey, OH0443. Vietnam Center and Sam Johnson Vietnam Archive, September 19, 2005, Lieutenant General Richard E. Carey Collection, Vietnam Center and Sam Johnson Vietnam Archive, Texas Tech University, accessed June 10, 2021, https://www.vietnam.ttu.edu/virtualarchive/items.php?item=OH0443.

22 Lieutenant General Richard E. Carey, interview with the author, June 15, 2021.

23 Lieutenant General Richard E. Carey, interview with the author, November 3, 2021.

24 Billy C. Mossman, *United States Army in the Korean War Ebb and Flow November 1950–July 1951* (Washington, D.C.: Center of Military History United States Army, 1990), 100.
25 Lieutenant General Richard E. Carey, interview with the author, February 9, 2022.
26 Smith, *The U.S. Marines in the Korean War*, 274.
27 "Veterans' Memoirs—Orace Leon Edwards," Korean War Educator, accessed September 27, 2021, http://www.koreanwar-educator.org/memoirs/edwards_orace/index.htm.
28 McLaughlin remained a POW until September 1953, a month and half after the signing of the armistice. He received the Legion of Merit "for exceptionally meritorious conduct in the performance of outstanding services to the Government of the United States in Korea while interned as a Prisoner of War." A World War II veteran of the Pacific where he earned the Silver Star for actions at the Peleliu Airfield, McLaughlin remained in the Marine Corps until 1977. He rose to the rank of lieutenant general and commanded the Fleet Marine Force Pacific (FMFPAC) when he retired after 36 years of service. "John N. McLaughlin," Wikipedia, accessed November 22, 2021, https://en.wikipedia.org/wiki/John_N._McLaughlin.
29 Lieutenant General Richard E. Carey, telephone interview with the author, November 22, 2021.
30 Email from Gordon Payne to the author, December 30, 2021.
31 Email from Gordon Payne to the author, August 19, 2021.
32 http://4mermarine.com/USMC/quotes.html, accessed October 10, 2022.
33 Email from Gordon Payne to the author, August 19, 2021.
34 Lieutenant General Richard E. Carey, interview with the author, August 25, 2021.
35 George Company 3/1, V*olume II Majoni-Hagaru-Ri, 1950*, August 6, 1989, 21.
36 "Rocco A. Zullo—Obituary," accessed October 15, 2022, https://www.stringerfh.com/obituary/3323573.
37 1st Marine Regiment 3rd Battalion—Special Action Report—August 28, 1950 – December 15, 1950, Korean War Project-USMC-1357.
38 "Chapter 1 Cover, Concealment, and Camouflage," accessed October 10, 2022, https://www.globalsecurity.org/military/library/policy/army/fm/21-75/Ch1.htm.
39 Interview with Richard E. Carey, OH0443. Vietnam Center and Sam Johnson Vietnam Archive, September 19, 2005, Lieutenant General Richard E. Carey Collection, Vietnam Center and Sam Johnson Vietnam Archive, Texas Tech University, accessed June 10, 2021, https://www.vietnam.ttu.edu/virtualarchive/items.php?item=OH0443.
40 Carey, "Post November 23 – December 6, 1950."
41 Interview with Richard E. Carey, OH0443. Vietnam Center and Sam Johnson Vietnam Archive, September 19, 2005, Lieutenant General Richard E. Carey Collection, Vietnam Center and Sam Johnson Vietnam Archive, Texas Tech University, accessed June 10, 2021, https://www.vietnam.ttu.edu/virtualarchive/items.php?item=OH0443.
42 Lieutenant General Richard E. Carey, interview with the author, June 24, 2021.
43 Interview with Lieutenant General Richard E. Carey, United States Marine Corps History Division GRC Archives, by Dr. Fred Allison, November 1, 2012, accessed September 27, 2021.
44 Bob Harbula, telephone interview with the author, June 22, 2021.
45 Interview with Richard E. Carey, OH0443. Vietnam Center and Sam Johnson Vietnam Archive, September 19, 2005, Lieutenant General Richard E. Carey Collection, Vietnam Center and Sam Johnson Vietnam Archive, Texas Tech University, accessed June 10, 2021, https://www.vietnam.ttu.edu/virtualarchive/items.php?item=OH0443.
46 Ibid.

47 Captain Sitter's efforts in Hell Fire Valley and East Hill earned him the Medal of Honor. He retired as a full colonel after 30 years that also included service in World War II and Vietnam.
48 Lieutenant General Richard E. Carey, interview with the author, January 5, 2022.
49 1st Marine Regiment 3rd Battalion—Special Action Report—August 28, 1950 – December 15, 1950, Korean War Project-USMC-1357.
50 Interview with Lieutenant General Richard E. Carey, United States Marine Corps History Division GRC Archives, by Dr. Fred Allison, November 1, 2012, accessed September 27, 2021.
51 Lieutenant General Richard E. Carey, interview with the author, January 5, 2022.
52 Lieutenant General Richard E. Carey, interview with the author, August 6, 2021.
53 Carey, "Post November 23 – December 6, 1950."
54 "How Tootsie Rolls Accidentally Saved Marines During War," Marine Corps Community Services, accessed July 5, 2021, https://www.usmc-mccs.org/articles/how-tootsie-rolls-accidentally-saved-marines-during-war/.
55 "Forgotten: The Arkansas Korean War Project—The Veterans," accessed November 26, 2021, http://bc-digital.org/koreanwarproject/veterans.html#p.
56 Peterson, a native of General Carey's hometown of Columbus, Ohio, later served in Vietnam and retired from the Marine Corps in 1967. "Forgotten: The Arkansas Korean War Project—The Veterans," accessed November 26, 2021, http://bc-digital.org/koreanwarproject/veterans.html#p.
57 Steve Liewer, "UNL professor: Marine killed in Frozen Chosin battle was starving, too," *Omaha World Herald*, accessed November 22, 2021, https://omaha.com/news/state-and-regional/unl-professor-marine-killed-in-frozen-chosin-battle-was-starving-too/article_d3e09c68-d2e0-11eb-99df-63e671af2c52.html.
58 Carey, "Post November 23 – December 6, 1950."
59 "Max Hastings on Oliver P. Smith's 'advancing in another direction'," Entersection, accessed July 6, 2021, http://entersection.com/posts/915-max-hastings-on-oliver-p-smiths-advancing-in-another-direction.
60 Before he headed to Korea, Lieutenant Carey met Lieutenant Colonel Ray Davis. Colonel Davis joined the Marine Corps through the Reserve Officers Training Corps after graduating from Georgia Tech University in 1939. As a major, he earned the Navy Cross during World War II while serving on Peleliu in the Palau Islands. During the summer of 1950, Davis led the 9th Marine Corps Reserve Infantry Battalion in Chicago. He held the position of Inspector-Instructor known as I & I. While at Camp Lejeune for a planned two-week training period, the battalion Davis led received orders for Korea. Many members of the battalion had not even been through boot camp, due to budget cuts. Much of their training took place on the ship heading to Korea. Colonel Davis led that training. In Korea, he earned the Congressional Medal of Honor for leading efforts to pull out a "beleaguered rifle company" surrounded by Chinese soldiers at Toktong Pass in North Korea. After serving as the commanding general of the 3rd Marine Division in Vietnam, General Davis assumed the position of commanding general, Marine Corps Development and Education Command at Quantico in 1970. Nine months after arriving at Quantico, General Davis earned his fourth star when he became assistant commandant of the Marine Corps (ACMC). General Davis retired in 1972.
61 Interview with Richard E. Carey, OH0443. Vietnam Center and Sam Johnson Vietnam Archive, September 19, 2005, Lieutenant General Richard E. Carey Collection, Vietnam Center and Sam Johnson Vietnam Archive, Texas Tech University, accessed June 10, 2021, https://www.vietnam.ttu.edu/virtualarchive/items.php?item=OH0443.

62 "Forgotten: The Arkansas Korean War Project—The Veterans," accessed November 26, 2021, http://bc-digital.org/koreanwarproject/veterans.html#p.
63 Smith, *U.S. Marines in the Korean War*, 312.
64 Watson Crumbie, interview with the author, December 12, 2021.
65 Hal Baker (ed.), *Transcripts—Robert B. Gault—Inchon—Chosin—10 July 1951 Korean War Project Record USMC 1025*, (Maryland: United States Marine Corps History Division), 15.
66 Jim G. Lucas, "Leathernecks dump out frozen dead," *The Pittsburgh Press*, December 6, 1950.
67 Baker, *Transcripts—Robert B. Gault*, 41.
68 Lieutenant General Richard E. Carey, interview with the author, January 5, 2022.
69 Baker, *Transcripts—Robert B. Gault*, 38–9.
70 According to Mrs. Carroll, her father volunteered to fly the Treadway bridge drop sortie from Japan, a round trip of approximately 1,300 air miles. Mrs. Carroll said that her father earned the Legion of Merit for leading his squadron's Treadway bridge drop. Flying into danger was not new for her father. In World War II, Thompson flew a C-47 with paratroopers from the 82nd Airborne Division to Normandy on D-Day. In 1969, Colonel Thompson retired after serving as the base commander at Travis Air Force Base, California.
71 Colonel Partridge received a gold star, in lieu of a second Legion of Merit. The award covered the period in Korea between November 3, 1950, and April 20, 1951, including the placement of the Treadway bridge over Funchilin Pass.
72 Marc D. Bernstein, "Americans Faced Blown Out Bridge During Retreat To 38th Parallel," Warfare History Network, accessed July 15, 2021, https://warfarehistorynetwork.com/americans-faced-blown-out-bridge-during-retreat-to-38th-parallel/.
73 Watson Crumbie, interview with the author, December 12, 2021.
74 Interview with General Robert H. Barrow United States Marine Corps (Ret), Oral History Transcript, History Division United States Marine Corps, Quantico, VA. Released 2015. Interview conducted by BG Edwin H. Simmons, accessed January 13, 2022.
75 Interview with Richard E. Carey, OH0443. Vietnam Center and Sam Johnson Vietnam Archive, September 19, 2005, Lieutenant General Richard E. Carey Collection, Vietnam Center and Sam Johnson Vietnam Archive, Texas Tech University, accessed June 10, 2021, https://www.vietnam.ttu.edu/virtualarchive/items.php?item=OH0443.
76 Keyes Beech, "Marines just 'attacked to the rear'," *Pittsburgh Press*, December 12, 1950.
77 Fred Sparks, "Courageous withdrawal was like a modernized caravan of covered wagons—warmed up men ready to avenge their lost comrades," *The Commercial Appeal* (Memphis, TN), December 12, 1950.
78 Email from Gordon Payne to the author, January 17, 2022.
79 Lieutenant General Richard E. Carey, interview with the author, January 12, 2022.
80 Intelligence reports gathered by the U.S. concluded that Chinese casualties at Chosin totaled an estimated minimum of 50,000 including those killed, wounded, and suffering non-battle injuries. (Estimates vary, although captured Chinese documents acknowledged 48,000 casualties. American intelligence sources believe the number could have been significantly more.)
81 Interview with Richard E. Carey, OH0443. Vietnam Center and Sam Johnson Vietnam Archive, September 19, 2005, Lieutenant General Richard E. Carey Collection, Vietnam Center and Sam Johnson Vietnam Archive, Texas Tech University, accessed June 10, 2021, https://www.vietnam.ttu.edu/virtualarchive/items.php?item=OH0443.
82 Lieutenant General Richard E. Carey, interview with the author, September 22, 2021.

83 "Forgotten: The Arkansas Korean War Project—The Veterans," accessed November 26, 2021, http://bc-digital.org/koreanwarproject/veterans.html#p.

Chapter 4: Reflections on Chosin Reservoir

1 "History," Marines, accessed June 18, 2021, https://www.marfork.marines.mil/About/History/#:~:text=In%201950%2C%20the%20Korean%20War%20saw%20the%20Marine,days%2C%20from%20July%2020%20to%20Sept.%2011%2C%201950.
2 Carey, "Post November 23 – December 6, 1950."
3 Before Arthur left for Korea, he was on Mediterranean cruise that took him to Lebanon in the summer of 1950. Twenty-six days and 9,000 miles later, the 21-year-old sergeant participated in the landing at Inchon. Chief Warrant Officer-2 Margarette Chavez, 4th Marine Air Wing/4th Marine Division, "Chosin: An 'advance to the sea'," *Marines*, September 1985, 27.
4 Russell Roemmele, "Build a Monument or We Will," *Bloomfield (NJ) Life*, June 18, 1992.
5 Diana Sevanian, "SCV Vet Remembers the Forgotten War," *The Signal* (Santa Clarita, CA), July 10, 2010.
6 Candace Page, "The Frozen Chosin," *Burlington (VT) Free Press*, November 28, 2010.
7 Walter T. Ham IV, "Veterans mark 60th anniversary of legendary reservoir battle," United States Army, accessed November 23, 2021, https://www.army.mil/article/47908/veterans_mark_60th_anniversary_of_legendary_reservoir_battle.
8 Gary Carter, "A 'Chosin Few' Marines mark wartime experience," *Herald Democrat* (Sherman, Texas), September 10, 2000.

Chapter 5: After Chosin Reservoir

1 Interview with Richard E. Carey, OH0443. Vietnam Center and Sam Johnson Vietnam Archive, September 19, 2005, Lieutenant General Richard E. Carey Collection, Vietnam Center and Sam Johnson Vietnam Archive, Texas Tech University, accessed June 10, 2021, https://www.vietnam.ttu.edu/virtualarchive/items.php?item=OH0443.
2 Ibid.
3 Interview with Richard E. Carey, OH0443. Vietnam Center and Sam Johnson Vietnam Archive, September 19, 2005, Lieutenant General Richard E. Carey Collection, Vietnam Center and Sam Johnson Vietnam Archive, Texas Tech University, accessed June 10, 2021, https://www.vietnam.ttu.edu/virtualarchive/items.php?item=OH0443.
4 General Ridgway headed the 82nd Airborne on D-day during World War II. He later succeeded General MacArthur as commander of UN forces when President Truman relieved MacArthur of his command on April 11, 1951. General Ridgway became the Army chief of staff in 1953 during the administration of President Dwight D. Eisenhower and retired in 1955. Bart Barnes, "Gen. Matthew B. Ridgway Dies," *The Washington Post*, July 27, 1993, https://www.washingtonpost.com/archive/local/1993/07/27/gen-matthew-b-ridgway-dies/0a190e34-8b09-4de5-9db7-8d1619102863/.
5 Interview with Richard E. Carey, OH0443. Vietnam Center and Sam Johnson Vietnam Archive, September 19, 2005, Lieutenant General Richard E. Carey Collection, Vietnam Center and Sam Johnson Vietnam Archive, Texas Tech University, accessed June 10, 2021, https://www.vietnam.ttu.edu/virtualarchive/items.php?item=OH0443.

6 Simmons also served in World War II and Vietnam and eventually rose to the rank of brigadier general. He later held the post as director of Marine Corps History and Museums. His awards and decorations include the Distinguished Service Medal, Silver Star, and Purple Heart. General Simmons wrote six books about the Marine Corps. "Edwin H. Simmons," Wikipedia, accessed July 8, 2021, https://en.wikipedia.org/wiki/Edwin_H._Simmons.

7 Interview with Richard E. Carey, OH0443. Vietnam Center and Sam Johnson Vietnam Archive, September 19, 2005, Lieutenant General Richard E. Carey Collection, Vietnam Center and Sam Johnson Vietnam Archive, Texas Tech University, accessed June 10, 2021, https://www.vietnam.ttu.edu/virtualarchive/items.php?item=OH0443.

8 Richard E. Carey (Lieutenant General USMC, Ret), written for *Battle Stories of the Korean War Heroes, My Last Mission*, (The Sae Eden Presbyterian Church, 2011), 21.

9 Interview with Richard E. Carey, OH0443. Vietnam Center and Sam Johnson Vietnam Archive, September 19, 2005, Lieutenant General Richard E. Carey Collection, Vietnam Center and Sam Johnson Vietnam Archive, Texas Tech University, accessed June 10, 2021, https://www.vietnam.ttu.edu/virtualarchive/items.php?item=OH0443.

10 Carey, *Battle Stories of the Korean War Heroes, My Last Mission*, 22.

11 Interview with Richard E. Carey, OH0443. Vietnam Center and Sam Johnson Vietnam Archive, September 19, 2005, Lieutenant General Richard E. Carey Collection, Vietnam Center and Sam Johnson Vietnam Archive, Texas Tech University, accessed June 10, 2021, https://www.vietnam.ttu.edu/virtualarchive/items.php?item=OH0443.

12 Lieutenant General Richard E. Carey, interview with the author, July 8, 2021.

13 Captain Fisher earned a Silver Star for his actions at Iwo Jima during World War II. He received the Navy Cross for leadership at Chosin Reservoir. Fisher later served in Vietnam commanding, among other units, 2/4 and retired from the Marine Corps as a full colonel in 1968.

14 Email from Colonel James Pendergast to the author, March 2, 2022.

15 Interview with Richard E. Carey, OH0443. Vietnam Center and Sam Johnson Vietnam Archive, September 19, 2005, Lieutenant General Richard E. Carey Collection, Vietnam Center and Sam Johnson Vietnam Archive, Texas Tech University, accessed June 10, 2021, https://www.vietnam.ttu.edu/virtualarchive/items.php?item=OH0443.

16 Ibid.

Chapter 6: Aviation Career Begins

1 President Truman awarded Lieutenant Commiskey the medal in an August 1, 1951 White House ceremony. Attendees at the event included his wife, children, parents, and brother, an Army master sergeant who served as a paratrooper. General Clifford B. Cates, the commandant of the Marine Corps, also attended. "President Truman Presents Medal of Honor to Commiskey," National Archives, accessed October 10, 2022, https://www.trumanlibrary.gov/photograph-records/73-3696.

2 Regarding the term SNJ, the S stood for scout advanced, the N stood for trainer and the J stood for North American, the aircraft's manufacturer. "North American SNJ-4 (AT-6)," National Air and Space Museum, accessed July 15, 2021, https://airandspace.si.edu/collection-objects/north-american-snj-4-6/nasm_A19610123000.

3 "Instrument Procedures Handbook (IPH)," accessed October 5, 2022, https://www.faa.gov/regulations_policies/handbooks_manuals/aviation/instrument_procedures_handbook.

4 Interview with Richard E. Carey, OH0443. Vietnam Center and Sam Johnson Vietnam Archive, September 19, 2005, Lieutenant General Richard E. Carey Collection, Vietnam Center and Sam Johnson Vietnam Archive, Texas Tech University, accessed June 10, 2021, https://www.vietnam.ttu.edu/virtualarchive/items.php?item=OH0443.

5 Interview with Richard E. Carey, OH0443. Vietnam Center and Sam Johnson Vietnam Archive, September 19, 2005, Lieutenant General Richard E. Carey Collection, Vietnam Center and Sam Johnson Vietnam Archive, Texas Tech University, accessed June 10, 2021, https://www.vietnam.ttu.edu/virtualarchive/items.php?item=OH0443.

6 "AD/A-1 Skyraider Bomber," Boeing, accessed July 20, 2021, https://www.boeing.com/history/products/ad-a-1-skyraider-bomber.page.

7 Interview with Richard E. Carey, OH0443. Vietnam Center and Sam Johnson Vietnam Archive, September 19, 2005, Lieutenant General Richard E. Carey Collection, Vietnam Center and Sam Johnson Vietnam Archive, Texas Tech University, accessed June 10, 2021, https://www.vietnam.ttu.edu/virtualarchive/items.php?item=OH0443.

8 Ibid.

9 Ibid.

10 "Quonset Hut History: From World War II & Beyond," Steelmaster, accessed July 23, 2021, https://www.steelmasterusa.com/quonset-huts/history/.

11 Lieutenant General Richard E. Carey, interview with the author, July 22, 2021.

Chapter 7: Mid 1950s to 1960s

1 "F7U Cutlass," National Naval Aviation Museum, accessed January 27, 2022, https://www.history.navy.mil/content/history/museums/nnam/explore/collections/aircraft/f/f7u-cutlass.html.

2 Interview with Richard E. Carey, OH0443. Vietnam Center and Sam Johnson Vietnam Archive, September 19, 2005, Lieutenant General Richard E. Carey Collection, Vietnam Center and Sam Johnson Vietnam Archive, Texas Tech University, accessed June 10, 2021, https://www.vietnam.ttu.edu/virtualarchive/items.php?item=OH0443.

3 Interview with Richard E. Carey, OH0443. Vietnam Center and Sam Johnson Vietnam Archive, September 19, 2005, Lieutenant General Richard E. Carey Collection, Vietnam Center and Sam Johnson Vietnam Archive, Texas Tech University, accessed June 10, 2021, https://www.vietnam.ttu.edu/virtualarchive/items.php?item=OH0443.

4 Howard Norton, "3-man team on moon by 1967 is eyed," *The Baltimore Sun*, May 26, 1961.

5 "110 candidates chosen as U.S. space pioneers," *The Spokesman Review* (Spokane), January 28, 1959.

6 Lieutenant General Richard E. Carey, interview with the author, August 25, 2021.

7 Lieutenant General Richard E. Carey, interview with the author, August 25, 2021.

8 Colonel Bangert, during World War II, landed the first American airplane at Guadalcanal. He also aided in the sinking of the first Japanese battleship. Bangert retired from the Marine Corps as a full colonel after 30 years of service. "COL Douglas Albert Bangert (1918–1992)," Find A Grave, accessed August 9, 2021, https://www.findagrave.com/memorial/34669584/douglas-albert-bangert.

9 Interview with Richard E. Carey, OH0443. Vietnam Center and Sam Johnson Vietnam Archive, September 19, 2005, Lieutenant General Richard E. Carey Collection, Vietnam Center and Sam Johnson Vietnam Archive, Texas Tech University, accessed June 10, 2021, https://www.vietnam.ttu.edu/virtualarchive/items.php?item=OH0443.

10 Ibid.
11 Ibid.
12 "The Philippine-American War, 1899–1902," Office of the Historian, accessed February 15, 2022, https://history.state.gov/milestones/1899-1913/war#:~:text=After%20the%20Spanish%2DAmerican%20War,of%20the%20independent%20Philippine%20Republic.
13 "United States military casualties of war," Wikipedia, accessed October 17, 2021, https://en.wikipedia.org/wiki/United_States_military_casualties_of_war.
14 Interview with Richard E. Carey, OH0443. Vietnam Center and Sam Johnson Vietnam Archive, September 19, 2005, Lieutenant General Richard E. Carey Collection, Vietnam Center and Sam Johnson Vietnam Archive, Texas Tech University, accessed June 10, 2021, https://www.vietnam.ttu.edu/virtualarchive/items.php?item=OH0443.
15 Gene Wilson, "The Origin of Chu Lai, 1965," 220th Aviation Company, accessed December 1, 2021, https://www.catkillers.org/history-chu-lai-name.html.
16 Lieutenant General Richard E. Carey, interview with the author, June 16, 2021.
17 Lieutenant General Richard E. Carey, interview with the author, June 16, 2021.
18 Lieutenant General Richard E. Carey, interview by Bob Porter, January 22, 1995. Oral History Collection/The Sixth Floor Museum at Dealey Plaza, Dallas, accessed September 7, 2021. JFK.org.
19 Lieutenant General Richard E. Carey, interview by Bob Porter, January 22, 1995. Oral History Collection/The Sixth Floor Museum at Dealey Plaza, Dallas. JFK.org, accessed September 7, 2021.
20 Ibid.
21 Ibid.
22 Ibid.
23 Appointed commandant in 1960 by President Dwight D. Eisenhower, Shoup held the position during the Kennedy administration and retired in December 1963 shortly after Johnson succeeded Kennedy. Shoup received the Medal of Honor for his leadership at Tarawa during World War II. "Shoup, David M.," accessed January 27, 2022, https://www.history.navy.mil/our-collections/photography/us-people/s/shoup-david-m.html.
24 Lieutenant General Richard E. Carey, interview with the author, September 8, 2021.
25 Interview with Richard E. Carey, OH0443. Vietnam Center and Sam Johnson Vietnam Archive, September 19, 2005, Lieutenant General Richard E. Carey Collection, Vietnam Center and Sam Johnson Vietnam Archive, Texas Tech University, accessed June 10, 2021, https://www.vietnam.ttu.edu/virtualarchive/items.php?item=OH0443.
26 Tad Szulc, "U.S. asks OAS to create Dominican Neutral Zone," *The Courier Journal* (Louisville, KY), April 30, 1965.
27 Associated Press, "We can win Vietnam," *Arcadia(CA) Daily News-Post*, April 30, 1965.
28 Interview with Richard E. Carey, OH0443. Vietnam Center and Sam Johnson Vietnam Archive, September 19, 2005, Lieutenant General Richard E. Carey Collection, Vietnam Center and Sam Johnson Vietnam Archive, Texas Tech University, accessed June 10, 2021, https://www.vietnam.ttu.edu/virtualarchive/items.php?item=OH0443.
29 Ibid.
30 "The Flying Nightmares, A History of VFMA-513, 1944–1967," 4.
31 Ibid., 9.
32 "Top honors for Col. Carey and the Flying Nightmares," *Windsock* (newspaper of MCAS Cherry Point, NC), June 1, 1967.
33 "Welcome," Marines, accessed August 22, 2021, https://www.mcasyuma.marines.mil/Welcome/.

34 Interview with Richard E. Carey, OH0443. Vietnam Center and Sam Johnson Vietnam Archive, September 19, 2005, Lieutenant General Richard E. Carey Collection, Vietnam Center and Sam Johnson Vietnam Archive, Texas Tech University, accessed June 10, 2021, https://www.vietnam.ttu.edu/virtualarchive/items.php?item=OH0443.
35 "Top honors for Col. Carey and the Flying Nightmares," *Windsock* (newspaper of MCAS Cherry Point, NC), June 1, 1967.
36 Lieutenant General Richard E. Carey, interview with the author, August 25, 2021.

Chapter 8: Fighter Pilot in Vietnam

1 Interview with Richard E. Carey, OH0443. Vietnam Center and Sam Johnson Vietnam Archive, September 19, 2005, Lieutenant General Richard E. Carey Collection, Vietnam Center and Sam Johnson Vietnam Archive, Texas Tech University, accessed June 10, 2021, https://www.vietnam.ttu.edu/virtualarchive/items.php?item=OH0443.
2 Speech by General David M. Shoup, United States Marine Corps (Ret) at the 10 Annual Junior College World Affairs Day at Pierce College, Los Angeles, California. *Congressional Record*, Senate, February 20, 1967, 3976.
3 Jack Shulismson, Lieutenant Colonel Leonard A. Blasiol, U.S. Marine Corps, Charles R. Smith, and Captain David A. Dawson, *U.S. Marines in Vietnam: The Defining Year 1968* (Washington, D.C.: History and Museums Division, Headquarters U.S. Marine Corps, 1997), 460.
4 Lieutenant General Richard E. Carey, interview with the author, July 29, 2021.
5 Lieutenant Colonel Ray Cushman, USMC (Ret), email to the author, December 20, 2021.
6 Lieutenant Colonel Ray Cushman, USMC (Ret), email to the author, January 17, 2022.
7 Gerald Ruud, email to the author, October 6, 2021.
8 After retirement from the Marine Corps with 20 years of service, Horne went to college and earned a law degree. In his civilian career, Horne worked as a contractor with Naval Air Systems Command on F/A-18 and AV-8B (Harrier) programs. Master Sergeant Dave Horne, USMC (Ret), email to the author, October 26, 2021.
9 Lieutenant Colonel Ray Cushman, USMC (Ret), email to the author, January 17, 2022.
10 1st MAW, Marine Command Chronology, January 1968.
11 Interview with Richard E. Carey, OH0443. Vietnam Center and Sam Johnson Vietnam Archive, September 19, 2005, Lieutenant General Richard E. Carey Collection, Vietnam Center and Sam Johnson Vietnam Archive, Texas Tech University, accessed June 10, 2021, https://www.vietnam.ttu.edu/virtualarchive/items.php?item=OH0443.
12 "U.S. Involvement in the Vietnam War: The Tet Offensive, 1968," Office of the Historian, accessed July 23, 2021, https://history.state.gov/milestones/1961-1968/tet.
13 Interview with Richard E. Carey, OH0443. Vietnam Center and Sam Johnson Vietnam Archive, September 19, 2005, Lieutenant General Richard E. Carey Collection, Vietnam Center and Sam Johnson Vietnam Archive, Texas Tech University, accessed June 10, 2021, https://www.vietnam.ttu.edu/virtualarchive/items.php?item=OH0443.
14 United Press International, "Communist infiltration, tenacity, alter Hue from bright to bloody battleground," *The Palladium-Item and Sun Telegram* (Richmond, IN), February 25, 1968.
15 Bernard Weinraub, "Hue battle is over—but there's no escape from death," *The Calgary Herald*, March 2, 1968.
16 Gavin Young, "Hue, murder of a city," *The Age*, Melbourne, Victoria, Australia, March 16, 1968.
17 Major George R. Dunham and Colonel David A. Quinlan, *U.S. Marines in Vietnam, The Bitter End 1973–1975* (Washington, D.C.: History and Museums Division, Headquarters U.S. Marine Corps, 1997), 1990, 150.

18 Lieutenant General Richard E. Carey, remarks prepared for address to Marine Vietnam veterans, July 4, 2004.
19 Interview with Richard E. Carey, OH0443. Vietnam Center and Sam Johnson Vietnam Archive, September 19, 2005, Lieutenant General Richard E. Carey Collection, Vietnam Center and Sam Johnson Vietnam Archive, Texas Tech University, accessed June 10, 2021, https://www.vietnam.ttu.edu/virtualarchive/items.php?item=OH0443.
20 J. David Barron, "Rep. Johnson honors local veterans: combatants recognized for valor on battlefield," *Allen American* (TX), October 12, 2012.
21 Interview with Richard E. Carey, OH0443. Vietnam Center and Sam Johnson Vietnam Archive, September 19, 2005, Lieutenant General Richard E. Carey Collection, Vietnam Center and Sam Johnson Vietnam Archive, Texas Tech University, accessed June 10, 2021, https://www.vietnam.ttu.edu/virtualarchive/items.php?item=OH0443.
22 Lieutenant Colonel Gary W. Parker and Major Frank M. Batha, *A History of Marine Observation Squadron Six* (Washington, D.C.: History and Museums Division, Headquarters, U.S. Marine Corps, 1982), 47.
23 Interview with Lieutenant General Richard E. Carey, United States Marine Corps History Division GRC Archives, by Dr. Fred Allison, November 1, 2012, accessed September 27, 2021.
24 After his return home, Puller earned a law degree from the College of William and Mary. He joined the Department of Defense as an attorney. In 1992, Puller wrote *Fortunate Son, the Healing of a Vietnam Vet.* His autobiography outlined his life as Chesty Puller's son, his service in Vietnam, and the personal struggles he faced with depression and alcohol. The book earned Puller a Pulitzer Prize in 1992. That same year, he took a leave of absence from the Defense Department. Puller then joined the faculty at George Mason University in Fairfax, Virginia, as a writer in residence. Unfortunately, the demons of alcohol and depression followed him and in 1994, he took his life at the age of 48.
25 Interview with Richard E. Carey, OH0443. Vietnam Center and Sam Johnson Vietnam Archive, September 19, 2005, Lieutenant General Richard E. Carey Collection, Vietnam Center and Sam Johnson Vietnam Archive, Texas Tech University, accessed June 10, 2021, https://www.vietnam.ttu.edu/virtualarchive/items.php?item=OH0443.
26 President Lyndon B. Johnson's March 31, 1968, speech.
27 "U.S. Involvement in the Vietnam War: The Tet Offensive," Office of the Historian, accessed July 23, 2021, https://history.state.gov/milestones/1961-1968/tet/1961-1968/.
28 "Tet Offensive," History.com, accessed July 17, 2021, https://www.history.com/topics/vietnam-war/tet-offensive.
29 "In Memoriam: Corporal James C. Marshall," Marine Embassy Guard Association, accessed March 29, 2022, https://embassymarine.org/events/inmemoriam-cpljcmarshall/.
30 Interview with Richard E. Carey, OH0443. Vietnam Center and Sam Johnson Vietnam Archive, September 19, 2005, Lieutenant General Richard E. Carey Collection, Vietnam Center and Sam Johnson Vietnam Archive, Texas Tech University, accessed June 10, 2021, https://www.vietnam.ttu.edu/virtualarchive/items.php?item=OH0443.
31 Associated Press, "Air attacks limited to DMZ Area," *St. Louis Post-Dispatch*, April 1, 1968.
32 Interview with Richard E. Carey, OH0443. Vietnam Center and Sam Johnson Vietnam Archive, September 19, 2005, Lieutenant General Richard E. Carey Collection, Vietnam Center and Sam Johnson Vietnam Archive, Texas Tech University, accessed June 10, 2021, https://www.vietnam.ttu.edu/virtualarchive/items.php?item=OH0443.
33 Lieutenant General Richard E. Carey USMC (Ret), remarks prepared for address to Marine Vietnam veterans July 4, 2004.

34 Congressional Record Volume 141, Number 129 (Friday, August 4, 1995), H8514-H8515. From the Congressional Record Online through the Government Publishing Office, accessed September 10, 2021, https://www.govinfo.gov/content/pkg/CREC-1995-08-04/html/CREC-1995-08-04-pt1-PgH8514.htm.
35 Ibid.
36 Lieutenant General Richard E. Carey, USMC (Ret) speech to Veterans Administration North Texas Veterans' Forum: "What is Tet?" on January 31, 2006.

Chapter 9: Vietnam Media Coverage

1 Interview with Richard E. Carey, OH0443. Vietnam Center and Sam Johnson Vietnam Archive, September 19, 2005, Lieutenant General Richard E. Carey Collection, Vietnam Center and Sam Johnson Vietnam Archive, Texas Tech University, accessed June 10, 2021, https://www.vietnam.ttu.edu/virtualarchive/items.php?item=OH0443.
2 https://freerepublic.com/focus/f-news/1230436/posts, accessed October 10, 2022.
3 McGovern flew 35 B-24 Liberator sorties over Europe and received the Distinguished Flying Cross and three Air Medals.
4 File scanned from "Vietnam (23)" Box 20, National Security Advisor, Presidential Country Files for East Asia and the Pacific, Gerald R. Ford Presidential Library.
5 "Number of daily newspapers in the United States from 1970 to 2018," Statista, accessed August 29, 2021, https://www.statista.com/statistics/183408/number-of-us-daily-newspapers-since-1975/#:~:text=The%20number%20of%20daily%20newspapers%20in%20the%20U.S.,many%20might%20expect.%20Daily%20newspapers%20in%20the%20U.S.
6 Interview with Richard E. Carey, OH0443. Vietnam Center and Sam Johnson Vietnam Archive, September 19, 2005, Lieutenant General Richard E. Carey Collection, Vietnam Center and Sam Johnson Vietnam Archive, Texas Tech University, accessed June 10, 2021, https://www.vietnam.ttu.edu/virtualarchive/items.php?item=OH0443.
7 "Tet Offensive," accessed August 30, 2021, https://www.history.com/topics/vietnam-war/tet-offensive.
8 Major Richard P. Holk, U.S. Army, "Print Coverage of Military Conflict: the *Los Angeles Times* and the Vietnam War (A content analysis, 1964–1972)" written as a thesis for his Master of Arts degree in communication at California State University, Fullerton, in 1979.
9 Augusta Denita Minor, "A content analysis: attitudes of *The New York Times* and the *Washington Post* toward the Vietnam War, as expressed in their editorials (1968)" (1981). Retrospective Theses and Dissertations. 18583. https://lib.dr.iastate.edu/rtd/18583.
10 Robert W. Merry, "Cronkite's Vietnam Blunder," accessed August 28, 2021, https://nationalinterest.org/commentary/cronkites-vietnam-blunder-7185.
11 Major Christopher Nelson, "The Tet Offensive 1968: A 50-Year Reflection on the Impact of Information, Influence, and Culture," accessed August 29, 2021, https://www.usmcu.edu/Portals/218/LLI/MLD/Tet%20Offensive%20Case_FINAL.pdf?ver=2019-02-26-152753-987.
12 Lieutenant General Richard E. Carey, USMC (Ret) letter to Brigadier E.H. Simmons, February 6, 1995.

Chapter 10: Post-Vietnam War

1 Interview with Richard E. Carey, OH0443. Vietnam Center and Sam Johnson Vietnam Archive, September 19, 2005, Lieutenant General Richard E. Carey Collection, Vietnam Center and

Sam Johnson Vietnam Archive, Texas Tech University, accessed June 10, 2021, https://www.vietnam.ttu.edu/virtualarchive/items.php?item=OH0443.

2 Lieutenant General Richard E. Carey, interview with the author, August 25, 2021.

3 Lieutenant General Richard E. Carey, interview with the author, September 1, 2021.

4 Associated Press, "General McCutcheon, Marine General," *The New York Times*, July 14, 1971.

5 Lance Corporal Steve Hoffman, "MAG-24 observes its 29th year of service to the Corps," *Windward Marine*, Kaneohe Bay, Oahu, HI, March 5, 1971.

6 Interview with Richard E. Carey, OH0443. Vietnam Center and Sam Johnson Vietnam Archive, September 19, 2005, Lieutenant General Richard E. Carey Collection, Vietnam Center and Sam Johnson Vietnam Archive, Texas Tech University, accessed June 10, 2021, https://www.vietnam.ttu.edu/virtualarchive/items.php?item=OH0443.

7 Associated Press, "Submarines Rescue Six from Downed B-52," *The New York Times*, July 9, 1972.

8 "Progress in Vietnam," Defense POW/MIA Accounting Agency, accessed August 31, 2021, https://www.dpaa.mil/Resources/Fact-Sheets/Article-View/Article/569613/progress-in-vietnam/.

9 Lieutenant General Richard E. Carey, interview with author, January 31, 2022.

10 "US Prisoners of War who returned alive from the Vietnam War," Defense POW/MIA Accounting Agency, accessed January 29, 2022, https://www.dpaa.mil/portals/85/Documents/VietnamAccounting/pmsea_returnee.pdf.

11 Ibid.

12 "John Howard Dunn," Veteran Tributes, accessed January 29, 2022, http://www.veterantributes.org/TributeDetail.php?recordID=136.

13 Lieutenant General Richard E. Carey, interview with author, September 8, 2021.

14 Interview with Richard E. Carey, OH0443. Vietnam Center and Sam Johnson Vietnam Archive, September 19, 2005, Lieutenant General Richard E. Carey Collection, Vietnam Center and Sam Johnson Vietnam Archive, Texas Tech University, accessed June 10, 2021, https://www.vietnam.ttu.edu/virtualarchive/items.php?item=OH0443.

15 Lieutenant General Richard E. Carey, interview with author, September 8, 2021.

16 Lieutenant General Richard E. Carey, interview with author, September 1, 2021.

17 Interview with Richard E. Carey, OH0443. Vietnam Center and Sam Johnson Vietnam Archive, September 19, 2005, Lieutenant General Richard E. Carey Collection, Vietnam Center and Sam Johnson Vietnam Archive, Texas Tech University, accessed June 10, 2021, https://www.vietnam.ttu.edu/virtualarchive/items.php?item=OH0443.

18 Ibid.

19 "About 1st Marine Aircraft Wing," Marines, accessed August 31, 2021, https://www.1stmaw.marines.mil/Unit-Home/About/.

Chapter 11: Evacuation from Vietnam

1 "Brig. Gen. Carey returns to duty after the holidays," *The Bonham (TX) Daily Favorite*, January 5, 1975.

2 Dunham and Quinlan, *U.S. Marines in Vietnam*, 66.

3 Digitized from Box 9 of the White House Press Releases at the Gerald R. Ford Presidential Library. Courtesy of Ford Museum and Library, Ford, Gerald, "April 3, 1975: Statement by the President."

4 "Remembering the downed first flight of operation baby lift," NPR, April 26, 2015, accessed August 15, 2021, https://www.npr.org/2015/04/26/402208267/remembering-the-doomed-first-flight-of-operation-babylift.
5 Interview with Richard E. Carey, OH0443. Vietnam Center and Sam Johnson Vietnam Archive, September 19, 2005, Lieutenant General Richard E. Carey Collection, Vietnam Center and Sam Johnson Vietnam Archive, Texas Tech University, accessed June 10, 2021, https://www.vietnam.ttu.edu/virtualarchive/items.php?item=OH0443.
6 Ibid.
7 Ibid.
8 Dunham and Quinlan, *U.S. Marines in Vietnam*, 141.
9 Interview with Richard E. Carey, OH0443. Vietnam Center and Sam Johnson Vietnam Archive, September 19, 2005, Lieutenant General Richard E. Carey Collection, Vietnam Center and Sam Johnson Vietnam Archive, Texas Tech University, accessed June 10, 2021, https://www.vietnam.ttu.edu/virtualarchive/items.php?item=OH0443.
10 Interview with Richard E. Carey, OH0443. Vietnam Center and Sam Johnson Vietnam Archive, September 19, 2005, Lieutenant General Richard E. Carey Collection, Vietnam Center and Sam Johnson Vietnam Archive, Texas Tech University, accessed June 10, 2021, https://www.vietnam.ttu.edu/virtualarchive/items.php?item=OH0443.
11 6015. Carey, BGen R.E. Headquarters Marine Corps (HQMC) debrief of former CG, 9th Marine Amphibious Brigade (MAB) in Apr-May 75 Operation FREQUENT WIND.
12 Interview with Richard E. Carey, OH0443. Vietnam Center and Sam Johnson Vietnam Archive, September 19, 2005, Lieutenant General Richard E. Carey Collection, Vietnam Center and Sam Johnson Vietnam Archive, Texas Tech University, accessed June 10, 2021, https://www.vietnam.ttu.edu/virtualarchive/items.php?item=OH0443.
13 Dunham and Quinlan, *U.S. Marines in Vietnam*, 143–5.
14 Ibid, 145–7.
15 Ibid, 148.
16 Cable from Secretary of State Dr. Henry A. Kissinger to Ambassador Graham Martin, April 29, 1975.
17 Tom Bartlett, "Frequent Wind," *Leatherneck*, September 1975, 28.
18 Dunham and Quinlan, *U.S. Marines in Vietnam*, 151–4.
19 Colonel Anthony A. "Tony" Wood USMC (Ret), telephone interview with the author, February 11, 2022.
20 Colonel Anthony A. "Tony" Wood, telephone interview with the author, August 18, 2021.
21 Dunham and Quinlan, *U.S. Marines in Vietnam*, 179–83.
22 Four months after his service during the evacuation, Lyons earned a meritorious promotion to corporal. He completed his Marine Corps duty as a Sergeant (E-5) and received an honorable discharge from the service in March 1980. Lyons is an attorney in the Dallas area. Anthony D. Lyons, interview with the author, February 16, 2022.
23 Citation of Navy Achievement Award presented to Lance Corporal Anthony D. Lyons on March 18, 1976.
24 Dunham and Quinlan *U.S. Marines in Vietnam*, 198.
25 In 1944, the Green Bay Packers made him a ninth-round choice in the National Football League draft. Whitmire graduated from the Naval Academy in 1946. One of his classmates was the nation's future 39th President, Jimmy Carter.
26 Dunham and Quinlan, *U.S. Marines in Vietnam*, 199.

27 "Helicopter pilot radio transmissions during the Saigon evacuation, April 29, 1975," President Ford Foreign Policy.org, accessed January 28, 2022, https://presidentfordforeignpolicy.org/wp-content/uploads/2018/03/Helicopter-radio-messages.pdf.
28 Lieutenant Colonel Ismael (Junior) Ortiz (USMC) (Ret), telephone interview with the author, February 14, 2022.
29 Ibid.
30 Jim Kavanagh, "Buddies, hometowns honor last two Marines killed in Vietnam War," CNN, April 29, 2010.
31 Captain Nytsul, 29, from Coronado, California, was the son of a retired Navy captain. Nytsul's wife and 23-month-old son survived him. Lieutenant Shea, 25, lived in El Paso, Texas. Lieutenant Shea left behind his wife. Shea's high school coach described him as "leader."
32 https://www.kpbs.org/news/military/2018/07/03/first-african-american-command-us-navy-aircraft-ca. Accessed November 17, 2022.
33 John Burlage, "Daring '75 landing on *Midway* made heroes of CO, Vietnamese pilot," *Navy Times*, July 3, 1989.
34 Bui Tin, "How North Vietnam Won the War," Viet-Myths, accessed January 30, 2022, http://www.viet-myths.net/buitin.htm.
35 "Coffee Break," *Washington C.H. Record-Herald*, (Washington Court House, OH) May 7, 1975
36 Then Brigadier General Richard E. Carey's undated hand-written notes following the evacuation of Saigon.
37 Letter from Ambassador Graham Martin to General Robert E. Cushman, USMC commandant, May 6, 1975.
38 Brigadier General Richard E. Carey, "Supplement to Command Chronology on *Frequent Wind*," August 5, 1975, 110.
39 Associated Press, "Both words of welcome, protests greet refugees," *The Owensboro (KY) Messenger-Inquirer*, May 3, 1975.
40 Ray Henderson, "Folks around Eglin wary," *The Miami Herald*, May 1, 1975.
41 "Indochinese Refugee Camps in the U.S. in 1975," Arcgis.com, accessed September 2, 2021, https://storymaps.arcgis.com/stories/89ef306b0f24468fbab7cae2dc0cd379.
42 Tom Bartlett, "Frequent Wind," *Leatherneck*, September 1975, 30.
43 Tim Stanley, "'Fate put us together:' Decorated Vietnam veteran from Tulsa, former refugee discover they share some history and an alma mater," *Tulsa World*, March 30, 2019.
44 Lieutenant General Richard E. Carey, telephone interview with the author, March 8, 2022.
45 Richard E. Carey, "U.S. and Vietnam: a 10 year perspective," *The Columbus Dispatch*, April 29, 1975.
46 "The Fall of Saigon," news release, The Discovery Channel, April 10, 1995.
47 Letter from Renee K. Gardner, Discovery Communications, Inc. to Lieutenant General Richard E. Carey, March 29, 1995.
48 Harry Summers, "Reliving heartbreak of Saigon's fall, plight of those left," in television preview of "The Fall of Saigon," *The Washington Times*, April 23, 1995. Summers was a retired U.S. Army colonel who participated in the evacuation of Saigon.
49 Letter from The Discovery Channel Communications Department (unsigned) to Lieutenant General Richard E. Carey, May 10, 1995.
50 Vernon Scott, "America's Darkest Hour," United Press International, *Arts and Entertainment—Scott's World*, April 25, 1995.
51 Beryl Chong, "Nevadan recalls harrowing days as refugee," *Reno Gazette Journal* (Nevada), April 30, 2005.

52 Chris Vaughn, "Heroes of a hasty exit," *Fort Worth Star-Telegram*, April 30, 2005.
53 Colonel Tony Wood, USMC (Ret), telephone interview with the author, February 11, 2022.
54 Interview with Richard E. Carey, OH0443. Vietnam Center and Sam Johnson Vietnam Archive, September 19, 2005, Lieutenant General Richard E. Carey Collection, Vietnam Center and Sam Johnson Vietnam Archive, Texas Tech University, accessed June 10, 2021, https://www.vietnam.ttu.edu/virtualarchive/items.php?item=OH0443.
55 Jim Webb, "Afghanistan: A Requiem for an Avoidable Disaster," The National Interest, accessed September 2, 2021, https://nationalinterest.org/feature/afghanistan-requiem-avoidable-disaster-192727?fbclid=IwAR2dtmqRkI2UfgXWmPHRc-6sAgsMyxIAXx7S-XKIWF-9fLg-FWHMQzuwD5nI.
56 Alan E. Mesches, "Commentary: Have we learned nothing from history?" *The Post and Courier* (Charleston, SC), August 14, 2021.
57 Lieutenant General Richard E. Carey, interview with the author, September 15, 2021.

Chapter 12: General Carey's Supplement to the Command Chronology on *Frequent Wind*

1 Brigadier General Richard E. Carey, "Supplement to Command Chronology of *Frequent Wind*," 107.
2 Ibid., 108.
3 Lieutenant General Richard E. Carey, interview with the author, January 26, 2022.
4 Brigadier General Richard E. Carey, "Supplement to Command Chronology of *Frequent Wind*," 114–15.
5 Ibid., 115.
6 Ibid., 116.
7 Ibid., 117–18.
8 Ibid., 93.
9 Ibid., 87.

Chapter 13: *Mayaguez* Rescue

1 "Rescue of SS *Mayaguez* and the 'Last Battle'," Ford Library Museum, accessed September 6, 2021, https://www.fordlibrarymuseum.gov/museum/exhibits/mayaguez/index.html.
2 Men Kimseng, "45 Years Later, U.S. Military Personnel Recall SS Mayaguez Rescue," VOA Cambodia, accessed September 6, 2021, https://www.voacambodia.com/a/5424477.html.
3 "*Mayaguez* Incident," Military Wiki, accessed September 6, 2021, https://military-history.fandom.com/wiki/Mayaguez_incident.
4 "Rescue of SS *Mayaguez* and the 'Last Battle'," Ford Library Museum, accessed September 6, 2021, https://www.fordlibrarymuseum.gov/museum/exhibits/mayaguez/index.html.
5 Dunham and Quinlan, *U.S. Marines in Vietnam*, 265.
6 RCA Marine telegram from Captain Charles T. Miller to President Gerald R. Ford, May 15, 1974.
7 "Rescue of SS *Mayaguez* and the 'Last Battle'," Ford Library Museum, accessed September 6, 2021, https://www.fordlibrarymuseum.gov/museum/exhibits/mayaguez/index.html.
8 Dunham and Quinlan, *U.S. Marines in Vietnam*, 242 and 250.

9 Interview with Richard E. Carey, OH0443. Vietnam Center and Sam Johnson Vietnam Archive, September 19, 2005, Lieutenant General Richard E. Carey Collection, Vietnam Center and Sam Johnson Vietnam Archive, Texas Tech University, accessed June 10, 2021, https://www.vietnam.ttu.edu/virtualarchive/items.php?item=OH0443.

10 Interview with Richard E. Carey, OH0443. Vietnam Center and Sam Johnson Vietnam Archive, September 19, 2005, Lieutenant General Richard E. Carey Collection, Vietnam Center and Sam Johnson Vietnam Archive, Texas Tech University, accessed June 10, 2021, https://www.vietnam.ttu.edu/virtualarchive/items.php?item=OH0443.

11 Dunham and Quinlan, *U.S. Marines in Vietnam*, 265.

Chapter 14: HQMC and Senior Leadership

1 Lieutenant General Richard E. Carey, interview with the author, September 13, 2021.

2 "CH-46 Sea Knight," Boeing, accessed September 10, 2021, https://www.boeing.com/history/products/c-46-sea-knight.page.

3 "McDonnell Douglas AV-8B Harrier II," Weapons and Warfare, accessed September 10, 2021, https://weaponsandwarfare.com/2020/07/16/mcdonnell-douglas-av-8b-harrier-ii/.

4 "F/A-18 A-D Hornet," NAVAIR, accessed September 10, 2021, https://www.navair.navy.mil/product/FA-18-D-Hornet.

5 Lieutenant General Richard E. Carey, interview with the author, September 13, 2021.

6 Richard Whittle, "Inspection keeps jets on ground," *The News and Observer* (Raleigh, North Carolina), July 28, 1977.

7 "Harrier jet is death machine," *The News and Observer* (Raleigh, North Carolina) July 28, 1977.

8 Memo for the record, summary of activities of CBS Atlanta Bureau by Cherry Point MCAS Public Affairs Office, July 28, 1977.

9 Memo for the record, summary of activities of WITN (Channel 7, Washington, North Carolina), by Cherry Point MCAS Public Affairs Office, July 29, 1977.

10 Aspin, a Democrat, chaired the House Armed Services Committee in the 1980s. President Bill Clinton named him as his first secretary of defense in 1993. He resigned in February 1994 and died in 1995.

11 Robert Hodierne, "The Harrier: does it need elite pilots?" *The Charlotte Observer*, July 31, 1977.

12 Richard Whittle, "General says Harrier not unsafe craft," *The News and Observer* (Raleigh, North Carolina), August 3, 1977.

13 Lieutenant General Richard E. Carey, interview with the author, September 22, 2021.

14 "Harrier record requires grounding," *The News and Observer* (Raleigh, North Carolina), August 5, 1977.

15 "Harrier loss figures incredible," *The News and Observer* (Raleigh, North Carolina), August 13, 1977.

16 Richard Whittle, "Harrier crash rate cited," *The News and Observer* (Raleigh, North Carolina), August 10, 1977.

17 Richard Whittle, "Harrier cut from air show," *The News and Observer* (Raleigh, North Carolina), August 24, 1977.

18 Lieutenant General Richard E. Carey, interview with the author, September 15, 2021.

19 Richard Whittle, "Marines halt low-level Harrier flights," *The News and Observer* (Raleigh, North Carolina), September 10, 1977.

20 Ferrell Guillory, "Marines to resume low Harrier flights," Washington correspondent, *The News and Observer* (Raleigh, North Carolina), September 14, 1977.
21 "Top Marine: Commandant tours Point with wife and Sergeant Major," *Windsock*, Cherry Point's base newspaper, September 23, 1977.
22 Lieutenant General Richard E. Carey, interview with the author, September 22, 2021.
23 Email from Colonel James Pendergast, USMC (Ret) to the author, March 2, 2022.
24 Jan Solum, interview with author, July 9, 2022.

Chapter 15: Atlantic Command

1 Both the admiral's father, Harold C. Train, and daughter, Elizabeth L. Train, served as Navy rear admirals.
2 Howard Troxler, "Umpire says live or die in war gems," *The News and Observer* (Raleigh, North Carolina), May 22, 1978.
3 P. J. Budhans, "Foreign policy a top focus at CINCLANT," *Daily Press* (Newport-News, Virginia), September 7, 1980.
4 "Iran Hostage Mission Report, Special Operations Review," August 1980, iii. https://www.history.navy.mil/research/library/online-reading-room/title-list-alphabetically/i/iran-hostage-rescue-mission-report.html, iii.
5 Ibid., v.
6 Ibid., iv.
7 Lieutenant General Richard E. Carey, interview with author, September 29, 2021.

Chapter 16: Final Assignment Quantico

1 Lieutenant General Richard E. Carey, interview with the author, October 6, 2021.
2 Ibid.
3 https://www.runnersworld.com/races-places/a29196504/marine-corps-marathon-faq/, accessed November 17, 2022.
4 "Marine Corps Values," Marines, accessed September 19, 2021, https://www.marines.com/life-as-a-marine/standards/values.html.
5 Lieutenant General Richard E. Carey, interview with the author, September 13, 2021.
6 "Sports etc.," *The St. Petersburg Times*, November 8, 1982.
7 Associated Press, "Marines' Marathon Runs Today," *The Charlotte Observer*, November 7, 1982.
8 Lieutenant General Richard E. Carey, interview with the author, September 29, 2021.
9 Lieutenant General Richard E. Carey, interview with the author, October 6, 2021.
10 "Letter from Chief of Staff and Assistant to the President James A. Baker III," accessed March 24, 2022, https://www.reaganlibrary.gov/public/digitallibrary/smof/cos/bakerjames/box-011/40-028-6914303-011-007-2016.pdf.
11 Lieutenant General Richard E. Carey, interview with the author, January 5, 2022.
12 Email from Colonel Warren Wiedhahn, USMC (Ret) to the author, August 21, 2021.
13 Email from Michael Pinckney NARA at the Reagan Library, September 27, 2021.
14 "The Daily Diary of President Ronald Reagan," accessed October 10, 2022, https://www.reaganlibrary.gov/public/digitallibrary/dailydiary/1981-03.pdf, https://www.reaganlibrary.

gov/public/digitallibrary/dailydiary/1981-04.pdf, https://www.reaganlibrary.gov/public/digitallibrary/dailydiary/1981-06.pdf, https://www.reaganlibrary.gov/public/digitallibrary/dailydiary/1981-07.pdf, https://www.reaganlibrary.gov/public/digitallibrary/dailydiary/1982-05.pdf.

15 "President, King Ride Horses of a Different Color," *The Washington Post*, accessed September 27, 2021, https://www.washingtonpost.com/archive/local/1982/05/22/president-king-ride-horses-of-a-different-color/ba34e8cd-5952-4ac8-af6b-481c21ee2b7e/.

16 Lieutenant General Richard E. Carey, interview with the author, September 29, 2021.

17 Lieutenant General Richard E. Carey, interview with the author, October 13, 2021.

18 Email from Colonel James Pendergast, USMC (Ret) to the author, March 2, 2022.

19 Lieutenant General Richard E. Carey, interview with the author, September 29, 2021.

20 Chuck Lloyd and Rick Llinares, "HMX-1 'The First and Finest'," *Naval Aviation News*, accessed November 17, 2022, https://www.hqmc.marines.mil/hmx-1/About/.

21 "Marines plan assault with equipment and awards," *The Arizona Daily Star*, August 13, 1981.

22 Pendergast, a retired colonel and Vietnam veteran, worked for General Carey during the General's late 1970s assignment at Cherry Point. In January 1981, the General requested Pendergast to join him at Quantico. Pendergast received his undergraduate degree from Louisiana State University, then the Marine Corps sent Pendergast to Syracuse University to study for his master's degree in journalism. Pendergast served in the Marine Corps from 1967 to 1992 when he retired from his last assignment as Public Affairs Officer, Fleet Marine Force, Atlantic, in Norfolk, Virginia. In retirement, he and a partner owned a golf practice facility for five years. Between 1993 and 2007, Pendergast served as executive director and CEO of Virginia Beach Visions, Inc. That organization worked with local leaders to help the city's "economic vitality and quality of life." Email from Colonel James Pendergast, USMC (Ret) to the author, March 2, 2022.

23 Email from Colonel James Pendergast to the author, March 2, 2022.

24 Associated Press, "Hinckley wrote of assassination interest," *Daily Press* (Newport News, VA), August 19, 1981.

25 Email from Colonel James Pendergast to the author, March 2, 2022.

26 Associated Press, "Government Sends Hinckley to Quantico," *Daily Press* (Newport News, VA), April 1, 1981.

27 Michael Sullivan, "Marines 'elite of elite' protect embassies," *Daily Press* (Newport News, VA), May 17, 1981.

28 Lieutenant General Richard E. Carey, interview with the author, September 29, 2021.

29 Lieutenant General Richard E. Carey, interview with the author, September 29, 2021.

30 Sergeant Chris Fordney, "Ceremony marks LtGen Carey's retirement," *The Quantico Sentry*, February 25, 1983.

31 Letter to Lieutenant General USMC (Ret) Richard E. Carey from Acting Secretary of the Navy James F. Goodrich, January 13, 1983.

32 Letter to Lieutenant General Richard E. Carey, USMC (Ret) from General Robert H. Barrow, Commandant, United States Marine Corps, February 10, 1983.

33 Letter to Lieutenant General Richard E. Carey, USMC (Ret) from General Robert H. Barrow, Commandant, United States Marine Corps, March 7, 1983.

34 Letter to Lieutenant General Richard E. Carey, USMC (Ret) from Supreme Court Justice Harry A. Blackmun, March 1, 1983.

35 "Retirement", Melody Carey, February 28, 1982.

Chapter 17: A Brief Entry into Politics

1 Lieutenant General Richard E. Carey, interview with the author, October 6, 2021.
2 "Anti-Saloon League of America," Ohio History Connection, accessed October 19, 2021, https://ndnpohio.ohiohistory.org/wp-content/uploads/2019/08/AntiSaloonLeague.pdf.
3 Department of Liquor Control Employee Newsletter, October 1983.
4 Associated Press, "Ohio has monopoly," *The Marion Star*, November 17, 1983.
5 "Ohio Liquor Stores Now Permit Display of Ads," *Cincinnati Enquirer*, November 20, 1983.
6 Richard E. Carey, "In defense of state liquor control," essay and comment in "Forum" *The Plain Dealer* (Cleveland), June 25, 1985.
7 "Ohio and John Barleycorn," editorial in *The Plain Dealer* (Cleveland), June 25, 1985.
8 Associated Press, "Cameras to monitor state liquor stores," *Marysville Journal Tribune*, February 7, 1984.
9 Jack Hicks, "Ohio expends questionable effort to protect monopoly," *Cincinnati Enquirer*, December 19, 1985.
10 "'Economic Blackmail', mayor says," *Dayton Daily News*, August 16, 1985.
11 "GOP wants Celeste to probe fund raising," *The Akron Beacon Journal*, March 14, 1984.
12 Lieutenant General Richard E. Carey, interview with the author, October 6, 2021.
13 Sam Perdue, "Some can be ruthless when they play politics," *The Columbus Citizen Journal*, August 5, 1985.
14 Lieutenant General Richard E. Carey, interview with the author, February 23, 2022.
15 Sam Perdue, "State personnel tact questionable but legal," *The Columbus Citizen Journal*, August 12, 1985.
16 Sam Perdue, "Hiring of a relative not deeply probed," *The Columbus Citizen Journal*, August 29, 1985.
17 Sam Perdue, "Politics is tough, a general finds out," *The Columbus Citizen Journal*, August 19, 1985.
18 Lieutenant General Richard E. Carey, interview with the author, December 3, 2021.
19 Joel Rutchik, "Ohio Cocktail: liquor stores and politics," *Dayton Daily News*, September 28, 1986.
20 Lieutenant General Richard E. Carey, interview with the author, October 13, 2021.
21 T. C. Brown, "Airport top post goes to Carey," *The Columbus Citizen-Journal*, December 7, 1985.
22 "Carey on the flight deck," *The Columbus Citizen Journal*, December 10, 1985.
23 "Carey at the helm," *The Columbus Dispatch*, December 12, 1985.
24 Joe Dirck, "Peace 'n good will at Fort Columbus," *The Columbus Citizen Journal*, December 18, 1985.
25 Lieutenant General Richard E. Carey, interview with the author, December 3, 2021.
26 Letter to Richard E. Carey from Ralph L. Warne, July 21, 1986.
27 Letter to Richard E. Carey from Ralph L. Warne, August 7, 1986.
28 Alan Johnson, "Former Columbus mayor Dana 'Buck' Rinehart dies," *The Columbus Dispatch*, February 18, 2015.
29 Lieutenant General Richard E. Carey, interview with the author, October 13, 2021.
30 Johnson, "Former Columbus Mayor Dana 'Buck' Rinehart dies."
31 Lieutenant General Richard E. Carey, interview with the author, October 13, 2021.
32 Associated Press, "Port Columbus airport administrator dismissed," *News-Journal* (Mansfield, Ohio), December 31, 1986.
33 Lieutenant General Richard E. Carey, interview with the author, December 3, 2021.

34 Associated Press, "Candidate may have to pull out," *The Tribune*, Coshocton, Ohio, February 6, 1987.
35 Lieutenant General Richard E. Carey, interview with the author, October 20, 2021.
36 Sherrod Brown, after his time as Ohio secretary of state, served as a member of the United States House of Representatives from 1993 to 2007. In 2006, he won election to the United States Senate. He won reelection in 2012 and 2018.
37 Lieutenant General Richard E. Carey, interview with the author, October 13, 2021.
38 Joel Rutchick, "Developer has left a trail of trouble," *Dayton Daily News*, January 25, 1988.
39 Lieutenant General Richard E. Carey, interview with the author, October 20, 2021.

Chapter 18: Aiding the Dallas District Courts

1 Mr. Semos served in the Texas House of Representatives for 16 years and on the Dallas County Commissioners Court for 12 years. "Chris Semos Obituary," *The Dallas Morning News*, accessed October 29, 2021, https://obits.dallasnews.com/us/obituaries/dallasmorningnews/name/chris-semos-obituary?id=9713064.
2 Lieutenant General Richard E. Carey, interview with the author, October 20, 2021.
3 Hellace Weiner, "Courthouse echoes somber mood," *Fort Worth Star-Telegram*, August 2, 1989.
4 "What does a Court Administrator do?" Spiegato, accessed October 29, 2021, https://spiegato.com/en/what-does-a-court-administrator-do.
5 Lieutenant General Richard E. Carey, interview with the author, October 20, 2021.
6 Lieutenant General Richard E. Carey, interview with the author, November 17, 2021.

Chapter 19: General Carey Continues to Serve in Retirement

1 Ed Fitzmaurice interview with the author, July 23, 2021.
2 "PFC Cloyde C. Pinson," obituary, *The Dallas Morning News*, May 24, 1967.
3 "Cloyde C. Pinson, Sr.," obituary, *The Dallas Morning News*, April 16, 2006.
4 Email from Larry Williams, Director of Dallas Fort Worth National Cemetery to the author, March 21, 2022.
5 Ken Watterson first became involved with helping Marine veterans of the Vietnam War after a chance meeting with his former forward observer during their first Vietnam tour, Lieutenant Colonel H.C. "Barney" Barnum. Barnum, a Medal of Honor recipient for his actions in Vietnam, served as deputy assistant secretary of the Navy for reserve affairs. Barnum encouraged Watterson to "get involved" with combat veterans. Watterson took Barnum's suggestion to heart. He became the "go to guy" for all veterans and veteran support organizations in North Texas. He created the Veterans Resource Center and served as its volunteer manager since 2011.
6 Interview with Richard E. Carey, OH0443. Vietnam Center and Sam Johnson Vietnam Archive, September 19, 2005, Lieutenant General Richard E. Carey Collection, Vietnam Center and Sam Johnson Vietnam Archive, Texas Tech University, accessed June 10, 2021, https://www.vietnam.ttu.edu/virtualarchive/items.php?item=OH0443.
7 Rick Atkinson and Barton Gellman, "U.S. confirms 'friendly fire' killed 7 Marines," *The Washington Post*, February 4, 1991.

8 Lieutenant General Richard E. Carey, telephone interview with the author, March 21, 2022.
9 Colonel Charles J. Quilter II, U.S. Marine Corps Reserve, *U.S. Marines in the Persian Gulf, 1990–1991: With the I Marine Expeditionary Force in Desert Shield and Desert Storm* (Washington, D.C.: History and Museums Division, Headquarters United States Marine Corps, 1993), 62–3.
10 Letter to Lieutenant General Richard E. Carey from General M. W. Hagee, Commandant, United States Marine Corps, May 19, 2003.
11 Ben "Chip" Filer, Executive Director, Wichita Falls (Texas) Bicycling Club, telephone interview with the author, October 21, 2021.
12 David Tarrant, "'It's like Halley's Comet': The remains of a Dallas Marine missing in action in the Korean War nearly 70 years ago come home," *The Dallas Morning News*, accessed November 24, 2021, https://www.dallasnews.com/news/politics/2019/09/27/it-s-like-halley-s-comet-the-remains-of-a-dallas-marine-missing-in-action-in-the-korean-war-nearly-70-years-ago-come-home/.
13 Sherri Steward Ganz, interview with the author, June 25, 2021 (71st anniversary of the start of the Korean War when North Korean troops moved south of the 38th parallel).
14 In addition to General Pitman's wartime achievements, New Orleans residents remembered him for his efforts to end a 1973 rooftop sniper attack. Without authorization, Pitman flew a CH-46 helicopter from NAS New Orleans to the shooting site. He put New Orleans police officers on the helicopter, flew over the rooftop, and positioned the CH-46 so police could take out the sniper. Despite preventing further loss of life, Pitman faced a court martial that could have ended his career. Louisiana Congressman and House Armed Services Chairman F. Edward Herbert took up Pitman's cause and there was no court martial. Pitman died following a lengthy battle with cancer, according to his family. "The decorated Marine pilot whose heroics helped stop the 1973 New Orleans sniper attack has died at 84," accessed March 31, 2022, https://taskandpurpose.com/news/marine-new-orleans-sniper-attack-pitman-obituary/.
15 Woody Williams Foundation—Gold Star Families Memorial Monument projects, accessed October 14, 2021, https://woodywilliams.org/monument-projects.html.
16 Williams died June 29, 2022. His flag-draped casket was placed in honor at the United States Capitol in Washington, D.C.
17 Lieutenant General Richard E. Carey, interview with author, September 13, 2021.
18 J. David Barron, "Rep. Johnson honors local veterans: combatants recognized for valor on battlefield," *Allen American* (TX), October 12, 2012.
19 "Richard Carey Presented with the Albert Nelson Marquis Lifetime Achievement Award by Marquis Who's Who," accessed September 14, 2021, https://www.24-7pressrelease.com/press-release/457537/richard-carey-presented-with-the-albert-nelson-marquis-lifetime-achievement-award-by-marquis-whos-who.

Chapter 20: The Chosin Few Monument Project

1 "Chosin Few Memorial Gate," Marine Military Academy, accessed December 6, 2021, https://www.mma-tx.org/blog/12847/chosin-few-memorial-gate/.
2 "New monument to honor Chosin Few," LI Herald, accessed December 6, 2021, https://www.liherald.com/stories/new-monument-to-honor-chosin-few,18803.
3 "The Chosin Few—Cape Coral, Florida USA," Waymarking, accessed December 6, 2021, https://www.waymarking.com/waymarks/WMWYM1_The_Chosin_Few_Cape_Coral_Florida_USA.

4 Lance Corporal Michelle S. Mattei, "'Chosin Few' honored with new monument," Pendleton Marines, accessed December 6, 2021, https://www.pendleton.marines.mil/DesktopModules/ArticleCS/Print.aspx?PortalId=98&ModuleId=35527&Article=537237.
5 "Stretch of Route 35 in Monmouth County Named for 'Chosin Few' Vets of Korean War Battle," Belmar/Lake Como, NJ News TAPinto, accessed January 19, 2022, https://www.tapinto.net/towns/belmar-slash-lake-como/sections/transportation-2/articles/stretch-of-route-35-in-monmouth-county-named-for.
6 Mark Austin Byrd, sculptor, telephone interview with the author, December 21, 2021.
7 Staff Sergeant Art Markey (Ret), "Our Memorial: the beginning," *The Guidon* (publication of members of Baker Company, 1st Battalion, 5th Marines), October 1986.
8 Lieutenant General Richard E. Carey, interview with the author, December 8, 2021.
9 Bud Gillet, "New national memorial to honor Korean War Veterans," CBS 11 Dallas, Texas, May 23, 2014.
10 Fran Woodward Kreekon, interview with the author, December 16, 2021.
11 Ibid.
12 Ibid.
13 Maddie Shepherd, "12 Direct Mail Statistics You Should Know in 2021," Fundera Ledger, accessed December 26, 2021, https://www.fundera.com/resources/direct-mail-statistics.
14 Lieutenant General Richard E. Carey, interview with the author December 16, 2021.
15 Lieutenant General Richard E. Carey, interview with the author, December 8, 2021.
16 Amanda Cicinazo, "South Korean President visits Marine Museum to honor Americans who saved his parents," *The Free Lance Star*, (Fredericksburg, VA) June 28, 2017.
17 "Meredith Victory—the Ship of Miracles," New Jersey Maritime Museum, accessed March 20, 2022, https://njmaritimemuseum.org/meredith-victory-the-ship-of-miracles/.
18 As for Captain LaRue, the man who led the rescue, he continued a life of service and became a Benedictine monk in New Jersey. His name as a monk—Brother Marinus. Marinus is Latin for "of the sea." "SS Meredith Victory: The 'Ship of Miracles'," accessed December 20, 2021, https://kwmf.org/ss-meredith-victory-the-ship-of-miracles/.
19 Fundraiser by Mark Austin Byrd: Chosin Reservoir Battle Memorial, gofundme.com, accessed December 20, 2021, https://www.gofundme.com/f/chosin-reservoir-battle-memorial-monument.
20 Email from Larry Williams, Director of Dallas Fort Worth National Cemetery to the author, March 21, 2022.
21 "Texas veterans make up 6.8% of state's population, study finds," accessed October 10, 2022, https://www.thecentersquare.com/texas/texas-veterans-make-up-6-8-of-state-s-population-study-finds/article_0f2271ea-e816-11ea-af12-5325a0b3d1dc.html.
22 "United States History Studies Since 1877, Crosswalk from 2010 TEKS to 2018 Streamlined TEKS," accessed October 10, 2022, https://tea.texas.gov/sites/default/files/US%20History%20Since%201877%20Crosswalk_rev.pdf.
23 Jenny Gaona, Texas Education Agency social student content specialist, interview with the author, December 9, 2021.
24 Frisco, a Dallas suburb of 220,000 people, refers to itself as "Veteran Ready." The school district fully funds the Navy National Defense Cadet Corps program first offered for high school students in the fall of 2021.
25 Dr. Kelly Crager, Texas Tech University, in email to the author, January 5, 2022.
26 Professor Andrew Mitchell, Grove City College, in email to the author, April 6, 2022.

27 Professor Stephen F. Taafe, Stephen F. Austin University, in email to the author, January 5, 2022.
28 Lieutenant General Richard E. Carey, interview with the author, January 5, 2022.
29 Mark A. Byrd, interview with the author, December 27, 2021.
30 Mary D. Karcher, "Sculptor Mark Byrd: Standing Tall in Bronze," *Leatherneck—Magazine of the Marines*, September 2018, 52.
31 Ibid., 52–3.
32 Mark A. Byrd, interview with the author, December 27, 2021.
33 Ibid.
34 Ibid.
35 "Stephen Goodwin Olmstead—Obituary," accessed July 25, 2022, https://legacy.suntimes.com/us/obituaries/washingtonpost/name/stephen-olmstead-obituary?id=35968899.
36 2020 Membership Directory of the Chosin Few, president's message.
37 John Y. Lee email to the author, July 14, 2022.
38 Ibid.

Chapter 21: Family

1 "20 Years Ago Today: Ronald Reagan Announces He Has Alzheimer's," accessed October 16, 2022, https://www.ecumen.org/blog/20-years-ago-today-ronald-reagan-announces-he-has-alzheimer-s/.
2 Bettina Boxall and Deborah Schoch, "Reagan says he is in early stages of Alzheimer's," *Los Angeles Times*, November 6, 1994.
3 That organization provided support to families with an Alzheimer's patient. Among the support options were the following: early-stage support groups, caregiver and professional education, and case management from a social worker designed to help families identify available services. "North Central Texas office offers resources for families dealing with Alzheimer's," *Fort Worth Star Telegram*, October 29, 2004.
4 Alzheimer's Association email to the author, October 22, 2021.
5 Daniel Q. Haney, "Ailment afflicts millions in the U.S.," *Fort Worth Star-Telegram*, June 5, 2004.
6 "Early diagnosis key to fighting Alzheimer's disease," *The Monitor* (McAllen, TX), February 23, 2003.
7 "When Was Alzheimer's Disease Discovered?" Devoted Guardians, accessed November 19, 2021, https://devotedguardians.com/when-alzheimers-was-discovered/.
8 Lieutenant General Richard E. Carey, interview with the author, November 17, 2021.
9 "Stages of Alzheimer's," Alzheimer's Association, accessed November 15, 2021, https://www.alz.org/alzheimers-dementia/stages.
10 Lieutenant General Richard E. Carey, interview with the author, November 24, 2021.
11 "Carey, Maudine 'Dena' E.," Aria Cremation Service & Funeral Homes, accessed November 10, 2021, https://www.ariacremation.com/obituary/18379/.
12 The Arizona-based organization has four pillars that include the following: diet, stress management, exercise, and spiritual fitness. ARPF's diet recommendations follow closely healthy heart guidelines including a low-fat food diet, eating complex carbohydrates, lean protein, and super foods such as blueberries and spinach, along with taking vitamin C and A supplements. Exercise includes a combination of 150 minutes a week of physical exercise and brain exercises.

Brain exercises consist of reading, writing, and puzzles. The ARPF also recommends reducing stress. Finally, the group urges that people have sense of spirituality, regardless of religion. That includes socialization, patience, and volunteering without any thought of self-reward. Further information is available at https://alzheimersprevention.org/.

13 "Michael Ramsey Carey," Tribute Archive, accessed November 23, 2021, https://www.tributearchive.com/obituaries/18221085/Michael-Ramsey-Carey/Candler/North-Carolina/A-Simple-Cremation.

14 Lieutenant General Richard E. Carey, interview with the author, December 3, 2021.

Epilogue

1 Lieutenant General Richard E. Carey video interview with the author, May 25, 2022.

Index